How to Get a Job
with a
Cruise Line

How To Sail Around The World
On Luxury Cruise Ships
And Get Paid For It

Mary Fallon Miller

Ticket to Adventure
St. Petersburg, Florida, USA

FIFTH EDITION

How To Get A Job With a Cruise Line:
Adventure-Travel-Romance;
How to sail around the world on luxury
cruise ships and get paid for it.

Cover Design: Randy Hall
Cover Photo Credit: Princess Cruises.

Although the author and publisher have exhaustively
researched all sources to ensure accuracy and completeness
of information in this book, we assume no responsibility for
errors, inaccuracies, omissions, or any inconsistency herein.
Any slights of people or organizations are unintentional.

Fifth Edition 2001

Library of Congress Cataloging-in-Publication Data

Miller, Mary Fallon, 1963-
    How to get a job with a cruise line : how to sail around the world on luxury
cruise ships and get paid for it : adventure, travel, romance/ Mary Fallon
Miller.- -5th ed.
    Mary Fallon Miller. -- 5th ed.
        p. cm.
    Includes bibliographical references and index.
    ISBN 0-9624019-3-5 (pbk.)
    1. Cruise ships--Vocational Guidance. 2. Cruise ships--Job descriptions. I.
Title.
    HE566.E9 M55 2000
    387.5'42'02373–dc21

00-044301

Printed in the United States of America

How to Get a Job with a Cruise Line

is the *only* cruise employment guide

Recommended by

New York Times
U.S. News & World Report
Conde Nast Traveler
Cosmopolitan
Miami Herald

and the 25 Cruise Line Members

of Cruise Lines International Association, CLIA

"...whenever we get a question regarding
how to find a job in the cruise industry,
your book is our first reference point..."
James G. Godsman, President, CLIA

"The interviews with cruise line professionals, and the tips they
offer, provide invaluable 'insider's information'...
It's truly like having a friend in the cruise business."
Director of Personnel, American Hawaii Cruises

"I wrote my resume according to the directions in the book ...
I was hired as a gift shop manager with Carnival Cruise Lines."
Shawn Lennox, Gift Shop Manager, *Ecstasy*

Here's what job seekers and people who have found jobs say:

"Your book was a tremendous help ... I joined Royal Caribbean Cruise Line as an asst. purser."

Cynthia Whan, Asst. Purser
Royal Caribbean Cruise Line

"It's great not having to pay a high agency fee to get this information."

V. Durej, Student

"I currently work in a cruise line office, and this book will help me if I ever consider changing jobs. Thank you for doing all the research."

J.S.

"I read each cruise line profile and sent my resume to 15 cruise lines. I was offered five different positions! I'm now a social hostess ."

J.B. Owen, Social Hostess

"I got an interview with Premier Cruise Lines! Thank you for all of your help!"

Melinda Dominic

"Thanks - I finally left my boring 9-5 job... I'm traveling and I get paid for it."

Jennifer Hansen

Here's what travel industry executives & career advisors say:

" ... the book travels well."
Joyce Lain Kennedy
Career Columnist, Author

" ... the travel standard..."
Travel Weekly

" The in-depth interviews give the reader a real world look at the cruise industry .... this book will not only help the cruise lines attract more qualified personnel, but will also upgrade the candidates the cruise lines interview."
John Dalton
Director of Training, Travel Trade Magazine

"Excellent. Any faculty member in a tourism school would appreciate having copies of How to Get a Job with a Cruise Line *available.*"
Bob McIntosh, Ph.D. Academic Council Member Emeritus
Institute of Certified Travel Agents

"I consistently receive letters and phone calls from students or recent graduates who are interested in a job in the cruise industry and are looking for advice. I'll steer them toward your book in the future."
Director of Public Relations,
Commodore Cruise Line

"An extensively researched book...packed with valuable inside information ... a must for job seekers, and for career libraries!"
Anita Wofford
University of Florida Career Resource Center

" The personal accounts of cruise employees and the Cruise Line Directory, are just two of the resources that I find most helpful for our students."
Tony Procaccino, Career Advisor
American Airlines Travel Academy

Dedication

To Charles & Rini Miller

Acknowledgments

Thanks to Janet L. Harris, the 7am,
the Mayor and Council of Northshore Park,
Cautie DuFais, Susie & Bongo Walsh.

Members of CLIA
Cruise Lines International Association

American Cruise Line

American Hawaii Cruises

Cape Canaveral Cruises

Carnival Cruise Lines

Celebrity Cruises

Commodore Cruise Line

Costa Cruise Lines

Crystal Cruises

Cunard Line, Ltd.

Disney Cruise Line

First European Cruises

Holland America Line

Mediterranean Shipping

Norwegian Coastal Voyages

Norwegian Cruise Line

Orient Cruises

Premier Cruise Lines

Princess Cruises

Radisson Seven Seas Cruises

Regal Cruises

Royal Caribbean
International

Royal Olympic Cruises

Seabourn Cruise Line

Silversea Cruises

Windstar Cruises

"*Our doubts are traitors, and make us lose the good we oft' might win, by fearing to attempt.***"**

William Shakespeare

TABLE OF CONTENTS

New 5th Edition
Completely Revised, Updated and Expanded

★ TOP 15 QUESTIONS & ANSWERS

★ 180 JOBS

★ EXCLUSIVE JOB CONTACTS

★ EMPLOYEES PERSONAL STORIES

Our Guarantee: You will save time & money. We've done the homework for you!

1 ADVENTURE-TRAVEL-ROMANCE
Expert Answers to the Top 15 Questions about Cruise Line Jobs.

2 JOB DESCRIPTIONS
FROM PEOPLE ON THE JOB
Cruise Ship Lifestyles: The Inside Story
Accurate answers to your questions about duties, responsibilities and ideal qualifications for shipboard and shoreside jobs. Real life stories of people on the job. Stories of how they got their position, what they do and advice on how you can land your dream job.

JOB DEPARTMENTS

Casino	Host
Cruise Staff	Gift Shop
Deck & Engine	Lecturer
Entertainment	Medical
Food & Beverage	Photography
Gentleman Host	Salon & Spa

3 THE TOP SIX FIRST JOBS

Here's how to get your first job. Why these positions are available and when is the best time to get hired. Ideal qualifications, exclusive insider's tips.

4 JOB APPLICATION TIPS FROM PEOPLE IN THE KNOW

The best way to get hired - Advice from top executives, industry experts and cruise line personnel directors.

5 THE 10 BEST WAYS TO APPLY FOR YOUR CRUISE LINE JOB

Specific Tips on Your Resume, Cover Letter and Application from Cruise Line Personnel Directors and Top Executives.

6 CRUISE LINE PROFILES

What cruise lines should I apply to?
Where can I go?
When can I travel?
What new ships are planned?
Here are all the answers! **We've done your homework for you.** These profiles show you how to match your education, work experience, skills and talents to a specific job. Detailed information on 40 major cruise lines will help you travel around the world and get paid for it.

FEATURES: **Cruise Line Classification**
Destinations
Fleet
Nationality of Crew
Passenger Profile
Programs and Facilities
Job Contact

PLUS Insider's Info: - hiring policies, new developments; special programs, facilities & job opportunities; job hotlines, Web sites.

1

EXPERT ANSWERS TO THE TOP 15 QUESTIONS ABOUT CRUISE SHIP JOBS

1. What types of jobs are there?

Cruise ships are floating resorts, a complete city at sea. Whether you've just returned from a cruise or you've seen *Love Boat* or *Titanic*, you know what a cruise vacation is about: fun, entertainment, service and worldwide travel. Working with a cruise company gives you the best of both worlds - Travel, Adventure, Romance *and* a Steady Paycheck.

Did you know there are **more than 180 types of jobs** aboard ship plus dozens of opportunities at cruise company headquarters around the world?

Imagine yourself traveling to places you've always dreamed of - and getting paid for it. Which of these jobs would be best for you? Review our list of 180 jobs.

Jobs are listed alphabetically. Several job titles may be used to describe the same position. 'Assistant' is abbreviated as Asst.. The following is a partial list of possible jobs aboard cruise ships and at cruise line headquarters.

CRUISE LINE JOBS

Able Bodied Seaman
Accountant
Activities Coordinator
Administrative Asst.
Aerobics Instructor
Air/Sea Agent
Air/Sea Manager
Audio Visual Technician
Auditor, Chief
Auditor, Asst.
Baggage Handler
Baker, 1st, 2nd, 3rd
Baker, Asst. Supervisor
Barman
Bar Manager
Bartender
Bar Waiter
Beautician
Boatswain
Boatswain, Mate
Buffet Man
Busboy
Butcher
Butcher Staff
Cabin Steward
Carpenter
Cashier
Casino Manager
Casino Manager, Asst.
Casino Staff
Catering Manager
Cellar-man
Chef
Chaplain
Chef
Chef de Partier
Confectioner
Cook, 1st, 2nd, 3rd
Comedian
Computer Specialist
Controller
Cook Helper
Cosmetologist
Croupier
Cruise Director
Cruise Director, Asst.
Cruise Staff
Cruise Staff Captain
Cruise Staff Steward
Cruise Terminal Staff
DJ
Dance Instructor
Dancer
Data Manager
Dealer
Deck & Engine Staff
Dentist
Disc Jockey

District Sales Manager
Dishwasher
Electrician, Chief
Engineer, 1st, 2nd, 3rd
Engineer,Chief
Engineering
Entertainer
Expedition Leader
Fitness Instructor
Food & Beverage Staff
Food & Bev. Manager
Gentleman Host
Gift Shop Manager
Gift Shop Staff
Group Sales Manager
Group Sales Staff
Guest Services Coord.
Head Waiter
Host/Hostess
Hotel Manager
Hotel Manager, Asst.
Hotel Staff
Housekeeper
Ice Carver
Instructor
   Bridge
   Chess
   Cards
   Dance
   Yoga
   Diving
   Golf
   Tennis
Janitorial Staff
Laundry
Lecturer

Lounge Performer
Machinist
Magician
Maintenance Engineer
Maitre d
Marketing
Masseur/Masseuse
Massage Therapist
Master
Maitre D
Mate, 1st, 2nd, 3rd
Medical Doctor
Musician, Solo
Musician, Duo
Musician, Group
Nurse, Registered
Officer, 1st, 2nd, 3rd
Officer, Chief
Ordinary Seaman
Painter
Pastry Cook
Pianist/Harpist
Photographer
Photo Manager
Plumber
Port Lecturer
Printer
Production Manager
Program Coordinator
Provision Master
Purchasing Agent
Purser
Purser, Asst.
Purser, 1st, 2nd, 3rd
Purser, Chief
Purser's Staff

3

Public Relations
Psychic
Physician
QMEDs
Radio Officer, Chief
Receptionist
Refrigeration Tech.
Restaurant & Bar Staff
Reservationist
Reservations Manager
Restaurant Manager
Restaurant Waiter
Sales Agent
Salon Manager/Staff
SCUBA Instructor
Security Officer
Server
Shore Excursion Mgr.
Shore Excursion Asst.
Slot Technician
Stage Manager
Stage Manager, Asst.
Singer
Slot Technician
Social Host
Social Hostess
Sound & Light Tech.
Sous Chef
Sports Director
Staff Captain
Steward/Stewardess
Steward, Chief
Storekeeper/Storeman
Swimming Pool Attend.
Television Technician

Upholsterer
Videographer
Vocalist
Youth Counselor
Water Sports Instructor
Waiter/Waitress
Wine Steward

2. Who are cruise lines hiring?

Cruise lines want to hire 'People-persons' - the type who love working with others. Do you have experience in hospitality, tourism, entertainment, restaurants and bars, teaching, childcare, sales or customer relations? The cruise lines are looking for you. They also need people with experience in gaming, marketing, fitness, health and beauty, healthcare, administration, and banking.

Did we mention entertainment? That's the name of the game aboard cruise ships! Your #1 priority as a cruise line employee is to provide a safe, fun and memorable vacation experience. Cruise lines hire dependable, competent people with outgoing, positive attitudes.

3. How do I get hired?
The A-B-C's of getting hired:

A. **Get to know the players** and you'll find the cruise lines most likely to hire you. Who are the most successful cruise lines? Who is adding new ships? Apply there first.

Familiarize yourself with your prospective employer's "product. Where do their ships travel?

For what programs and facilities are they best known? Most importantly - what kind of people will you find aboard their ships? The passengers are your ultimate employer, the customers you'll serve, inform and entertain.

Know the Players: Royal Caribbean International, Princess Cruises, Carnival Cruise Lines and Star Cruises/NCL are now known as the 'Big Four', with the largest fleets in the industry, these employers should be at the top of your list. There are also unique job opportunities with smaller, specialty cruise lines like Delta Queen Steamboat Co., and Special Expeditions.

The type of programs and facilities offered by each cruise line define who gets hired. Companies with state-of-the-art spas, salons and fitness centers hire more stylists, cosmetologists, massage therapists and fitness instructors. Entertainment jobs vary from line to line. Crystal Cruises and Seabourn hire lecturers, pianists, classical quartets and duos; while NCL's popular sports and theme cruises create openings for theme entertainers, lecturers and celebrities. Comedians, production dancers and Rock N Roll bands are most likely to be hired by lines such as Carnival, Princess, Royal Caribbean International, Celebrity, and Holland America Line.

A cruise line's 'primary market' or type of guest also determines job opportunities: Youth Counselors will find employment with Disney Cruise Line and Carnival Cruise Lines, which boast the largest year-round youth counselor staffs. Gentlemen Hosts will find openings with lines that cater more to the mature traveler.

B. **Choose several jobs which interest you** and compare your qualifications to the required duties and responsibilities. You many find your previous work or education can easily translate into a job that offers world-wide travel. You'll also learn what skills or certifications you need to add to your resume to get aboard. Hot Tip: Practice public speaking whenever possible, study a foreign language or get your CPR or Lifesaving Certification.

C. **Sell yourself!** Make it easy for the personnel director to hire you - target your resume and cover letter towards one specific job. Show how you can contribute to the passenger's cruise experience. Include on your resume: previous work experience, duties, responsibilities, awards, promotions and salary history. Include educational achievements, degrees and certifications, hobbies, awards and membership in organizations.

Hot Tip: Apply early and often - but don't pester personnel by phone - send follow up letters and resume updates.

4. Are there short-term, holiday and summer jobs?

Yes, the cruise industry hires year-round and seasonally. Most employees work for a period of six to nine months with one to two months off. Many departments add staff for holiday cruises and peak sailings through winter and spring.

Doctors and nurses can find year-round employment or assignments as brief as two to three months.

Peak hiring times for youth counselors? Holidays and summer - perfect for students or teachers who love to travel. Hot Tip: (from a leading executive of Carnival Cruise Lines) List your specific dates of availability (example: Dates of Availability: May 1 - Sept. 15 ,) so personnel knows how to schedule you.

> **Tami** teaches Kindergarten in Indianapolis during the school year. She travels as a youth counselor over Christmas & summer break.
> **Karina** saves her tips and salary from eight months work as a massage therapist -then backpacks across Europe for two months.
> **David**, a retired widower, now dances his way around the world as a gentleman host.

5. How's the Pay?

Cruise ship pay compares to good jobs shore - Plus you save a lot of money because most expenses are left behind. Onboard ship, your accommodations and meals are included. No more rent, grocery, electric, or gas bills! You can bank your salary and tips, or blow it all in ports

7

of call. You'll want to negotiate your pay based on your own salary history and demand for the job.

Sample current pay ranges:

Casino Manager: $2,000-3,000 per month.

Gift Shop Staff $1,000-1,500 per month

Hairstylist/Beautician: $1,000-1,300 per month

Shore Excursion Mgr. $1,800 - $3000/month

Linda, a shipboard gift shop manager, met her husband-to-be, a handsome Finnish officer, on her first assignment. Now they own homes in Finland and Florida.

Andy, a casino manager, banked his salary and opened his own business back home.

6. What other benefits are included?

Your room and board are free! No rent, utility or grocery bills. Transportation to the ship, as well as medical, dental, long-term disability, and life insurance are usual benefits. Holland America Line -Westours benefits are a good example:

Medical & Dental Coverage

401(k)

Profit Sharing

Life Insurance

AD&D and Long Term Disability

Vacation and Personal time off

Commuting subsidies

Tuition Assistance

After one year of employment, Holland America Line employees become eligible for a free cruise.

7. How much do crew members work?

You may work 72-75 hours per week. Shifts are varied and are defined by your type of work. Entertainers may perform nightly while practicing during the day. Youth counselors may have time off while the ship's in port; when parents take their children ashore. Deck and engine staff work a 12-month contract, 6 days per week,12 hours per day. Housekeepers and servers work a 4-month rotation, 7 days per week, 10 hours per day. Chefs de Partie work a 3-month rotation, 7 days per week, 12-14 hours per day.

8. Whatever shall I wear? Are there uniforms?

You'll wear a designated uniform, determined by your position. The cruise line provides the uniforms and crew members usually pay half of the cost. A monthly uniform charge may be deducted from your base pay. Replacements are provided by the cruise line. Crew members are responsible for doing their own laundry (washers and dryers, soap, starch, etc., are provided).

9. Where will I live? Will I share a room?

You'll live in designated crew cabins on board the ship. Most of the crew cabins are located on the lowest decks. There are usually two crew members per cabin and each cabin has a private bathroom.

10. How do I keep in contact with friends and family?

On most itineraries, the ship is docked 3-4 days per week, with phones available near each dock. Crew members use phone cards and cellular phones are becoming more popular. Mail is usually forwarded from the cruise line office and distributed once per cruise.

11. What should I bring?

When you're hired, you'll receive a list of suggested personal items. In general, crew members are responsible for supplying personal clothing, personal and uniform shoes, toiletries, etc. All linens are supplied. Bring all prescriptions; eyeglasses, sunscreen, swimsuits, workout clothes, a VCR, CD player, favorite music, board and card games, camera, laptop, etc.

12. Do crew members need a passport?

When you are hired you'll receive a list of passport and visa requirements.

13. How many crew members are there?

Ship's personnel range from less than 100 aboard boutique and adventure ships to more than 900 aboard the mega ships.

14. How can I spend my time off?

Go Shopping! Sightsee, sunbathe on the beach, parasail, snorkel, Scuba dive, visit new friends in exotic ports of call, explore your world! All crew members work on split shifts and have time off at various times.

Crew members usually spend time in the crew mess, on the crew sun deck or in a crew cabin. Several ships are adding more crew facilities including a pool!

15. How do I get started? What steps do I take to travel & get paid for it?

We've done the homework for you! Everything you need to get started on your job search is in this book. *How to Get a Job with a Cruise Line* is recommended by the cruise line personnel directors, executives and employees.

This is the guide recommended by Cruise Lines International Association, CLIA, the *New York Times, Conde Nast Traveler, US News & World Report, Miami Herald* and more. College career resource centers rely on the step-by-step guidelines on applications and the personal stories of employees.

Follow the practical tips from people just like you who have used this book to get their job. Begin today with *Job Application Tips from People in the Know* and *Job Descriptions from People on the Job.*

2

JOB DESCRIPTIONS FROM PEOPLE ON THE JOB

CRUISE SHIP LIFESTYLES: THE INSIDE STORY

*"You enjoy what you do, therefore it's not work.
It becomes your way of life."*

Louise Chattell-Castleman
Dancer, Assistant Cruise Director

You'll be prepared when you apply to cruise lines - you'll know the inside story - as told by cruise line employees. These true life stories tell you what to expect from the cruise ship lifestyle and how to prepare yourself for your new job. These are stories of how people like you got hired; what they do and specific, practical advice on how you should apply.

Now you can feel confident when you apply for your job. This chapter will help you save time and money on your job search. It's the next best thing to having a relative in the business. Employees are candid in their evaluation; They tell all: Travel, adventure and day to day duties; what they like most or least or worst about their jobs and practical tips to help you find your job.

13

Each job title is followed by a description of salary range and benefits; ideal qualifications; duties and responsibilities and personal interviews with employees.

What type of jobs are available? You'll find that job opportunities aboard a cruise ship are similar to those at your local shopping center, a five-star hotel or a fine resort. Your employment experience, education, skills and talents may qualify you for several positions. Here are some of the jobs cruise lines hire for:

There are many opportunities within the growing cruise industry, both aboard ship and at shoreside head-quarters. We've organized 180 jobs by department. Use these descriptions to help find the right job for you.

DEPARTMENTS
SHIPBOARD OPERATIONS
CASINO

CRUISE STAFF

ENTERTAINMENT

FOOD & BEVERAGE

DECK & ENGINE

HOTEL/PURSER

MEDICAL

SALON & SPA

SHORESIDE/CORPORATE OPERATIONS

SALES & MARKETING

PURCHASING/FINANCIAL

ADMINISTRATIVE

CRUISE LINE JOBS INCLUDE:

Able Bodied Seaman
Accountant
Activities Coordinator
Administrative Assistant
Aerobics Instructor
Air/Sea Agent
Air/Sea Manager
Audio Visual Technician
Auditor, Chief
Auditor, Asst.
Baggage Handler
Baker, 1st, 2nd, 3rd
Baker, Asst. Supervisor
Barman
Bar Manager
Bartender
Bar Waiter
Beautician
Boatswain
Boatswain, Mate
Buffet Man
Busboy
Butcher
Butcher Staff
Cabin
Steward/Stewardess
Carpenter
Cashier
Casino Manager
Casino Manager, Asst.
Casino Staff
Catering Manager
Cellar-man
Chef

Chaplain
Chef
Chef de Partier
Confectioner
Cook, 1st, 2nd, 3rd
Comedian
Computer Specialist
Controller
Cook Helper
Cosmetologist
Croupier
Cruise Director
Cruise Director, Asst.
Cruise Staff
Cruise Staff Captain
Cruise Staff Steward
Cruise Terminal Staff
DJ
Dance Instructor
Dancer
Data Manager
Dealer
Deck & Engine Staff
Dentist
Disc Jockey
District Sales Manager
Dishwasher
Electrician, Chief
Engineer, 1st, 2nd, 3rd
Engineer,Chief
Engineering
Entertainer
Expedition Leader
Fitness Instructor
Food & Beverage Staff
Food & Beverage

JOB DESCRIPTIONS FROM PEOPLE ON THE JOB

Manager
Gentleman Host
Gift Shop Manager/Staff
Group Sales
Manager/Staff
Guest Services
Coordinator
Head Waiter
Host/Hostess
Hotel Manager
Hotel Manager, Asst.
Hotel Staff
Housekeeper
Ice Carver
Instructor
    Bridge
    Chess
    Cards
    Dance
    Yoga
    Diving
    Golf
    Tennis
Janitorial Staff
Laundry
Lecturer
Lounge Performer
Machinist
Magician
Maintenance Engineer
Maitre d
Marketing
Masseur/Masseuse
Massage Therapist
Master

Maitre D
Mate, 1st, 2nd, 3rd
Medical Doctor
Musician, Solo
Musician, Duo
Musician, Group
Nurse, Registered
Officer, 1st, 2nd, 3rd
Officer, Chief
Ordinary Seaman
Painter
Pastry Cook
Pianist/Organist/Harpist
Photographer
Photo Manager
Plumber
Port Lecturer
Printer
Production Manager
Program Coordinator
Provision Master
Purchasing Agent
Purser
Purser, Asst.
Purser, 1st, 2nd, 3rd
Purser, Chief
Purser's Staff
Public Relations
Psychic
Physician
QMEDs
Radio Officer, Chief
Receptionist
Refrigeration Technician,
Chief

16

Restaurant & Bar Staff
Reservationist
Reservations
Manager/Staff
Restaurant Manager
Restaurant Waiter
Sales Agent
Salon Manager/Staff
SCUBA Instructor
Security Officer
Server
Shore Excursions
Manager
Shore Excursion
Manager, Asst.
Slot Technician
Stage Manager
Stage Manager, Asst.
Singer
Slot Technician
Social Host
Social Hostess
Sound & Light Technician
Sous Chef
Sports Director
Staff Captain
Steward/Stewardess
Steward, Chief
Store Keeper/Storeman
Swimming Pool/Deck
Attendant
Television Technician
Upholsterer
Videographer
Vocalist
Youth Counselor

Water Sports Instructor
Waiter/Waitress
Wine Steward

Job descriptions and interviews with employees are organized by department.

CASINO

The Jet-Set parties here. Enter a world of tuxedos and sequined gowns, gold and diamonds. High stakes create an intoxicating atmosphere few can resist. If you have worked in a casino or resort, try your luck aboard a cruise ship. Many cruise ships have large, fantastic casinos or are expanding their current gaming facilities.

Shipboard casinos usually employ a few people to do the job of many. The more gaming skills you have to offer, the more likely you'll get the job.

Casino staff should have experience at a major gaming location such as Atlantic City, Curacao, Monte Carlo, Nassau, Tahoe, Vegas, etc. **17**

LARRY KAVANAGH
Director of Casino Operations

*"When I said good-bye to my friends in Lake Tahoe,
I could tell they were envious of my new job."*

Larry Kavanagh has been in the casino business for more than fifteen years and worked aboard the Princess fleet for six years. "I was originally hired by Princess as a dealer," says Larry. "I had worked the casinos in Lake Tahoe for six years and I was ready for something new. Princess Cruises ran an advertisement in my local newspaper for casino positions. I sent Princess my qualifications and they interviewed me in Tahoe. I was a little nervous about the interview; I felt confident about my casino skills; but I'd never worked aboard a ship before.

"The interview went very well - they wanted me to start in one week! When I said good-bye to my friends in Lake Tahoe, I could tell they were envious of my new job. I loved it from the start. It's a good life. I traveled the Mexican coast, mostly in the winter, and Alaska in the summer; my favorite port of call is Vancouver. It was a tremendous experience. You have to be a people person, and be able to get along with everybody because it's such close quarters. It's a tradeoff. You trade some privacy and space for a chance to travel the world - and you do see the world!

"Normally you're on the ship for a year and then if you want to transfer to another ship, it's up to you. People move around so they can see different parts of the world. I found that it wasn't difficult to live aboard ship and still take care of business at home. I had a home and a business in Acapulco. You're not isolated; the world is getting smaller everyday. It's easy to keep in contact with your friends and family. Another benefit is that you can really put some money away. You also get a minimum of two months off a year, paid. Our contract is for five months, so you work five months, take a month off.

"For your first couple of years, you'll like the travel best. Anything beyond a year and a half and it's the savings - the money you make. You've got to be ready to do much more than just your own job. The casino operations are small and understaffed. You'll be working with a very grass roots organization. There's a lot of teamwork. That's the essential thing that brings it all together."

Casino Manager

Oversees entire operations of the casino; accounting, all casino-related revenue activities, supervises staff.
Three to five years casino managerial experience required. Salary Range: $2,000-3,000 per month with percentage of revenues. Length of contract 6-9 months on board, vacation: 4-8 weeks. Benefits: Room & Board, Medical Insurance, Single cabin facilities, Dining with passengers & officers.

Assistant Casino Manager

Oversees operations of the casino. Supervises staff and accounting activities. One to two years casino experience required. Salary Range: $1,600-2,000 per month plus tips. Length of contract: 9-12 months on board, vacation: 4-8 weeks. Benefits: Room & Board, Medical Insurance, Single or shared cabin facilities, Dining with officers.

Croupier

Conducts gambling activities. 1-2 years casino experience or casino school graduate certificate required. Salary Range: $1,200-1,800 per month plus tips. 9-12 months on board, 4-8 weeks off, Benefits: Room & Board, Medical Insurance, Single or shared cabin.

Slot Technician

Repairs and maintains all casino devices and machines.Comprehensive mechanical and electrical experience and/or education required. Slot technicians must have three to five years experience on different machines.Salary Range: $2,000-2,500 per month Length of contract: 9-12 months on board, vacation: 4-8 weeks. Benefits: Room & Board, Medical Insurance, Single or shared cabin facilities, Dining with officers.

Cashier

Customer service and accounting of revenue. Entry-level. Accounting experience preferred. Salary Range: $1,000-1,200 per month plus some tips from croupiers. Length of contract: 9-12 months on board, vacation: 4-8 weeks. Benefits: Room & Board, Medical Insurance, Single or shared cabin facilities, Dining with officers.

Dealer

Dealers need three years experience with two games. Casino staff should have experience at a major gaming location. $1,000-1,200 per month plus some tips from croupiers. Length of contract: 9-12 months on board, vacation: 4-8 weeks.

CRUISE STAFF

The cruise staff are the cheerleaders of the 'cruise experience,' a winning combination of manager, entertainer; the cruise director and his staff develop and coordinate passenger activities.

As the liaison between passengers and crew, the best cruise director can speak well in public, delegate responsibilities and work well with officers, crew and passengers. An entertainment and public relations background is preferred along with strong organizational, coordination and creative abilities.

"You won't be Julie on the LoveBoat, standing around with a clipboard," says Jeff Charron, former personnel director of the Delta Queen Steamboat Company.

"You might do that for four hours a day and then go out and sing a four hour show."

The cruise staff consists of entertainers, shore excursion managers, hosts and hostesses, water sports directors and youth counselors. Cruise staff members assists the cruise director and assistant cruise director with passenger activities and entertainment.

"The cruise director position is something you work up to," says Mary Ann, in marine personnel.

"We don't hire new people on as cruise director even if they have loads of experience. You have to start off as cruise staff, because you need to get a feel for the cruise line. You start as an assistant, then promote to shore excursion manager, first assistant, and next perhaps cruise director. It's a division - head position. Ninety-nine times out of one hundred you have to be promoted from within the ranks."

LOUISE CHATTELL-CASTLEMAN
Dancer, Assistant Cruise Director

"Cruising is contagious...When I returned home from the ships, I no longer felt satisfied with 9 to 5... I wanted more!"

Louise is one remarkable young woman. Focused and multi-talented, she traveled to more than 100 countries during her eight years as a dancer and cruise director.

"I started dancing when I was two years old. At age sixteen, I finished school and left home. I moved to London, where I attended a dancing college for three years. I had to grow up very quickly, by leaving home so soon. I wanted to get out, I wanted to see the world.

"You dance all your life with the goal of attending a superior dance college. The standards for acceptance are high and the competition is intense. Each annual class is made of 60-70 people that are chosen from auditions held each Thursday, every week of the year - the pressure - you're dancing every day, all day. I was doing ten ballet classes a week, jazz, tap, drama, voice. You learn the business is tough, very competitive.

"At age eighteen, I did not feel I had the hard shell you need to compete and succeed in entertainment. But I promoted myself and worked hard to gain an equity card. To get good work you need to be an equity member. I left college at age eighteen and started traveling the world. My first job was in an ice show aerial act. There I was, forty feet in the air, over an ice rink and afraid of heights. But I got over the fear and I earned my equity card.

"I used to watch the *Loveboat*, and I decided I wanted to travel aboard a cruise ship. Of course, these

22

were all dreams and you never actually think that you're going to do it. You never think you will achieve your dreams, that they'll always be dreams. But they don't have to stay dreams. Not only did I land my dream job, I worked aboard ships for eight years. People at home think I'm lucky, but it's not luck, It's promoting your self, and having the confidence to say 'I've got to try it!'

"I answered an advertisement in the publication *Stage* for dancers aboard ship. It was a great opportunity to travel to the United States and get paid for it. At my first cruise ship audition, I was chosen to be one of three dancers. At eighteen years old, all I wanted to do was travel, and there I was in Jamaica and Grand Cayman!

"Cruising is contagious. As soon as you've traveled with one ship, it's 'What's next?!' It's a very easy life and a very pleasing life. After my first job; I returned home and then worked in Italy; but it didn't offer the travel or the prestige of being a ship's entertainer.

I auditioned with Royal Caribbean through Miller Reich, a concessionaire that auditions in London twice a year for dancers. When I went for that audition, there was four hundred dancers and only ten would be hired. Most auditions are like cattle markets and employers are often interested in a particular 'look' or persona. You may be the best dancer, but not have the hair color or height they're looking for. My previous experience helped me win the job. I was one of ten dancers chosen from four hundred candidates."

Louise has traveled with several cruise lines, promoting from dancer to line captain and lead choreographer to assistant cruise director.

"Aboard Royal Caribbean Cruise Line's *Sun Viking* I performed both as a dancer and as cruise staff. I've also worked for a Greek cruise line in the Mediterranean and

I helped bring out Carnival's *Fantasy* on her inaugural voyage. I worked with Carnival Cruise Lines for five years.

"People who work aboard ships are either running away from something or looking for something. I was doing a little bit of both. I was looking for my niche in life- what I could become. When I would return home from traveling, I no longer felt satisfied with the 9 to 5, lifestyle; looking forward to one week's vacation in Spain. I wanted more.

"Cruising is like an intermission in life - it may not be what you're going to do for the rest of your life. But it's easy to get hooked on cruising. It's an easy life. You have no responsibilities, you have no car, no house to worry about. You work all day, you have your cabin cleaned for you, your meals prepared. There's other stresses, it's not all a bed of roses.

"You are 'on stage' 24 hours. I didn't find it that difficult, because that's my personality - happy. If I felt down, I could get away, you do have your privacy. If you are a person who requires a lot of time all alone, cruising's not for you. It can be a long day. If you're just dancing, you'll be performing at night and rehearsing in the day. If you're also on cruise staff, your duties may start early morning with debarking for tours; pool games at 2 p.m.; and if you're not doing shows that evening you may be leading bingo or masquerade. It's certainly not 9 to 5.

"You enjoy what you do - therefore it's not work. It becomes your way of life. You've got to enjoy it. I love it. It's a challenge, you've got passengers coming on for vacation, not knowing what to expect. I've had passengers who just want to complain, and that's a challenge, I'll want to turn it around so at the end of the day, they thank me for a wonderful time.

"It's personally gratifying. When you're up there on stage and the audience applauds, it's a rush!"

Louise offers these tips for a bon voyage:

Friends: "Aboard ship, you're a family. You're each there to make the passenger happy. There may be people aboard who you wouldn't choose as friends on land. Just as in any corporate office. Get along with everybody, and you'll have friends to go out with while you're in port."

Romance: "When you meet someone aboard ships, the dating process accelerates. It's so romantic, no everyday hassles of bills and money. It's a fairy tale romance. It can be very glamorous. But you must be careful in becoming involved. You'll be spending a lot of time with your shipmates."

Favorite Port: "I like some ports for beaches, others for culture. My favorite -Grenada - the island of spice. Stepping off the ship, the scent of cinnamon and cloves would welcome me. It was so beautiful and natural."

And the best part of cruising the world and getting paid for it?

"I learned so much, not only about other people, but about myself. Because you have a lot of time to understand your own goals, morals and expectations. I learned more in the cruise industry, than I could ever learn through college. You travel and meet different cultures. Aboard ship, you may be working with as many as 32 different nationalities. There's been wars going on between the countries of my shipmates - but we all worked together. I think politicians ought to come aboard and see how real cooperation works!"

JOYCE GLEESON
Assistant Cruise Director

*"Don't be afraid of learning,
step right into a new job."*

In her crisp white cruise staff uniform and white heels, Joyce Gleeson is a woman in charge. Her gold necklaces and emerald rings tell of travels around the world, and the way she gives exclusive attention to each passenger tells of her sincere concern. Joyce Gleeson is excited about her job and it shows.

Joyce started her travel career in San Diego, California, as a travel agent.

"I met some people from Greece who asked me to travel to Greece and work. I wanted to learn their culture, and try to learn the language, so I moved to Athens, and worked in a travel agency."

"It wasn't challenging enough," says Joyce

"That's when I decided to get into cruising."

Joyce went to one of the cruise line companies in Piraeus, Greece; home to all the major Greek shipping lines; completed an application and told them what she could do.

"I was a little nervous when I applied. I was fortunate that an employee had just left the ship, so I was needed right away. I walked in on a Thursday and was on a ship that Saturday. That took guts!," she laughs.

"Being a travel agent helped me understand what people are looking for in their vacation. Knowing what the passengers expect has helped me do a better job. Good timing is the key in this business - and who you know. You've got to have the right name or someone who knows somebody. You'll find that a lot of ship personnel

26

know personnel in other companies. I worked with one chief purser eight years ago on a different line, and here we are together eight years later. People who work together on ships take care of each other."

Joyce assists the cruise director in creating the activities and atmosphere on the ship.

"If the cruise director is an energetic person it is contagious. The assistant will be energetic and get people involved," she says.

She is the liaison between the cruise director and the crew. She keeps things running; makes sure the staff is on schedule and activities are held on time.

"In other words, I can't sleep in. I have to be there. I oversee whatever the cruise director schedules. If you work closely with a cruise director you will intuitively know what he wants. You get it done and then you report. Staff and passengers come to you for help and advice, where and how to do something, and it's up to you to have the answers and to see it through.

"You'll need a strong personality, but not overbearing. You must be able to survive in small quarters and get along well with people. Be energetic and always willing to learn, because it's a job where the type of passengers change faster than the seasons change.

You must be a very flexible and free spirited person," says Joyce. "I could set the schedule for the entire staff and something will happen at the last minute; someone higher up will call and say 'I need this,' and I have to rearrange the schedule to fit the new request.

"You need to be sure of yourself and confident that you can do the job well. Don't be afraid of learning, step right into a new job."

The Assistant Cruise Director is also responsible for getting passengers involved. Joyce advises cruise staffers to be direct, because you may be working with over a thousand people.

"Involve passengers in a way they enjoy. You have to know which ones want to be part of the show. There are those who want to stay in the background and watch and you can really make them angry by bringing them into the spotlight."

"It sounds corny, but I love the people. One day I tried to figure out how many passengers I'd met within eight months. Almost 30,000 people. We've had movie stars and celebrities and we keep in touch. You meet a variety of people, and you begin to learn personalities, cultures and nationalities. This just makes your character better because you can begin to relate to these people. You know that an Italian does this and a Greek does that and you can get along better. I really like that.

"You learn languages too. Before, I couldn't speak a word of Italian. Now I speak conversational Italian, and also conversational Greek. I can speak to passengers in their own language and let them know that I care. I'm not just somebody doing a job."

Joyce advises the newcomer to:

"Get some kind of training, don't just walk in off the street. Cruise lines want people with certificates showing professional training. If you have skills, experience or special education, the cruise line will interview you first. Fluency in languages in addition to English is valuable. It helps that I speak English, conversational Greek and conversational Italian. If you can speak English, French and Spanish, that's needed on all ships.

"I love my job. And all the staff members here enjoy their jobs. You have to love this business. If you don't, get out. If you really think that you can't stay on a moving hotel, be confined to a small cabin and deal with the constant stress of always having to be on the go, not phony but sincerely happy, then it's not worth getting into."

28

PAM JAYE
Cruise Staff

*"It's important that when you wake up
you're excited about
what you're going to be doing that day."*

Welcoming aboard new passengers, Pam Jaye exudes confidence. Her excellent posture, and warm smile project the professionalism cruise lines desire. Pam chose to change jobs when she tired of her career in the business world.

"I'm a people person, I love to work with people. Office jobs just are not for me. I tried that for ten years and it didn't work. I wasn't happy. I was not fulfilled. It's important that when you wake up that you are excited about what you're going to be doing that day. I don't ever want to wake up and say, "Oh my gosh, not another day, I hate this!," says Pam.

"My most recent position in the business world was executive director for a health aids corporation. Then I rediscovered my love for dancing. I was offered an opportunity to intern and teach at a dance school. It was at a time in my life when I could do it, so I trained and became a dance staff specialist at Arthur Murray in Orlando.

"I decided I wanted to get involved with the travel industry, so I looked for alternatives that would allow me to dance and travel. Cruising was one of the options. I sent Royal Caribbean my resume and within three days, they contacted me. They were interested in my entertainment and dance background."

Pam drove from Orlando to Miami, made an appointment and presented herself at the personnel office.

"I am a little more aggressive than the average person. I just showed up and said, 'Here I am, I want the job!' It happened very quickly. The whole secret is being in the right place at the right time when they need you. There's really no way to know when you're applying if there is a position available. The best thing to do is every month is to send them a resume; and follow up every month. Be professional! Cruise lines only look at the cream of the crop; the top of the line. Understand that your resume is your main contact with them, you're often hired without ever meeting your employer.

"The dancing is really only a very small part of it. The other responsibilities far outweigh the entertainment; although you are hired based on your entertainment value. So if you're writing your resume, highlight your entertainment talents. Your talent is what they're looking for. Education is also important. They look for people that have an education, because that's a sign of dedication and commitment. And they want you to be able to speak intelligently to passengers."

Cruise lines are also looking for confidence. Pam's secret is to find one thing that you're good at and use this to build your self-confidence.

"If you can find what your little niche is and perfect that; it will make you more self-confident," says Pam.

TESS BLAKE
Hostess/Cruise Staff

"You make a lot of good friends. I know people from all over the world!"

Tess Blake's navy skirt swirls as she turns to greet passengers starting their seven- night cruise.

"Welcome aboard!," says Tess with a smile.

"May I see your embarkation card? Thank you! Now, if you'll step to your right for a photo by Amy, our photographer."

As a hostess, Tess will welcome aboard more than 600 passengers per cruise, check embarkation cards and direct each passenger to their cabin, all within the first few hours of a cruise. Tess is a graduate of a cruise training institute in Florida. She got her job after graduating from the school's course on cruise staff.

"Embarkation is just one of my duties," says Tess. "I'm responsible for the Captain's cocktail parties; the port talk, a review of daily activities and I arrange shore excursions and parties for anniversaries, birthdays and reunions. I also write the ship's *Daily Gazette* - the passenger's activity guide. I do everything that a cruise director does, and soon I hope to be promoted so that when the cruise director is on vacation, I can jump right in."

Tess enjoys being the ship's hostess. She shares her cabin with Cathy the cruise director, Amy the photographer, and a young woman from the gift shop.

"You make a lot of good friends. I know people from all over the world! Many people apply at the right place and the right time. They come on as passengers and make the right contacts.

"I wouldn't have gotten this job unless I went to school. Especially if you don't have any experience. When you apply, I suggest you go directly to a cruise line office. If you send a resume, you're on this desk with twenty other resumes. You have to be able to offer the cruise line experience or education."

See *Travel and Tourism Training Programs*.

JEFF ADAMS
Cruise Staff

"I wondered how I would adapt to this new lifestyle - it was very different from work at the radio station. But I fit right in."

"Many of the promotional techniques and people skills I learned as a radio announcer helped me to be successful in cruising. When you go aboard ship, take your best people skills with you; your sense of humor, a good laugh and a ready smile. I've had more fun meeting people from all over the world, and now I'm traveling like I always wanted to.

"When I first started, I wondered how I would adapt to this new lifestyle - it was very different from work at the station. But I fit right in, and every day is different, never boring. I found my promotional and public relations experience really came in handy. Use the talents God gave you and have a blast."

MICHAEL JAMES JONES
Assistant Cruise Director

"It's good experience, you'll learn excellent management skills."

In a cool corner of the Britanis Fantasy Lounge, Michael James Jones burns with energy and excitement. Lean and wiry, wearing a royal blue blazer and sharp red tie, Michael takes advantage of a short break in his non-stop day. The Britanis Five band warms up for their embarkation show. Above the shrieks of clarinets, Michael speaks with passion of his life aboard ship.

"As assistant cruise director, I do everything!" says Michael. "I help the cruise director coordinate most of the ship's activities. The assistant cruise director is the front man for the cruise staff. I oversee every activity aboard ship. I make sure all staff is on time; that everyone wears proper name tags and attire and follows all ship's rules. As an assistant, I'm also in charge of the cruise staff supplies inventory. It's a big job!," says Michael.

"It takes a special type of person to be an assistant cruise director. You must be super flexible to work with a lot of different egos; officers, entertainers and room stewards alike. You must be friendly and have a nice on-stage persona.

"I've worked in the travel business with Chandris, Norwegian Cruise Line and TWA," Mike says. I was in charge of public relations and singles' programs aboard the Norwegian Cruise Line fleet. I've been an in-flight service manager for TWA and I've even earned a living as a stand-up comedian. My career goal is to become a cruise director."

Michael got his start in cruising through his family.

"My mother is in sales and marketing with NCL. Getting into the cruise industry often depends on who you know. And it never hurts to have a relative in the business. Just as with any success story there's a lot of chance, a lot of luck involved. I've been very lucky with the cruise lines I've worked with. The best part of my job is the travel. I like to travel and I like the stage work. Whenever I get a chance to slide in some of my comedy, I do."

"The most difficult part of the job can be the long hours. As an assistant cruise director I probably put in the most hours of anybody on this ship. A sixteen to seventeen hour day is not uncommon. Expect it. I've worked some ships where it is understood you will work for three months at a time, seventeen to eighteen hours a day. If you don't like it the common saying is "Sign-Off and Get Off."

"It's a nice way to cruise for free; bring the family on board for nothing. It's good experience and you'll learn excellent management skills.

"Once on board, however, eyes are everywhere," warns Michael.

"There's always somebody watching. You might be partying one night and had a few too many cocktails. Watch what you say, keep your nose clean and try to save what money you can. You also have to pace your partying. You can burn out real fast. Especially if you have nice ports of call."

Water Sports Instructor

Water sports instructors conduct daily dive and snorkeling programs, are responsible for the safety of passengers and the maintainance of diving equipment, Zodiac and dive boats. Dual dive instructor certification is preferred with lifesaving, CPR and First Aid certification. Cruise lines desire public relations and teaching experience plus Instructor-level experience with a dive operation or resort. Certification is required: National Association of Underwater Instructors NAUI, Professional Association of Diving Instructors PADI, or Scuba Schools International SSI offer instructor training.

Tip: Target your resume for cruise lines with private out-islands or shipboard retractable water sports platforms See *Cruise Line Profiles, International Directory of Concessionaires*

BRUCE GLOBERMAN
Water Sports Director/Divemaster

*"You need to prepare in two areas:
technical training and people skills"*
"The people I hire are experienced at the instructor level. Instruction experience is critical. It's best if you are dually- certified through two of the three largest agencies; PADI, NAUI and SSI.

"Prepare yourself in two areas: first and most important is your time in the water. Your confidence and comfort level shows right away. Secondly, I'm interested in your personal outlook or the amount of time that you've spent working in a social environment. As a diver, you're dealing with people constantly. It's a good idea to get involved in a resort diving operation."

Youth Counselor

The 'youthing of cruising' has created a demand for experienced youth counselors. The increase in families sailing with children has made youth programs a standard in the industry. Most ship's offer children's programs and facilities. Most youth counselors are hired for holiday and summer cruises, however several cruise lines hire year-round. See *Cruise Line Profiles* and *Cruise Guide for Children*.

Youth Counselors coordinate youth and children's activities. Activity programs cater to several age groups and include games; contests; scavenger hunts and parties; dances; and sports and fitness instruction. Cruise lines prefer supervisory experience; either as a counselor or instructor; and experience in education, fitness or psychology. Water safety certification is helpful.

35

RICK REINDERS
Youth Activities Staff

"I think my friends at the city recreation department
are probably jealous,
but what are they doing with their lives?"

Up and down zips the white yo-yo with the blue Royal Caribbean logo.

"This is my fourth one this week,' says Rick.

"On the previous cruise, I gave away three yo-yos. I'm studying at the University of Wisconsin for my degree in secondary education. I applied to Royal Caribbean with my resume three months ago and then talked to personnel on the phone.

"They were pleased with my application but they did not have a position open at that time. I took a job as a playground supervisor for the city parks and recreation and was set for the summer, when the cruise line called. They told me I was hired and gave me three days to quit my job. Wow! It was a big surprise.

"At first, it was a hard decision to make. I had just been promoted with the city recreation job. But then, after I thought about it for a whole 10 minutes, I realized that there wasn't a decision to make. I was going! My brother worked with RCI, so he helped me get my foot in the door. RCI recognized my last name, but what got me the job was the experience I have.

"Those long summers with the city parks and recreation department really paid off. I'm on contract with the cruise line for the summer, but I get to leave a little early because I need to return to school. I have one year until I graduate.

"Our hours vary depending on the ship's itinerary. The days we're at sea we work with the kids for twelve hours. Two of the four days in port the kids go sightseeing with their parents. The other days we have them for three or four hours during the day, and every night, from about eight-thirty to ten. You've got to be patient for my job. You've got to learn how to control your temper because sometimes you just want to throw them over the side of the ship.

"Every counselor has to be healthy, energetic, always smiling and ready to experience new things - I've never seen anything like what I'm seeing here. Every week I can do something new; snorkeling, scuba diving. You get a chance to do your thing. That's what surprised me. When we arrive in port, the kids go with their parents and we've got the day to ourselves. I've made some good friends on board. Four of us counselors do things together, because we have the same free time. Last week, a group of us went parasailing.

"When we're not doaling directly with the kids, we spend a lot of time preparing activities and we help out with Bingo. One thing I've noticed; I have these little gaps of time; not enough time to take a nap or workout. I used to think 'Well, I've got 45 minutes I'll go put some gas in my car.' I don't have to bother with that now.

"The pay is good when you consider you get your room and board for free. You get a paycheck and you put it in your pocket or send it home or to a bank. And all you have to worry about is tipping your room steward and waiter. And from what I hear, since it is a seasonal program, I may be hired again for Christmas, and I've got a month off from school so why not?

"My friends at the city recreation department were upset with me for leaving, and I sat them down and said, "Guys this is the greatest opportunity I've ever had." They understood, I think. I'm only gone a couple months and when I get back I'll see them all at school. I think they're probably jealous, but what are they doing with their lives?"

LYNDA SMITH
Youth Counselor

*"I did a lot of promotions for radio,
and after seventeen years, I had seen it all and
I was looking for a change."*

Petite and athletic; with an intense energy in her small frame; Lynda is easy to talk with. A natural with children, Lynda's previous jobs include radio broadcasting, marketing and promotions. She has also written several fiction books. "I did a lot of promotions for radio, and after seventeen years I had seen it all and I was looking for a change. In radio, a woman can often only promote so far.

"The best part of this job..." says Lynda, her voice softening, " ... is seeing a little child who is shy and reserved and they don't want to do anything. I get them involved by saying 'you come on and help me', or 'you come and keep score for the game or hand out the prizes!' The next thing - they're out running around with all the other kids having a good time.

"Respect from a child makes it all worthwhile. At the end of the cruise, all the kids know your name and they want to hug you. To me, children are the most honest things in the world. You know when a kid doesn't like you, but you also know when they do like you. As a youth hostess with Celebrity, I entertain the kids, supervise activities, and lay out a daily schedule with between 8-10 activities daily. The roughest day is Thursday, because it's a full day at sea. You're working, a full, long day.

"You have to have a great deal of patience because you're dealing with a wide array of people. You have to be able to run in several directions at one time, and deal politely with all kinds of people. It takes a lot of psychology to be able to relate with children, parents and staff.

"Start preparing in high school. Start dealing with people and polish your talent for singing or dancing or telling stories. Get involved with the public. I recommend that you consider a cruise employment school. Beware of those that charge a lot of money. If you're seriously thinking of getting into the industry I suggest you talk to the people who are doing the job. I chose to work with Ship's Services International. They told me the good and bad, so I was prepared.

"The competition for jobs is really rough. It is strong because everybody has this picture of the *Love Boat*. Just be prepared that this is not the *Love Boat* and it's a very cutthroat industry. You have to be tough-skinned a lot of the time, because there are going to be people on the ship who like you, and also some who won't. You have to take it with a grain of salt and just let it roll off you." See *International Directory of Concessionaires; Travel and Tourism Training Programs*.

ENTERTAINMENT STAFF

Now you can take your show on the road - and maybe around the world! The cruise experience on board revolves around entertainment. Are you a comedian, dancer, duo, soloist, vocalist, magician, juggler, musician or psychic? Be prepared to share the duties of the cruise staff. Expect to perform daily plus participate in a variety of passenger activities such as embarkation, deck games, contests and parties.

Qualifications: Extensive professional experience in your art. Previous cruise ship experience is preferred. There is always a need for seasonal and theme entertainers; Themes include Country Music, 50's Nostalgia, Big Band and Swing, Jazz, Health and Fitness, Mardi Gras and Ocktoberfest. Winter, spring and summer are peak hiring seasons.

Auditions may be held, but your first contact is usually via your resume and a brief two to three minute demonstration tape, either audio or VHS video. In your demonstration tape state your name, talent, height, weight etc. ('slate'). Use this demonstration to emphasize your people skills as well as your art. Show highlights of you as a performer.

Your demonstration tape need not be expensively produced. Make it professional and easy to view/listen to. Submit your resume with a headshot and or full body photograph showing you as an entertainer to the Entertainment Director/Coordinator or entertainment concessionaire. See *Cruise Line Profiles.*

MICHAEL ANDREW
Cruise Ship Fly-In Entertainer
*"Whenever you have a goal, set objectives
and figure out strategies to achieve it."*

How did Michael Andrew get started in entertainment? He earned a degree in theatre with a minor in promotions from the University of Wisconsin.

"I kept denying that I should be in show business. My major was undeclared. I'm a very practical person with a strong business sense. I felt a theatre major would be too frivolous.

"However, once I began performing as the lead in musicals, I chose theatre as a major and minored in a combination of disciplines; consumer psychology, marketing, advertising and graphic design. I wanted to know how to promote myself."

"I was fortunate to have Wil Denson as my college advisor. I wasn't sure where to go from college. Wil said, 'Why don't you get on a cruise ship?' With my promotions and advertising experience, I prepared a promotional package with a ten minute audio tape. This demonstration tape showcased my singing accompanied by a pianist. I sent my promotion to all the cruise lines."

"Carnival Cruise Lines hired me with my "Sinatra" singing act. My first contract was for a month as a ship board 'in-one' entertainer. There are two types of shipboard entertainers; the headliner or 'in-one' act is an entertainer with a self-contained act; their own show. You could be a comedian, juggler etc. The production entertainer will be a dancer or production singer in an existing show. These are the two slots for shipboard entertainers. Many people come aboard as a production entertainer."

"I learned to customize my performance for Carnival's audience, the baby-boomers just were not digging the Sinatra. I expanded my act to include humor and singing and began to get standing ovations. Carnival's audiences may be as large as 1,200 people - it's the ideal 'television audience' - you perform for every income level, age range, families, seniors, people from Idaho, people from New York City."

"I've chosen Orlando as my base of operations and one venture I'm involved with is Michael Andrew Orchestras. The orchestra caters to the corporate convention market with sophisticated entertainment; big band, swing, jazz, and humor. We've built up a good

41

following, and perform in several configurations with a six or ten - piece band or a twenty - piece orchestra appropriate for Walt Disney World and other venues.

"As my business became established, I contacted Carnival and promoted myself as a fly-in entertainer. I enjoy my relationship with Carnival. The cruise line flies me to whatever port the ship is in; I perform the next night and fly back to my business from the next port."

Focus, and everything you do will build toward making your dream happen," says Michael, and his focus continues to pay off in a successful artistic career.

Always 'pushing the envelope,' Michael continues to work with the Carnival family of ships and develop his own shoreside productions. Michael produced and starred in the popular musical *Mickey Swingerhead and the Earthgirls*, for which he wrote the script and lyrics as well as composed and arranged the musical scores. Mike has played the Rainbow Room in Rockefeller Center, New York and Disney World's Atlantic Dance Room on the Boardwalk. His original compositions are available on CD and cassette. Michael Andrew: *Overnight Success*, ©1993, and *A Little Out of Date*. ©1996 M.A. Records, 503 Westminster Street, Orlando, FL 32803. Visit Mike at www.swingerhead.com.

ROGER LAWSON
Entertainer

*"This is not a job for someone
who treasures their privacy, as I do.
But the money can be worth it."*

Roger Lawson took his show on the high seas. A vocalist, dancer and actor, he has sung with Rock and cabaret acts; worked as an artistic director for a New York City theatre company and has performed On and Off-Broadway.

"On the cruise, we perform some of my own music from my club act and much of the ship's material. When I started, there were just three entertainers aboard; two men and one woman. We had to work as a team to carry the show. I shared a cabin with the other male vocalist.

"We had been working on the ship for less than a month and were in port in Miami, preparing for the next cruise. I was just getting ready to take a shower, when I heard shouts and someone pounding on my cabin door. "Miami Police! Open up!" Before I could dress, my roommate was busted for possession of marijuana. He had taken drugs off the boat in Miami and the police caught him. All of his things were off the ship within an hour. Cruise lines do not tolerate drug use.

"For several months I was the only male performer. I had to carry the shows. We performed ten shows a week, with two nights off. In-between shows we helped out with other activities such as games and contests. On our night off we would sit around and talk, or crowd into my friend Sandy's cabin and watch videos. Sometimes those nights off could get pretty boring.

"My advice is to bring some kind of hobby with you.

43

Involve yourself in some kind of project. Otherwise you're bound to get into trouble. Sports, artwork, reading; anything, just bring along something to do. You are basically on call twelve hours a day and the work can sometimes be monotonous and confining, but there are gorgeous days and all you can eat. The passengers can be very nice and quite complimentary.

"The toughest thing for me was getting into the Port of Miami and not having enough time to really relax. You only get a few hours off before the ship sails again. If you're late to the ship you are fined, they take it off your pay. So be on time or you might literally miss the boat!

"Know the rules! There are extra duties and curfews, as well as crew restrictions. On some ships there are fines for various infractions of the rules. If you are fined, your misdeed is posted on a public bulletin board. It becomes the scuttlebutt of the day.

"This is not a job for someone who treasures their privacy, as I do. But the money can be worth it, since expenses are minimal. I advise you to bank your money. One singer had to stay on the ship for another contract because he had spent all his money on video and audio equipment.

"I was lucky. I've already had the experience of making a lot of money on tours and spending it all. I've learned to put my money in the bank, to save. I recommend that you watch your money. Always maintain your self-esteem, your sense of humor and an open mind!"

SHORE EXCURSION STAFF

"Sell, Sell and Sell some more... send every single guest ashore." The shore excursion staff advises guests on ports of call and sells shore excursions. You'll need to have all the answers - from the best place to buy emeralds to where to ride a moped. Customer relations, computer skills and sales experience is helpful.

NYRON PETERS
Assistant Shore Excursion Manager

"I am one of the happiest people in the world because I have the job of my dreams.

"I believe there is no better education than traveling! I have sailed Alaska, Europe, Hawaii, the Mexican Riviera, the East and West Coast, and now South America."

Nyron Peters' experience as a percussionist and band leader in his native Trinidad gave him the perfect skills for work as an assistant shore excursion manager: diplomacy, sensitivity towards his 'audience,' attention to detail and excellent managerial skills.

He began his cruise line career dockside in Port of Spain, Trinidad; playing for arriving passengers. In 1994, he joined Princess Cruises and played in a band for two years before taking a gig with Holland America Line. He joined the *Noordam's* cruise staff in 1997 and now sails in South America as an assistant shore excursion manager. (Source: *FCCA Newsletter*, Winter 2000)

EXPEDITION LEADER

The Expedition Leader is the liaison between the passengers, the ship's crew and the natural history staff.

Expedition leaders guide passenger shore excursions, lead discussion on local wildlife, culture and history and maintain friendly relations with local peoples. You may also coordinate excursions and activities.

45

DENNIS & SABINA MENSE
Expedition Leaders

For five months of the year, Dennis and Sabina Mense leave their scientific jobs to become lecturers and expedition leaders for Society Expedition Cruises. Dennis and Sabina work several months a year as lecturers and as an expedition leading team onboard cruise ships.

The couple travels to the Arctic, Amazon, Antarctica, Alaska and the South Pacific. A graduate of the University of Victoria, British Columbia, Sabina worked as a Marine Biology research technician and then founded Midsummer Day Enterprises, a marine education center.

Dennis graduated from the University of Hawaii to study coral reefs in Micronesia, Marshall Islands. His studies brought him to a Canadian Fisheries and Oceans field camp, and a research position at the University of British Columbia. Dennis and Sabina met on Vancouver Island, and married four months later. When they aren't cruising, they teach novice marine biologists about the marine environment at the Midsummer's Day center. They enjoy teaching and leading passengers on scientific expeditions while seeing the world. What could be better than traveling the world for free?

MIKE MESSICK
Expedition Leader

At age twenty-seven, Michael had visited more than 125 countries.

Michael has been traveling as long as he can remember. His family's international trading business caused him to move from Minnesota to Texas, California, and eventually Geneva, Switzerland. Mike had his first experience with cruises at age fourteen, on a family vacation aboard the *Lindblad Explorer*.

"I told the ship's dive master that I wanted to be an expedition leader," says Mike. "He told me to write him when I was twenty years old." Six years later, in his sophomore year of college, Mike wrote the dive master and asked him for a job. He landed his first cruise line job as a Zodiac driver aboard the *Lindblad Explorer*.

In his senior year of college, a month before graduation, Mike was promoted to a dive master position in Indonesia. Mike has done a lot of traveling with Society Expeditions. He has driven Zodiacs in Norway and explored the Amazon, Antarctica, the South Pacific and South America. At age twenty-seven, Mike had visited over one hundred and twenty-five countries.

(Source: Eric Elvejord)

LECTURER/SPECIAL GUEST

Pioneers of a new frontier, cruise lines are expanding their ship board activities to entertain and educate guests. Upscale, deluxe, premium and adventure cruise lines often hire guest lecturers. Topics of interest include fine arts, sports and fitness, health and beauty, music, business and finance, world affairs, gaming or cooking.

47

If you are an expert, published author or university professor, economist, nature and wildlife specialist or historian; you may be able to exchange your services for a discounted or free cruise. For a complete listing of topics, See *Wanted: Lecturers - Instructors and Gentlemen Hosts.*

Contact the Director of Entertainment or concessionaire with promotional material on your lecture, a photograph and a brief video or audio tape. See *International Directory of Concessionaires; Cruise Line Profiles.*

GREG CYLKOWSKI
Lecturer

"I'll sail the Western Caribbean
on the Costa Allegra this February.
What a break from frozen Minnesota!"

"An associate of mine told me, 'Greg, you should customize your corporate and sports presentations for a cruise ship audience - there's a big demand for it.' I'll be sailing on the *Costa Allegra* for Valentines' Day.

"My Life Skills Seminar blends the same techniques and skills used by successful corporate executives, entertainers or athletes. I customize my presentation to meet the needs of the passengers with specific illustrations and processes. I'll teach emotional control, personal identity, higher level performance, stress management, self-discipline and increased ability to focus. Skills any individual can use to excel.

"The cruise line is stringent on specific restrictions for your presentations. No distributing business cards or flyers and no solicitation of customers for future

48

presentations or personal consultations. In exchange for giving my presentation, I receive an excellent discount for both my wife and I.

"I've been pursuing the opportunity to lecture aboard a luxury liner for over a year. I saw an article in a tennis magazine about sports cruises like Norwegian Cruise Line's Sports Afloat and Royal Caribbean's Golf Ahoy program. I discovered that many cruise lines hire lecturers or presenters on a regular basis. I began researching who to contact, the timing and demand for presentations. *How to Get a Job with a Cruise Line* helped me get started on my contacts. I planted a lot of seeds and promoted myself."

Sample Clipper Cruise Line Lecturers

Susan Adie has a B.S. degree from Cornell University in environmental education and communication, and almost 25 years of experience as a naturalist. Susan is an avid birder, whale watcher, wildflower enthusiast and a three time winner of the Conservation Educator of the Year Award.

Robert Lippson has explored and studied the Chesapeake Bay for more than 20 years, and has served as senior scientist and assistant regional director of the National Oceanic and Atmospheric Administration's fisheries service. His research interests are blue crabs, fish, wetlands & ecology.

More ways to turn talk into travel: theme cruises:

Crystal Cruises Food & Wine Festival hired *Gourmet* magazine Wine Editor, Gerald Asher; best-selling author, John Jakes, and makeup artist, Michael Maron. Cigar Lovers cruises feature experts such as representatives of leading cigar makers and Avo Uvezian, "cigar composer". One Ultimate Rhythm & Blues Cruise promoted entertainers Marcia Ball, Katie Webster, & Louisiana Red. "Gin Rummy & Pinochle Tournament of the Sea" featured experts and instructors.

Seabourn Cruise Line has teamed up with the Wide World of Golf to offer a golf cruise with lecturers and clinics. RCI's shipboard enrichment program sponsors former ambassadors, professors, marine biologists and geologists. Their lecture schedule has featured such diverse topics as 'Europe's Economic and Political Development,' 'Ocean Liners of Today and Yesterday,' and 'Handwriting and What it Reveals.'

FOOD & BEVERAGE
GALLEY, RESTAURANT & BAR

Positions mirror those that you would find in a fine, expensive restaurant or resort. Master chefs, sous chefs, maitre' d and other leadership positions are held by people with extensive experience, training and knowledge. Cruise lines prefer substantial restaurant experience, hospitality and/or food and beverage training and skill. As with all shipboard positions, there is a hierarchy of experience and skill.

Food and beverage/Dining staff positions include (but are not limited to): food and beverage director, chef, sous chef, cook, food prep staff, maitre d', dining room captain, bar and wine steward/bartender, head server, server, assistant server, busboy and dishwasher.

Food and beverage/provisioning management positions are hired by cruise line personnel department/shipboard operations manager or through a food and beverage concessionaire. Galley, restaurant and bar staff originate primarily from Africa, Asia/Pacific, Caribbean, Eastern Europe, Europe and Central and South America. See *International Directory of Concessionaires.*

MICHEL ROUX
Master Chef, Culinary Consultant

Master Chef, Michel Roux, began his career at age 14, as an apprentice to M. Loyal of Paris. He later became head chef to society hostess Mme. Cecile de Rothschild. In 1967, Michel opened the Waterside Inn in the English village of Bray. Roux and his brother Albert starred in a BBC TV series. Roux has guided British Airways' Concorde and First Class food service for more than 15 years. His ongoing collaboration with Celebrity Cruises continues to bring the line superlative ratings for its cuisine and special food services.

SEVERINO SURACE
Food and Beverage Director

After competing his education as an accountant in Genoa, Italy, Severino went to sea as a Junior Provision Master. 28 years later, he directs food and beverage operations with Princess Cruises. His responsibilities include supervising and training hundreds of crew members and upholding US Health service standards.

The Chef and Maitre D' report to Severino and together they coordinate the activities of the galley and dining room staff. When he's not traveling the world, Severino lives in Calabria, Italy with his wife and two beautiful daughters.

All in a day's work: dining logistics. Cruise lines pride themselves on memorable dining experiences - made possible in part by careful selection of dining partners. Dining staff consider passenger's choices of first or second seating, smoking/non-smoking; traveling companions: family, friends, children; age, language, number in party. This complicated seating procedure serves 1,000 to 3500 passengers per week!

Snack Steward

Assists in set-up of buffets at all locations; serves passengers and explains buffet menu. Entry level position. Requires one to two years of hotel and/or restaurant or prior ship experience in a related position. Length of Contract: 9-12 months with 8 -12 weeks vacation. Salary Range & Benefits: $550-$800 per month, room & board, medical insurance, shared stateroom, dining with crew.

Dining Room Buffet Man

Supervises and sets up dining room buffet, serves passengers and explains buffet menu. Entry level position. Requires a minimum of one to two years hotel and/or restaurant experience or prior ship experience in a related position. Length of Contract: 9-12 months with 8 -12 weeks vacation. Salary Range & Benefits: $600-$850 per month, room & board, medical insurance, shared stateroom, dining with crew.

Busboy

Assists dining room waiters in passenger food and beverage service, explains menus to guests and attends to table settings. Entry level position. Requires a minimum of one to two years hotel and/or restaurant or prior ship experience in a related position. Length of Contract: 9-12 months, with 8 -12 weeks vacation. Salary Range & Benefits: $50 per month plus percentage of tips (average $1,100-$1,500 per month). Room & board, medical insurance, shared stateroom, dining with crew.

Wine Steward

Recommends and serves passengers alcoholic beverages. Entry level position. Requires a minimum of one to two years hotel and/or restaurant experience or prior ship experience in a related position. Expertise in wine and liquor. Length of Contract: 6-9 months with 4-8 weeks vacation. Salary Range & Benefits: $50 per month plus percentage of tips (average $1,450-$2,300 per month). Room & board, medical insurance, shared stateroom, dining with crew.

Dining Room Waiter/Waitress

Serves passengers, makes recommendations and explains menu, fulfills special requests, maintains table settings, serves and cleans during three daily meals and supervises busboys. Entry level position. Requires a minimum of one to two years hotel and/or restaurant or prior ship experience in a related position. Length of Contract: 6-9 months with 4-8 weeks vacation. Salary Range & Benefits: $50 per month plus percentage of tips (average $1,600-$2,300 per month). Room & board, medical insurance, shared stateroom, dining with crew.

Head Waiter

Supervises all waiters, busboys, and wine stewards at an assigned station. Oversees waiters and busboys maintenance of table settings. Promotes high standards of service. Requires one to two years minimum of hotel and/or restaurant experience or prior ship experience in a related position. Managerial experience preferred. Length of Contract: 6-9 months with 4-8 weeks vacation. Salary Range & Benefits: $50 per month plus percentage of tips (average $1,650-$2,400 per month). Room & board, medical insurance, shared stateroom , dining with crew.

Princess Cruises entire fleet is recognized by Chaine des Rotisseurs; the exclusive gastronomic society; for culinary excellence. With this designation, the fleet joins an exclusive list of fine hotels and restaurants around the globe whose chefs have been granted society membership. Princess ships proudly display the Chaine des Rotisseurs plaque, and executive chefs are eligible to wear the society's famous ribbons.

"Many of our chefs have held Chaine membership for some time," said Rick James, Princess' senior vice president of customer service and sales.
"It is quite unusual for a ship to be accepted into the society, let alone an entire fleet."

ALFREDO MARZI
Executive Chef

A native of Novara, Italy, Chef Marzi is fluent in French, English and Spanish and winnner of the Silver medal at the Culinary Olympics, San Francisco and Gold medal Annual American Chef's Cavalcade, NY 1998. He has produced official banquets for Queen Elizabeth II, Princess Diana, King Umberto of Italy, President George Bush, Prime Minister Margaret Thatcher and the leaders of Saudi Arabia, Brunei, Tonga, Jordan and Argentina.

Asst. Restaurant Manager

Supervises the restaurant staff; directs staff training and maintenance of food and service standards. Requirements: One to two years (minimum) hotel and/or restaurant experience. Prior ship experience in a related position preferred. Education or culinary background, food protection certificates suggested. Managerial experience preferred. Length of Contract: 4-6 months with 4-8 weeks vacation. Salary Range & Benefits: $1,650-$2,200 per month plus percentage of tips. Room & board, medical insurance, single or shared stateroom, Dining with officers.

Restaurant Manager

Supervises daily restaurant operations, staff training, maintenance of food and service standards. Requires managerial experience; two to three years (minimum) food and beverage experience with a hotel or restaurant. Prior ship experience in a related position preferred. Education or culinary background, food protection certificates suggested. Length of Contract: 4-6 months with 4-8 weeks vacation. Salary Range & Benefits: $1,900-$2,150 per month plus % of tips. Room & board, medical insurance, single stateroom, dining with officers.

Asst. Food & Beverage Manager

Supervises daily restaurant, bar and galley operations, staff training, maintains food and service standards. Managerial experience required: two to three years (minimum) food and beverage experience with a hotel or restaurant. Prior ship experience in a related position preferred. Education or culinary background, food protection certificates suggested. Length of Contract: 4-6 months with 4-8 weeks vacation. Salary Range & Benefits: $2,100-$2,500 per month, room & board, medical insurance, single stateroom, dining with officers.

Food & Beverage Manager

Manages and supervises restaurants, bar and galley. Responsibilities include training staff, maintaining food and service standards, food cost budgeting and safe handling of food supplies. Requires managerial experience, three to five years (minimum) food and beverage experience with a hotel or restaurant. Prior ship experience in a related position preferred. Education or culinary background, food protection certificates suggested. Length of Contract: 4-6 months with 4-8 weeks vacation. Salary Range & Benefits: $2,800-$3,300 per month, room & board, medical insurance, single stateroom, dining with passengers & officers.

Princess Cruises galleys are staffed with as many as 150 hardworking folks working round-the-clock throughout the fleet, preparing approximately 15,000 meals and snacks daily.

DECK & ENGINEERING STAFF

To apply for deck, engine positions, prepare by gaining some "time on the water" and hospitality experience. Previous cruise ship experience is preferred.

Begin locally by working with your seaman's union, port authority or a highly rated hotel or resort. To gain time at sea, begin in cargo/freight or one-day passenger cruises. Local one-day party, sightseeing or casino cruises are a great way to start.

Most cruise lines require that you have a round trip airline ticket to and from your home country valid for one year and a valid passport. Your ability to comprehend and speak conversational English is important.

Cruise lines hire deck/engineering and steward or hotel staff either direct through their marine operations department, a concessionaire or seaman's union. Licensing requirements vary. See *International Directories of Cruise Lines & Concessionaires*.

HOTEL

Gift Shop Staff

Bored with your local mall, shopping center or major department store? Why not 'see the sights' around the world on your time off?! Apply your retail, sales and customer service experience to a position in an international fashion designer's boutique, jewelry shop, perfume kiosk or souvenir shop.

One gift shop concessionaire representative says, "there is definitely a demand for people with experience who will live aboard ship for six months."

Responsibilities for shop managers or assistants include inventory, display, storage, coding, pricing and sales, sales, sales! Qualifications: three years full time experience in a department store or a specialty shop. Most gift shop personnel are hired through concessionaires such as Greyhound Leisure. Contact the concessionaire for specific employment arrangements and an application. See *International Directory of Concessionaires.*

LINDA MARSHALL
Gift Shop Manager

"It was love at first sight"

"I knew I wanted to travel, and the job opportunities locally just didn't offer much. "When I first took the job, I wasn't the 'outdoors' type; I didn't even know how to swim and I hated fishing. What I imagined was the opportunity to see the world and save a good amount of money. What I never could have imagined was that I'd make the best catch of my life - my husband. He's a Finnish officer; we met on my first ship - it was 'love at first sight'."

Linda married her shipboard sweetheart and the cruising couple have saved enough money to purchase a home in Finland and Florida.

SHAWN LENNOX
Gift Shop Manager

*"I've worked in retail with clothing stores
for seven years.
I was ready for a change."*

While in port at Key West, Shawn, 27, a native of Kelowna, BC, Canada telephoned and ordered a second copy of **How to Get a Job with a Cruise Line** for his cousin in Canada.

"It has everything you need to know to get a cruise line job," said Shawn. "I read the book front to back, and immediately called Carnival Cruise Lines' job hot-line which referred me to Greyhound Leisure. Greyhound Leisure's address and telephone number was listed in *How to Get a Job with a Cruise Line*. I wrote my resume according to the directions in the book, and after a successful telephone interview, I was hired as a gift shop manager aboard the *Ecstasy*. Greyhound Leisure told me they chose my resume over dozens of others.

"I've worked in retail, with clothing stores, for seven years. I was ready for a change. I love what I do, and I love to travel, so I thought I'd try working aboard a cruise ship. I haven't had a bad day, so far. My contract is for nine months, and I'm enjoying myself. The shops close while the *Ecstasy* is in port, so my friends and I go ashore to our favorite restaurants, or we hang out at the beach.

"My base salary is decent and I can earn an excellent commission on what I sell; plus I'm given an allowance for laundry and for tipping my cabin steward. Days at sea can be long; sometimes from 9 a.m. to midnight. But the travel more than makes up for it. My cousin can't wait to leave freezing Canada behind to join me in Key West!"

Hotel Manager/Chief Purser

The hotel manager/chief purser supervises all departments except deck and engine. He is responsible for both financial matters and human resources. The hotel manager/chief purser and his crew of assistant pursers handle all shipboard auditing and accounting, revenue reporting and other monetary duties. He also directs staff training and scheduling.

Requirements: Managerial experience: Five or more years with a hotel or cruise ship; a degree in hotel and restaurant management. Length of Contract: 3 to 4 months with 2 to 5 weeks vacation. Salary Range & Benefits: $3,000 - $5,500 monthly plus vacation pay. Room & board, medical insurance, single stateroom.

Assistant Hotel Manager

The assistant hotel manager acts as a liaison between hotel manager and crew and supervises the daily operations of crew. Requires a minimum of three years previous hotel managerial experience; prior cruise ship experience or a degree in hotel and restaurant management.

Purser's Staff

The Purser Department is the nerve center of passenger services. As a member of the purser's staff you are the front line. You represent cruise line policies and procedures. In addition to hospitality or finance experience, customer relations skills and computer skills will help you get a job on the purser's staff. Similar to duties at the front desk of a fine resort hotel, the purser's staff responsibilities are 50% administrative; dealing with official documents and financial matters and 50% passenger relations.

An Operations Manager of Carnival Cruise Lines describes the ideal qualifications: "I look initially at hospitality experience. Education, such as a hotel degree is helpful. A college degree is important. Experience with a financial institution is also important because you will be handling a great deal of money."

CHRISTOFOROS METAXAS
Chief Purser

*"Our ratings have been quite high and I'm proud...
I love my job or I wouldn't do it*

Christoforos began his cruise line career with Chandris Cruise Companies in 1968. He joined Sun Lines in 1973 and then returned to Chandris; now Celebrity Cruises; as Chief Purser.

Christoforos supervises hotel operations, passenger and crew accounting procedures, embarkation and passenger requests and complaints.

His duties include management of restaurant, bar, salon and casino staff. Christoforos' support team of four assistant pursers manage an information desk and a shore excursion office.

"My responsibilities are similar to those of an executive manager of a large hotel. I supervise many of the crew activities. To be chief purser you must have cruise ship experience. I now have twenty years working on cruise ships. When you're just beginning, you will take exams for a purser's certificate. You will work for four years as an assistant purser, another four years as a purser and then earn a special certificate.

61

"Next to experience, communication skills are most important. A purser needs to speak good English as well as other languages. I speak Greek, English and a little Spanish and Italian. I oversee so many different nationalities. It's unbelievable that things run so smoothly. We have Greeks, Koreans, and people from Bangladesh, India, Honduras and the Caribbean Islands. I have worked on other ships where there were only Greeks. Chandris is the most well organized Greek company.

"There are rules that each of us has to follow and comply with; but that's why the ship runs so smoothly. Our ratings have been quite high and I'm proud of that. I love my job or I wouldn't do it. I feel happy when a cruise goes well and passengers are saying good things about the ship."

1st Purser

Oversees daily operations of the purser's office/guest relations department. Supervises training of purser's staff. Managerial experience; previous hotel experience; a degree in hotel and restaurant management. Previous shipboard experience is preferred. Length of Contract: 4 to 6 months with 2 to 5 weeks vacation. Salary Range & Benefits: $2,000-$2,200 per month; room & board, medical insurance, single stateroom, dining with officers.

DARREN PARKER
First Purser

Bored with the social scene in his small village in England; and ready for better career opportunities; Darren Parker set his sights on a cruise ship job.

His background was ideal, as he had worked in a post office, Barclays Bank and Chase Manhattan Bank. He had the right combination of customer relations and money-handling skills.

Darren trained for a purser's staff position with a school in Florida, and landed his first job as purser's staff on a ship based in San Diego. He has since promoted to First Purser, denoted by two and one-half stripes on his uniform - just one-half stripe away from becoming Chief Purser!

Crew Purser

The crew purser supervises daily operations of crew and implements company policy and procedure. He acts as a liaison between officers and crew. His responsibilities include: arranging crew stateroom assignment; check-in by crew returning from shore; issuing crew ID cards, stateroom keys, lifejackets and uniforms and maintaining crew supplies

Requires a hotel and restaurant management degree and/or a university degree. Previous hotel experience or accounting experience is preferred. (Crew purser is promtoed from current staff.) Length of Contract: 6 months with 2-4 weeks vacation. Salary Range & Benefits: $1,400-$1,800 per month; room & board, medical. insurance, shared/single stateroom, dining with officers.

Hotel Controller

Supervises the auditing and accounting of the ship's supplies, inventory and cash flow. Supervises and trains the accounting staff. Requires a degree in accounting, finance or business; management experience, computer skills. Length of Contract: 4 - 6 months with 2 - 5 weeks vacation. Salary Range & Benefits: $1,800-$2,100 per month. Room & board, medical insurance, single stateroom, dining with officers.

Printer

Prints daily activities programs/newsletters and all shipboard announcements. Experience with desktop publishing, digital photography, graphics and design required. Experience with printing equipment preferred. Length of Contract: 6 months with 4-8 weeks vacation. Salary Range & Benefits: $1,300-$1,700 per month, room & board, medical insurance, shared stateroom facilities, dining with officers.

Program Coordinator

Coordinator produces a daily activities program or newsletter. Requirements: Experience with desktop publishing, digital photography, graphics and design. Length of Contract: 4 - 6 months with 2-5 weeks vacation. Salary Range & Benefits: $1,300-$1,700 per month, room & board, medical insurance, shared stateroom, dining with officers.

Photographer

Photographers are responsible for all photography aboard ship, at port, during embarkation and debarking. Qualifications: The ideal candidate has an outgoing personality; is well groomed; speaks clear English and has a basic knowledge of automated systems, color, printing and processing.

Photographers shoot posed shots of each and every passenger boarding and debarking; candid shots during cruise and ashore at ports of call. Photographers handle all developing in the on-board lab. Most photographers work through a concessionaire and may be assigned to one cruise line's fleet or work for several lines. All equipment is provided by the concessionaire.

PAUL DICKEN
Photographer

*"I sent in a resume and waited for a reply.
When that telephone call came, it was a mad dash.
I've been cruising the world ever since."*

Paul Dicken ushers groups of excited passengers up the gangway of the luxury cruise ship, and the embarkation photo session begins.

"Folks, let's get a picture, stand behind the line. Great, get a little closer there, that's good," says Paul.

It's three hours into embarkation and Paul and a co-worker have photographed over one thousand passengers. These "Welcome Aboard" photos become treasured souvenirs.

With the patience of a professional, Paul flips his camera up onto his shoulder, resting its weight for a moment. Paul is one of five ship's photographers on this cruise. He works with Sea Cruise Services, a photography concessionaire. Paul has only just started his one year tour and has traveled to Alaska with Costa Cruises and the Caribbean with Royal Caribbean International.

"The photography staff is responsible for embarkation photos, shipboard shots and ports of call," says Paul. "We must take somewhere between 10,000 and 20,000 photos over the week. And we do all of the developing." Before he started traveling, Paul had been shooting the social scene, weddings, portraits and headshots.

"There are a lot of concessions that advertise in the photography trade journals. That's how I heard about a job with Sea Cruise Services. I sent in a resume and waited about a month for a reply. When that telephone call came in, it was a mad dash. They told me I had to be in Puerto Rico in two days! That's right. Off I flew. And I've been cruising the world ever since."

Paul describes the qualities that make a successful photographer:

"You've got to be quite pushy, quite loud and pretty obnoxious," he laughs. "The best part of the job is the money, you can save money. The lifestyle is demanding. We seem to be working eighteen hours a day and getting five hours of sleep a night. If you're interested in photography and you want to make a bit of tax-free money fairly quickly, for a lot of hard work, then this is the area to get into."

MALCOLM HADDOCK
Ship's Photographer

Malcolm Haddock began his cruise ship photography career at age 19. As Operations Manager for The Cruise Ship Picture Company, a cruise line concessionaire, Malcolm looks for photographers with an ambition to travel, often with a college degree in photography, from 20-26 years of age, single with no dependents.

As a shipboard photographer with The Cruise Ship Picture Company, you will be using Nikon, Leica and Hasselblad photo equipment and Fuji developing equipment.

Janitorial/Maintenance

A cruise ship is a floating resort. High standards prevail: polished brass, crisp bed linens, spotless flooring - an atmosphere of perfection is upheld by an unobtrusive janitorial and maintenance staff. Positions include Stateroom Steward/Stewardess, Deck Staff, General Maintenance Staff.

Duties include: Daily maintenance, repair and cleaning of individual cabins, public areas; lounges, restaurants and overall structural maintenance; laundry and, yes, you will do windows. Helpful skills/experience: General housekeeping, janitorial/cleaning, painting, carpentry, miscellaneous "handy-man" skills.

When Crystal Cruises' Thomas Mazloum, Ship Hotel Manager, interviews prospective employees, he first asks himself whether he would feel comfortable buying a used car from the applicant.

Qualifications: Previous hotel/resort/cruise ship experience and affiliation with janitorial concessionaires, such as Marine and Mercantile. Apply first to the concessionaires or contact your local shipping/maritime union. Staff originate primarily from Africa, Asia/Pacific, Caribbean, Eastern Europe, Europe, Central and South America. Several cruise lines specifically employ Scandinavian stewardesses. See *International Directory of Concessionaires.*

MEDICAL

Registered Nurse

Nurses are on-call 24 hours for walk-in and hospital care. Applicants must have a minimum of three years recent hospital experience, with two or more years emergency room, trauma, or critical care. Advanced Cardiac Life Support (ACLS,) certification and a second language are helpful but not essential. Apply with copies of your curriculum vitae CV or resume; diploma from an accredited nursing school; current state license and recent passport size photo.

SUZANN CHRISTENSEN
Registered Nurse

*"Do it, because if you don't do it now
you may never have a chance.
Do it and enjoy it."*

Suzann just knew when she was a passenger aboard the *Song of America* - she couldn't wait to finish at the hospital, and travel as a shipboard nurse.

"I had just sailed on Royal Caribbean as a passenger; I returned to work and said 'I'm tired of this.' So, I sent in my resume to the medical staff I'd met on the cruise. Four days after I mailed my resume, Royal Caribbean called and asked me if I was interested in a position.

"I've had eighteen years of emergency room experience, so I feel qualified to be a ship board nurse. After graduating from nurses' training, I began working in a small emergency room outside of Chicago. My next job was with Massachusetts General in Boston for two years. I've also worked in the advanced cardiac life support unit and as a mobile intensive care nurse.

"The ship's hospital is set up to be a full emergency room. With Royal Caribbean there are two nurses aboard the ship, a North American nurse and a Scandinavian.

"The quality of the patient aboard ship is really different from on land. Working in a large emergency room outside of Chicago, you see more trauma accidents, alcoholism and drug overdoses. Aboard ship, you see more sunburn, some sea sickness and at most, passengers who have had motor scooter accidents in Cozumel and Grand Cayman.

"The passengers are here to enjoy themselves and they're more anxious about being ill because it's ruining their vacation. So you'll be doing a lot of public relations. You have to be outgoing, supportive and make them feel comfortable. It's different than what I had been used to. Before; I had to be very supportive; but it was more hustle-bustle. Now I have more time.

"The nurses are on call for twenty-four hours and then off duty for twenty-four hours. We're always available to help the other nurse. If there's a passenger who is a patient in the hospital for any length of time, we're on duty. The best part of my job is the travel and meeting people. I also love the shopping sprees in port. My favorite port of call for bargains is St. Thomas.

"I traveled aboard the *Nordic Prince* for four weeks and I'm finishing my six month contract aboard the *Sovereign of the Seas*. With all the benefits, the travel, the room and board; the pay comes out about equal to what you'd make on land. The most difficult challenge is being away from home."

Suzann is married and though her husband visited her last weekend, she misses him. She calls her family when she's in port.

"My husband and my brother have been supportive of me wanting to travel. When my chance came, they said 'Do it, because if you don't do it now you may never have a chance in the future. Do it and enjoy it.'

"This is something I've always wanted to do. I've always loved cruising. If you think you'd like to work on a cruise ship, get as much emergency room, intensive care, or operating room procedure as you can. Know life support and emergency techniques. Royal Caribbean recommends that you have five years experience in either emergency, intensive care or the operating room."

Suzann plans to return to a ship for another six months after her contract ends. After that - she'd like to do flight nursing aboard air evacuation medical helicopters!

Physician

Physicians are hired directly through a line's marine medical department or through a concessionaire. Physicians are hired from throughout the world. Industry-wide qualifications include a background in internal medicine or primary care medicine and experience in emergency room, trauma or cardiac care.

As the ship's physician, you provide emergency medical services for all passengers and crew. Expect to be on call 24 hours and hold minimum office hours each day. You will direct the ship's medical staff to provide general care and interim emergency care.

"Our physicians need to be Advanced Cardiac Life Support, ACLS, and preferably Advanced Trauma Life Support, ATLS certified," explains a director of medical services.

"We have doctors in their 30's and some who are retired physicians in their 50's and 60's. We don't hire people straight out of medical school," says Dr. William Heymann, Medical Director of ShipMed Health Care Systems.

"We staff ships with doctors who hold a Drug Enforcement Administration, DEA, certificate, a current United States license from any state and certification in

Advanced Cardiac Life Support, ACLS. We hire physicians who are trained in primary care specialties or emergency medicine."

Apply with a copy of your curriculum vitae, CV or resume; your diploma from an accredited medical school; a recent passport size photograph and your dates of availability. See *International Directory of Concessionaires.*

GEORGAKOPOULUS SPIROS, MD
Ship's Physician

"When I would return home from the ships,
I no longer felt satisfied with the hospital's routine"

"I have been working on ships since 1978. Two days after my Naval discharge, I walked down to Piraeus Port, looked at the ships and dreamed that one day, I might become a ship's physician. I visited several companies, and a few days later, received a telephone request to join a vessel. Since then, I have sailed the world as a ship's physician.

"I was treated as an officer; and we were married; my wife accompanied me onboard for several weeks. Some times we were 'skating', some times we were killing ourselves. Thank God, I had good nurses. I've heard that some companies, for economical reasons, do not hire nurses, and all the job is completely on you.

"My advice to physicians is to examine your contract terms carefully. Make sure the company pays your malpractice insurance. Are you considered a crew member or independent contractor? Make sure you have Intensive Care (ICU), and Critical Care (CCU) experience, you will need it. Minor surgery, gynecology, family practice, and emergency medicine is necessary.

71

On Alaskan cruises you must expect seniors, so geriatric experience is helpful. All cruise lines are OK as long as your department is well equipped.

"Life on board is fun and you will see exotic places. The only bad thing is that you make friends, and when you leave, you lose them. I wish all of you doctors and nurses smooth seas and have fun!"

Dr. Spiros has worked with Holland America Line, Carnival Cruise Lines and Celebrity Cruises.

DR. BRAD ENGLAND, DO
Ship's Physician

"My wife traveled with me.
I was a three stripe officer
and we were treated as VIP's."

"I started my career with my own private practice for eleven years. I worked with the US Coast Guard for four years as a ship's physician and started in the cruise industry with Norwegian Cruise Line, alternating between two NCL ships for three months. Because I was a three stripe officer, my wife and I had full run of the ship. We were treated as VIP's.

"I had one nurse on my staff who would screen the patients and she could handle most cases. My job was to take care of the passengers and my main duty was to care for the crew. There were always more crew than passenger injuries; from working in the kitchen, dining room and engine room.

"The average day was pretty easy, normally in the morning we would hold office hours from 9:30 a.m. to 10:45 a.m. and these hours were posted and announced to the passengers. I would hold office hours in the afternoon for another hour, but I did many things on an emergency basis; I was on call 24 hours.

"I treated sunburn, sea sickness, some of the chronic maintenance problems like diabetes, heart disease and high blood pressure. The crew injuries were usually falls, lacerations and flu. The illnesses were more varied among the crew than the passengers but most of them were routine cases. I had been a doctor for twenty years before I went on board, so nothing was remarkable.

"My extra duties, outside of medicine, were to inspect the galley and water purification systems. I also was expected to be cordial as a representative of the ship's officers. I was expected to work with the other officers in greeting and being sociable with the passengers. I was recognizable as an officer because I wore a white uniform with three stripes on the epaulets. All officers wore a short sleeve uniform during the day, but at night and at parties it was full dress uniform.

"I'd return to working aboard ship. The travel is worth it - my wife Jane's favorite port of call is Puerto Plata. It was a nice place to relax. Jane and I got to know some Dominican locals there, so we saw what the tourists miss.

"Our Dominican friends treated us royally and they always helped us buy things at the local price instead of the inflated tourist price. Jane was able to pick up some delicious coffee for next to nothing - it would have been outrageously expensive in the United States. It was fun to buy it like we were locals - we were 'insiders' in Puerto Plata. We still send Christmas cards and write.

"My advice to physicians considering working aboard ship is to be sure you like to travel and that you don't mind the confines of a ship. Be active in all types of medicine, Family Practice, Emergency Medicine, etc. Because if anything happens, you're the one they turn to.

Focus on Shipboard Medicine: Doctors of the Love Boat.

Dr. Sally Bell (England) Her experience includes five years with St. Mary's Hospital Medical School, London, joined Princess in 1988

Dr. Andrew John Iddles, (England) studied medicine at London University, 19 years with Princess, Dr. Iddles and his wife Denise, a Princess Purser, have a 7-year-old daughter.

Dr. Katrina Lewis (South Africa) entered the University of Capetown Medical School at age 16, and joined Princess in 1992. She married a Princess entertainer.

Focus on Loveboat doctors, continued...

Dr. Bruno Casaregola, (Italy) attended medical school in Rome for six years and practiced surgery in Parma for five years before joining Princess in 1988

Dr. Jason Reddy (Nigeria) studied at London's University College and originally wanted to be an astronaut!

Dr. Umberto N. Orazi (Italy) and his wife, Karen, met aboard ship, where she worked in the casino. They now have two children.

Source: *Captain's Circle* Newsletter, Princess Cruises

SALON & SPA

The new hot spot aboard ship is the health and fitness center or full facility spa. Can you imagine meeting new people from around the world at your next aerobics or step class? Health and fitness programs are popular on most ships with some cruise lines dedicating entire cruises to sports and fitness.

See *Cruise Line Profiles* and *Cruise Activity Guide*, for sports, health and beauty theme cruises and highlights of spas and salons.

Complete salon and fitness staffs manage spas on larger ships. Most lines now have full time fitness/aerobics instructors and massage therapists. Cruise lines are competing to offer specialty programs in aqua-aerobics, kickboxing, water sports, dance, yoga and stretching and nutrition.

Previous experience in coordinating activities, aerobics and sports instruction, sports medicine, lifesaving, exercise physiology, nutrition or physical education are required. Certification for your specialty is desired.

Employment experience and education or college course work will help you land your job. Gain the skills you'll need by working at a fitness center, spa, gym, resort or your local parks and recreation program. Enhance your chances of getting hired - add hospitality, travel and tourism or public speaking classes to your physical education or recreation studies.

Apply with your resume, photograph, sample of a proposed program/curriculum and a brief, simple video featuring your work. Apply to the Entertainment Director, Ship's Operations Manager, Cruise Director or appointed concessionaire.

ANNIE FRARACCIO
Fitness Director

*"I'm young and I want to travel,
but I didn't have the money. That's when
I got interested in combining work and travel."*

"Work that body, work that body! Ship-shape, ship-shape!," The *Sovereign of the Sea's* fitness program's theme song welcomes passengers to the fitness center. Annie Fraraccio, from Bricktown, New Jersey opens the center every morning at eight and instructs three to four aerobic classes daily. She also plans custom workout routines for the passengers.

"I've been a certified aerobics instructor for five years and I love teaching. I became interested in working for the cruise line when I took my first cruise last March. I loved it, I'm young and I want to travel, but I didn't have the money. That's when I got interested in combining work and travel."

Annie discovered an advertisement for ship-board aerobics instructor in an aerobics magazine. The ad was placed by Steiner, a salon and fitness concessionaire.

"They wanted a resume and a demonstration video. I didn't have a video so I just put it off. A few months went by and it was almost graduation time. I had made some videos of my teaching over Easter, so when I saw a similar ad for an aerobics instructor, I sent in my application.

"Meanwhile, I was getting my resume ready for jobs in health spas. I'd never dreamed I'd get a job working on a cruise ship. I couldn't believe my good luck when the cruise line called. Was I available?, they asked. Yes! I sent my audition video, and waited - they called the same week. It was the chance of a lifetime. Royal Caribbean International asked me to come down to Miami for an interview. We discussed the program and what the job entailed. They needed somebody right away. My ship had just come in."

Cosmetologist & Massage Therapist

Cosmetologists and massage therapists promote ship's fitness and beauty programs and schedule passengers for massage and beauty treatments. Many ships offer modern spas with complete facilities including several forms of massage therapy, facial and body treatments, manicures and pedicures, hair styling and makeovers. Massage therapists can expect a full day of giving massages. Relaxational massage is the most requested, although proficiency in other modalities including Neuro Muscular Therapy are often desired.

Qualifications: Previous employment and education in massage and/or beauty. On many ships you will need three years full time work experience after licensing or certification. A certificate showing completion of an educational program and board certification or licensing is required. Licenses and certification requirements for salon staff vary with your nationality and individual cruise line facilities/programs.

A Licensed Massage Therapist will have passed both written and practical examinations in anatomy, physiology, massage techniques, nutrition and professional ethics. For health and beauty programs See *Cruise Line Profiles*, See *International Directory of Concessionaires*

ANN TAYLOR
Cosmetologist

"I occasionally send post cards from the islands back to the girls at the salon. I don't miss my old job. I'm having too much fun here!"

"I've always wanted to travel around the world. It's been my life long dream. When I saw an advertisement for jobs with cruise lines, I knew it was for me, so I sent my resume and a photo to Steiner, a concessionaire for cruise ship cosmetology employees, and crossed my fingers!

"I couldn't believe it when Steiner called. They wanted me to start work that week! I quit my job, packed my bags and was ready to go. I told my old boss at the salon, 'Hey, later. I'm outta here, Anchors Aweigh.' I think the other girls were jealous as they watched me pack up my things.

"When I walked on board my first cruise ship, I noticed right away how nice the rest of the crew was. I felt at home, like I was part of a team. My days are very busy. My partner and I schedule appointments from early morning to seven at night. I enjoy designing new hairstyles and doing makeovers. My customers are in a good mood. They're on vacation and want to pamper themselves.

"And they tip good too. I love spending those tips on expensive perfumes in the ports of call. My hours on board ship may be long, but when I have time off and we're in port, I can shop 'til I drop. I especially like getting bargains on unusual jewelry. Stuff that would cost you a fortune at home.

"Yes, there are some shipboard romances. A lot of blonde, Norwegian men and attentive Italians. But I'm not serious about anyone yet. If you love to travel and enjoy meeting new people, you've got to try cruising. I occasionally send post cards from the islands back to the girls at the salon. But I don't miss my old job. I'm having too much fun here!"

MARIA EDWARDS & SARAH WELLS
Massage Therapists

"I forget I'm even on a ship when giving a massage, but each port we visit is a whole new world!"

Smiling faces of salon staffers and sparkling, state-of-the-art fitness equipment welcome passengers to the *Sovereign of the Seas* Spa and Fitness Center. Sarah and Maria answer questions from curious passengers. A new arrival rushes to their table to reserve her massage. Maria schedules a relaxational massage for the morning and describes the spa's sauna and other facilities.

Maria and Sarah were hired as massage therapists by a concessionaire. Maria has sailed with Cunard, Royal Viking and Royal Caribbean Cruise Line.

"In the ship's salon we mainly do massage. We also sell products used in massage, and make a commission on what we sell," says Maria. "You'll need at least two years of massage or beauty experience before cruise lines will consider you. My work with a health spa on land was my ticket out of England. I worked in the spa for over two years. I've always enjoyed working with people. Now I spend my time off visiting Caribbean ports of call."

A newcomer to cruising, Sarah is taking things one day at a time. It is her first week of a nine month contract.

In England; Sarah worked as a masseuse and technical sales representative for beauty products. She is surprised at the workout she gets from giving massages, but is looking forward to the next nine months.

"Finally, I get a chance to travel and see some of the world, and I'm getting paid to do it!" says Sarah.

"The most important quality you need for this job is patience. You deal with a lot of different personalities."

SHORESIDE/CORPORATE OPERATIONS

SALES AND MARKETING

The sales staff is responsible for promoting their cruise line's products via travel agents to prospective and experienced cruisers. Sales and marketing departments are expanding to represent new ships. Jobs in sales and reservations are the positions most often advertised in travel trade magazines. See *Bibliography*; travel trade magazines.

Positions include reservations, air-sea ticketing, group sales, incentive/ corporate sales, marketing coordinator, sales account executive, district sales manager DSM, regional sales manager and vice president of sales and marketing.

Sales account executives and DSM's visit travel agencies to promote new ships, itineraries, programs, special promotions and rates. Your goal is to motivate travel agents to recommend your cruise line's products to prospective cruisers. The successful sales manager will be flexible, resilient, reliable, enthusiastic, a good public speaker and have a good sense of humor.

Helpful previous experience includes: sales executive or cruise consultant for a travel agency, experience with airline reservations and sales/marketing, rental car sales and hotel and resort sales or promotions. Cruise lines prefer candidates with developed contacts within the travel agency community in a defined geographic region and experience with reservations systems.

Reservations Agent

"Reservations is a great place to start," says Vicki Moulinos, Director of Reservations. "We do promote from within, because you'll have the product knowledge that people coming off the street don't have. We promote into individual sales, group sales, tours and capacity control."

Tony Hernandez, Sales Account Manager, agrees.

"If you talk to any reservations manager, one of the hardest things for them to do is to keep good people. Because the best people always get promoted. There's a big turnover in reservations," .

"As reservations manager..." says Ms. Moulinos. "...I help reservationists build their selling skills. We train our reservationists to sell properly and communicate with travel agents."

She looks for applicants with the ability to be consistent, organized, dedicated, responsible and resourceful. "A good reservationist knows the product and can meet the customer's needs effectively and efficiently," says Moulinos.

"There is a certain amount of stress in this job because you are on the telephone all day," says a former Premier Cruise Lines personnel executive.

"The ideal reservation agent applicant has graduated travel or tourism school, has some computer background and a 'people person,' outgoing personality. The applicant must have some sales and telephone experience. Most cruise lines offer in-house reservations training."

Direct Response Marketing Manager

Manages existing direct marketing and database projects/processes; maintains full knowledge of existing projects; leads development of new projects; identifies processes that can be redesigned to achieve greater market/customer impact and/or greater process efficiency; affect greater integration of customer information with operational systems and leads development/dissemination of marketing database value as a corporate asset; Reports to director of marketing and works with Marketing, Sales, IT and call centers to achieve efficient tracking & ROI reporting.

Sales Vision 2000
Royal Caribbean & Celebrity Cruises Decentralize Sales Management Team

Royal Caribbean International. is decentralizing its sales management team and changing the structure of its field sales force to more closely align itself with today's distribution system.

"Consolidation, automation and specialization have all played a key role in how travel products are being sold today," said the senior vice president of Marketing and Sales for Royal Caribbean International.

Royal Caribbean and Celebrity currently have the largest field sales force in the industry with 100 district sales mangers and six regional sales managers to service the United States and Canada, based on territories.

"We will continue to have the largest sales organization deployed in the industry," said the vice president of Sales for Royal Caribbean International and Celebrity Cruises.

"As we begin to bring the first of nine new ships on line this fall, an efficient and productive sales force will be vital to filling the more than 21,000 new berths.

"The reasoning behind Sales Vision 2000 is to increase face-to-face contact between the sales team representing Royal Caribbean International and Celebrity Cruises and the travel community.

"We have defined the roles of each of the company's field representatives to more closely mirror today's segmented distribution system.

"The company will continue to have a national account team headquartered in Miami and six regions headed by directors. The regional teams will consist of key account mangers, incentive sales managers, district sales managers and regional automation managers. Overseeing the sales team will be six directors of sales located in five United States and one Canadian region.

"The total deployed sales force will be larger tomorrow than it is today."

PURCHASING & FINANCIAL

Purchasing Agent

Duties include the purchase of uniforms and other textile goods; locating of new sources; administration of contracts, and the maintenance of supplier relations, and interaction with Operations, Accounts Payable, Logistic and Ship Personnel. Successful candidates will be proficient in Word, Excel and AS400.

Qualified candidates must have a college degree plus a minimum of 3-4 years experience purchasing any of the following: uniforms, china, flatware, glassware, food & beverages, hotel consumables and replaceables. APP

(Accredited Purchasing Practitioner) certification is highly desirable.

Senior Purchasing Agent

Duties include the purchase of hotel consumables, marine and technical consumables, spare parts, and technical equipment; locating of new sources and administration of contracts, maintenance of supplier relations, and interaction with Operations, Accounts Payable, Logistic and Ship Personnel. Successful candidates will be proficient in Word, Excel and AS400 – JD Edwards a plus. Qualified candidates must have a college degree plus a minimum of 3-4 years purchasing experience and creative problem solving skills. Mechanical/technical background a plus.

Accountant

Accountants are needed to handle general accounting, payroll and financials. You will work with cruise line operations, sales and marketing, passenger services, ticketing and billing. Qualifications include a strong accounting background, bookkeeping and computer skills in Lotus or other database or spreadsheet programs. Banking, travel agency, restaurant, hotel or other tourism experience is preferred.

Senior Staff Accountant

Manages and obtains financial data for use in maintaining accounting records. The following are required: BS/BA Accounting, 4-5 years in corporate accounting, auditing, and systems experience. Working knowledge of AS400 or similar environment w/strong systems aptitude, including query skills. Proficiency with PC software & spreadsheet programs and experience with JD Edwards or similar accounting system.

EMILIANO PEREZ
Accounts Receivable

"I love my job."

A former mathematics teacher, Emiliano Perez enjoys working with the ticketing, and billing processes. "I love my job," says Emiliano. "Although I have to work some Sundays, because the ships sail seven days a week, I enjoy the organization and the diversity of my work."

ADMINISTRATIVE

Administrative Assistant

Administrative assistants are needed in all departments including sales and marketing, public relations, finance and accounting, reservations, ticketing, shore side and ship operations.

You will perform secretarial duties including typing reports & letters, scheduling meetings, answering phones, file maintenance and report distribution. Duties include: creating and maintaining databases; arranging travel and preparing presentations. Required skills: type 60 words per minute, perform well under deadline, proficient in Word, Excel, PowerPoint, and Lotus Notes. AA degree preferred. Recommended: 2+ years of secretarial experience.

SKILL & EXPERIENCE WORK SHEET

What do you do best? Which job is right for you?
List previous jobs. What duties were you most capable
of? Which experiences did you enjoy?. List your best
skills or abilities. Compare your notes to the requirements for a specific job. Use this list when preparing
your cover letter and application.

3

THE TOP SIX FIRST JOBS

Love to Travel? But can't afford the ticket? See how these people get paid to travel:

"I'm a people-person. I love to work with people," says **Pam**, cruise staff assistant. *"Office jobs are not for me. I tried that for nine years and I wasn't happy. Now I love what I do!"*

"I'm young, and I wanted to travel, but I didn't have the money," says **Annie**. *"That's when I got interested in combining work and travel."*

Want to know how you can travel and get paid for it? Cruise lines operate similar to most large corporations, you start at the bottom of the corporate ladder and work your way up. Your employment experience, talents and skills may qualify you for that dream job. Travel, Adventure, Romance *and* a Steady Paycheck are yours!

If you want to break into the cruise industry, prepare and educate yourself for these six first-time jobs:

1. **Youth Counselor**
2. **Gift Shop Staff**
3. **Purser's Staff**
4. **Reservationist**
5. **Cruise Staff/Host**
6. **Salon & Spa/Fitness Center Staff**

These six entry-level positions are your best bet for a first-time job. *Here's why:*

A. High turnover - jobs open when people promote up the ladder; employees leave the ship to travel or return home

B. Expansion of departments: As cruise lines compete in the areas of spa, salon and children's programming, more jobs are created. See the *Cruise Line Profiles* for companies offering these services.

C. Traditional starting positions - This is where you learn the cruise line's operations.

D. Seasonal hiring patterns. Peak cruising times require more cruise staff, youth counselors, entertainers and salon and spa staff. Review *Job Descriptions* for the best seasonal opportunities.

E. Theme cruises: Music, sports and other themes create opportunities for specialty entertainers, lecturers and instructors.

F. Growing fleets require complete staffing of each new ship plus expanding reservations, marketing and sales staffs ashore.

Job Descriptions: Top Six First-time Jobs

1. Youth Counselor

The 'youthing of cruising' has created a demand for experienced youth counselors. An increase in families sailing with children has made youth programs a standard in the industry. Most ship's offer children's programs and facilities. Youth counselors are hired for holiday and summer cruises, however several cruise lines hire year-round. See *Cruise Line Profiles and Youth Counselors; Childcare at Sea.*

Youth Counselors coordinate youth and children's age-specific activities: games, contests, scavenger hunts, parties, dances and sports and fitness instruction. Cruise lines prefer supervisory experience either as a counselor or instructor. Previous training in child education, physical education or child psychology is desirable. Water safety certification is helpful.

2. Gift Shop Staff

Bored with your local mall, shopping center or major department store? Why not see the sights around the world on your time off?! Apply your retail, sales and customer service experience to a position in an international fashion designer's boutique, jewelry shop, perfume kiosk or souvenir shop.

One gift shop concessionaire's representative says, "there is definitely a demand for people with experience who will live aboard ship for six months."

Responsibilities for shop managers or assistants include inventory, display, storage, coding, pricing and sales, sales, sales! Qualifications: three years full time experience in a department store or a specialty shop. Most gift shop personnel are hired through concession-aires such as Greyhound Leisure. Contact the concessionaire for specific employment arrangements and an application. See *International Directory of Concessionaires.*

3. Purser's Staff

The Operations Manager of Carnival Cruise Lines describes the ideal purser's staff member: "I look initially at hospitality experience. Education, like a hotel degree is helpful. A college degree is important. Experience with a financial institution is also important because you will be handling a great deal of money."

The Purser's Department is the nerve center of passenger services. As a member of the purser's staff, you are the liaison between passenger, crew and headquarters. You represent cruise line policies and procedures. In addition to hospitality or finance experience, customer relations skills and computer skills will help you get a job on the purser's staff.

Similar to duties at the front desk of a fine resort hotel, the purser's staff responsibilities are 50% administrative; dealing with official documents and financial matters and 50% passenger relations.

4. Reservationist

"If you talk to any reservations manager, one of the hardest things for them to do is to keep good people," says top sales representative, Tony Hernandez.

"The best people always get promoted. There's a big turnover in reservations."

As a reservationist, you're the cruise industry's front line of sales. Richard D. Fain, Chairman an CEO of Royal Caribbean International describes the goal of an effective reservations staff: "To help travel agents achieve success and provide their clients with fast, efficient service." Royal Caribbean, like many major cruise lines, employs several hundred professional reservation agents.

You'll provide travel agents with the facts and figures to close the sale; sailing dates, rates, itineraries, availability of cabins and special arrangements (dinner seating, honeymoons, birthdays, anniversaries and pre-cruise and post-cruise packages.)

Reservations manager Vicki Moulinos looks for applicants with the ability to be consistent, organized, dedicated, responsible and resourceful.

"I help reservationists build their selling skills. We train our reservationists to sell properly and communicate with travel agents," says Vicki.

"A good reservationist knows the product and can meet the customer's needs effectively and efficiently."

A former Premier Cruise Lines personnel executive describes the ideal reservation agent: "a graduate of a travel or tourism school, with computer experience and a 'people - person,' outgoing personality. It's also very important that the applicant have some sales experience and a pleasant telephone voice. Most cruise lines offer in house training on their reservations systems.

"Reservations is a great place to start, we do promote from within, because you'll have the product knowledge that people coming off the street don't have. We promote into individual sales, group sales, tours and capacity control."

5. Cruise Staff/Host

This catch-all cruise staffer is always on the run - assisting the cruise director, shore excursions staff, guest services and purser's staff. Customer relations and hospitality experience and an outgoing, 'can-do' personality are essential.

Get ready to learn something new everyday as you 'wear many hats' and perform a variety of tasks. Host duties will prepare you for future work on the cruise staff or purser's staff.

6. Salon & Spa/Fitness Center staff

Great opportunities exist for fitness/aerobics instructors, cosmetologists, hair stylists, massage therapists and nail technicians.

Salons aboard ship are expanding to offer complete health and beauty services; including aromatherapy, massage therapy, hydrotherapy and endless facials, body scrubs and wraps, makeovers, hairstyling and manicures/pedicures. Get certified and add 1-2 year's experience working with the public.

Spa/Fitness Centers need people with experience in coordinating activities, aerobics and sports instruction, sports medicine, lifesaving, exercise physiology, nutrition or physical education. Certification or licensing for your specialty is desired.

Employment experience and education or college course work will help you land your job. Gain the skills you'll need by working at a fitness center, salon, spa, gym, resort or your local parks and recreation program. Enhance your chances of getting hired - with hospitality, travel, tourism or public speaking classes.

Top Free-Travel Opportunities

1. Lecturer/instructor

Talk your way aboard and around the world: desirable topics include: gourmet cooking, wine, financial planning gaming, arts & crafts, history, ecology, self help, health and nutrition. See *Wanted: Presenters, Lecturers and Gentlemen Hosts* for a complete topic listing.

2. Gentleman host

Do you love to dance? Want to travel several times a year? Do you have what it takes to cruise as a Gentleman Host? See *Wanted: Presenters, Lecturers and Gentlemen Hosts.*

4

JOB APPLICATION TIPS FROM PEOPLE IN THE KNOW

NEW: Top 10 Interview Questions

Here are the **best ways to get hired** - again and again. Specific advice from people in the know; top executives, industry experts, employees and cruise line personnel directors.

PRACTICAL ADVICE - FROM THE TOP

Maurice Zarmati, Vice President of Sales for Carnival Cruise Lines recommends these strategies when applying for a cruise line job:

1. Make sure your resume is complete and to the point, stating specific dates (from-to) of employment.

2. Write to someone in particular, such as a department head, rather than 'to whom it may concern.'

3. Ask for an interview if you know a particular position you are interested in is available.

4. Do your homework about the particular cruise line. Find out as much as you can about the 'product' and how it is marketed.

95

5. During the interview, be positive, flexible & display all the enthusiasm you can.

6. Tell your interviewer you really need and want this job!

IS IT LIKE THE *LOVE BOAT*?

"It may not be the *Love Boat*," says one cruise executive, "but you can expect a lot of satisfaction. You get to see new places and you get to save money because you don't have to pay rent. Your room and meals are included. The only expenses you have are dry cleaning and shore expenses. Do expect to be in a great mood most of the time, it's somehow glamorous and exciting!"

THE EUROPEAN CONNECTION

If you're a college student spending a semester abroad, or if you're traveling for a summer, visit a cruise office while you're in town. Many lines do their hiring from offices in London, and Piraeus, Greece. European lines face the problem of how to interview Americans for a position. Cruise lines won't fly you to Europe for a job interview. You have to find your own way to the headquarters and fill out the application while you're in town, recommends a former manager of public relations for Paquet Cruises.

American lines face a similar problem in interviewing international job candidates. Cruise lines do not usually pay the travel expenses of prospective employees. Always submit your resume to the cruise line's main headquarters.

EVERYONE WANTS TO BE CAPTAIN

"We get a lot of requests for employment, for all kinds of positions: first and second mate; engineer; barman; waiter and receptionist; but the most requested position is Captain. However, to be considered for Captain, you need at least five years of nautical education to get your license, so think again if you're applying for the Captain's position," says a former vp of hotel operations.

Captain Cesare Ditel, Princess Cruises

"Coming from a seafaring family, it was inevitable that I would leave my home...and venture out to sea"

Cesare Ditel left his home on the island of Elba in 1953 to begin his maritime studies at the Nautical School in Leghorn, Italy. After attending the Italian Naval Academy and serving in the Navy for several years, Cesare began his Merchant Navy career in 1961 as a young officer on tankers.

He joined Sitmar Cruises in 1964, as a 3rd Navigating Officer and moved up the ranks until 1985, when was awarded command of his own ship. Captain Ditel has served on *Fair, Dawn, Regal* and *Sun Princess*, and now captains the *Ocean Princess.*

source: *Captain's Circle* , Princess Cruises

READ NEWSPAPER TRAVEL SECTIONS

Study your local newspaper travel section and those of cities with active cruise ports. These travel sections and the classified advertisements will keep you up to date on the cruise industry.

SHOW YOUR COMMITMENT AND ENTHUSIASM FOR THE JOB

"Personnel has a lot at stake when they hire you," comments a veteran personnel manager.

"When you hire your fleet personnel, these are the only people who can do the service. You don't walk out on the street and hire these people - not if you know what you're doing. You can't be in the middle of the Atlantic and change your mind. You don't wake up one night aboard ship, in the middle of the Caribbean and say 'Oops, we don't need these three people.'

Personnel can't afford to gamble when it comes to hiring. There's a lot of planning that goes into it. Prove to us that you will get the job done. If you can convince the interviewer that you are committed to the job, you'll have a good chance at getting hired."

SEE YOUR TRAVEL AGENT

Develop a friendly relationship with a local travel agent. Share your interest in working in cruising and your agent may have a personal contact with the cruise lines. Always ask for brochures and old copies of travel trade magazines.

READ TRAVEL INDUSTRY MAGAZINES

Travel trade magazines such as *Travel Trade: Cruise Trade, Cruise and Vacation Views, Travel Weekly, Travel Agent: Cruise Desk, Tour and Travel News, Travel Counselor, Leisure Travel News, ASTA Agency Management* may give you a job lead. Your agent may be able to supply you with a subscription business reply card so you can order your own copies. Invest in yourself by researching the cruise lines - the payoff can mean an exciting new job!

PROFESSIONALISM COUNTS

"Yesterday a girl called my office and said she's free for the summer and ready to have fun; what job could I give her? This girl didn't understand what was involved in getting a job with a cruise line. Business is business. Be professional when you apply and respect the people in personnel's time," says an executive with Royal Caribbean International.

PRESENT A STABLE WORK HISTORY

Royal Olympic Cruises' director of personnel looks for 'a stable track record,' not someone who jumps from job to job. Craft your resume to show dependability, stability.

RELATE YOUR QUALIFICATIONS
TO CRUISE LINE NEEDS

Emphasize specifically how your qualifications fit the requirements of the position you are applying for. Show how your work history has prepared you to be a valuable cruise staff member.

DO YOUR HOMEWORK

"Study the cruise line and know what it offers," advises the director of personnel for American Hawaii Cruises.

"We have received letters saying that they want to work in our casino and that they speak foreign languages and want to travel the world. We don't have a casino and we travel the Hawaiian Islands."

Tons of information on the cruise industry and specific cruise lines is available to you. We've done the research for you, see *Cruise Line Profiles and Cruise Guide for Active Adults; Cruise Guide for Children.*

STUDY A SECOND LANGUAGE

Many directors of marine personnel are experiencing a doubling of staff with each new ship.

"My duties as Director of Marine Personnel have shown me how important a second language can be. Now I look after twice as many employees and I'm always having to communicate with them, not just in English, but Greek and Spanish as well. Spanish is a must," says one top executive.

"It's helpful if you speak more than one language" advises Royal Caribbean International personnel director. "A good purser must speak Spanish, Italian, German, and English. One of our pursers speaks 8 languages."

GET THAT INTERVIEW

"It's important to meet your prospective employer face-to-face and really sell yourself," says a top district sales manager for a major line. "Do whatever you can to get a one on one interview. If you have to travel, do it. It will be worth it, because the interview will probably be what gets you the job."

IT'S NOT WHAT YOU KNOW - IT'S WHO YOU KNOW

Seasoned salesman Bruce Waters comments on connections: "A lot of people get the job because they are at the right place at the right time. They come on-board as passengers and talk to the right people. If you aren't getting the response you'd like from your applications, try taking a cruise and meet the people who work aboard ship."

"Don't be shy!" says a young woman from the midwest who now travels the Caribbean as an entertainer.

"Ask people you know for information about openings and opportunities. Network and let your friends know what you can do and what you're looking for. Give them copies of your resume so they can help you in your job search."

WORK HARD - PLAY HARD

With most cruise lines you must be willing to work your way up the ladder of success.

"American Hawaii Cruises promotes from within," comments American Hawaii's personnel director.

"You can start as a waiter or waitress and get pro-moted to steward. Unless you have cruise ship experience you will start at the bottom. Half of our applicants think they can be the cruise director right away, because they love people. It takes experience."

"You have to be realistic about your expectations," says a manager of shipboard operations.

"You will work a 4-6 month contract, seven days a week, 10-12 hours a day. You will work a seven day week because the ship's services don't stop when we're in port. It is sometimes difficult for new people to realize that they

101

are in the service business. You need to start telling yourself, 'I am in the service industry. I'm here to serve these passengers and make their cruise fun, safe and memorable. I'm not here necessarily to fraternize with them.' When you're reading the cruise line brochure you need to remember it was created for the passenger and not for the staff. Use the brochures to plan your time off in exotic ports around the world."

LOCALS ONLY?

Many people interested in cruising wonder if they need to be from a coastal state or live in a port city to get a job with a cruise line. Interviews with cruise line employees show that staff is hired from around the world.

"We hire throughout the world," says Carnival Cruise Lines' Manager of Operations.

"I'll interview over the phone if we have a qualified applicant who is seriously interested but cannot apply in person to Miami."

PERSISTENCE PAYS OFF!

As you begin your cruise line job search, understand that you are entering both the service industry and the entertainment business. Just as the actor in New York will wear out the soles of his shoes to get his first part, you must be willing to persist in your cruise line job search.

This requires a constant, relentless, and very polite campaign to keep your face in front of personnel. You want to say, 'Look at me, I'm enthusiastic, skilled, capable, and ready, willing, and able to work for your cruise line.'

Consistency, persistence, and politeness are the three keys to landing your dream job aboard a cruise ship.

"The people who are the most persistent are the ones I think of when a position comes open," says one personnel director. "It pays to be persistent, but not obnoxious or pushy. I simply won't deal with rude people," she says. Be polite, available, and persistent. Cruise employment instructor and former cruise director Beverley Citron, says it best: "Persistence breaks resistance!"

OOPS! NO ROOM FOR MISTAKES.

Carefully proofread your resume as if your job depends on its accuracy. It just might! A misspelling or typo brands you as careless and might cause a personnel director to reject your application. If you have access to a good computer system, use it! If not, spend the money and have your resume professionally typeset and printed.

You'll need 50-100 copies. Sounds like a lot? Don't cheat yourself. You will need to send your resume with each of your initial applications and any follow-up correspondence. Give copies of your resume to your friends and professional references - they can help you with your job search.

I'VE ALWAYS WANTED TO BE LIKE JULIE ON *LOVEBOAT*

"The most popular positions are on the cruise staff; cruise director or hostess," says a veteran shipboard entertainer. "It's glamorous, but there is a lot of

103

competition for these jobs. You can do well by applying for a specific cruise staff position such as a dancer, production entertainer, or youth counselor."

Beverley Citron says, "A good cruise staff member will stay with the passengers for 10-15 minutes after an activity, make the extra effort, be available and socialize. Always be punctual for setting up activities. Be a team player and get along with co-workers."

YOU GOT THE INTERVIEW! CONGRATULATIONS!

This is no time to be modest - sell yourself! Demonstrate you are a dedicated employee and a team player, with a sincere interest in serving that cruise line's passengers.

Prepare for the interview in advance. You'll need additional copies of your resume and cover letter, photos, and letters of reference. You'll also want to bring a list of questions about the position. Demonstrate your interest in the position and the cruise line. Be prepared with your own list of answers as to why you feel you are qualified for the position you desire.

Shake hands upon introducing yourself and before you leave the interview. Dress as if you already are a cruise line employee. Copy what cruise employees wear; a tailored dress, suit, jacket or blazer and tie. Appear professional, personable and happy! Listen carefully to all questions asked of you. If you don't understand the question, ask for clarification.

Answer all questions thoughtfully and directly. Cruise lines are looking for employees who are client-centered. Emphasize your commitment to the passengers, to the line, and to your co-workers.

"The passenger comes first," says Joyce Gleeson, Assistant Cruise Director.

Top 10 Interview Questions

1. How did you learn of this job opportunity?

2. What is your area of expertise? How many years of experience do you have in that area?

3. What is the best time for us to contact you?

4. Who is your current or most recent employer?

5. What is your current or most recent job title?

6. What are or were the dates of employment with the employer?

7. Who was your previous employer? What was your job title with that employer?

8. What is your highest degree? What is your major?

9. What salary range are you seeking?

10. When are you available to begin work? (Date)

GO GET THAT JOB!

5

THE 10 BEST WAYS TO APPLY FOR YOUR CRUISE LINE JOB

Amid the congested clutter of the mail room, Celebrity Cruises' personnel director gestures towards a chest-high stack of boxes, full of resumes.

"Those are just some of the resumes that we get every week."

It's fortunate that her office is close to the mail room. One by one, each resume will be reviewed.

"Only the best resumes are kept on file;" she says. "Unqualified or incomplete resumes are disposed of. I keep the promising ones on file for six months. We refer to these applications when a position comes open. This week, my department hired a new purser. We had received his application over a month earlier."

She opens a huge file cabinet, dumps an armload of resumes on her desk, and chooses a good example.

"This person really put a lot of effort into her application," the director says. "Her cover letter is polite and states a specific position. Her resume reflects experience in banking and customer relations. She is a good candidate for the purser's staff."

Amy M.'s resume is neatly typewritten in easy-to-read type on clean white bond paper. A light grey folder neatly holds Amy's resume, cover letter, and a professional looking photograph. Amy has succeeded in the first step to getting hired - her resume is placed in the 'approved' file for the next job opening.

Amy's resume was direct, specific and professional. She explained clearly how her skills and experience would be useful for a purser's staff position. Her good first impression with the personnel director could make her next in line to be hired.

The following advice summarizes suggestions repeated by top executives, industry experts and personnel directors. Prepare your application with this goal: *make it easy for personnel to hire you.* Our research will make it easier for you to succeed.

THE TOP 10 WAYS TO APPLY:

1. "The most important ingredient of your resume? **Emphasize passenger satisfaction!** You are selling your self as a member of a team, a team that exists to make the passenger's cruise experience a memorable and happy one. That's what cruising is all about - satisfied passengers.

To distinguish your self from thousands of star-struck hopefuls, emphasize how your employment experience, skills, education and talents can contribute to the passenger's cruise experience."

2. "**Details matter!**," says the Operations Supervisor for Carnival Cruise Lines. "I won't even look at those applications which are not signed by the applicant and I don't appreciate formula cover letters. Proofread and sign your cover letters. Address your application and cover letter to the appropriate person. People change jobs often in the cruise industry, it's important to submit your application to the current personnel director or department head. Avoid addressing your cover letter 'to whom it may concern.' Do some research!" *We've done your research for you. See Cruise Line Profiles.*

3. Make your resume easy to read.

What is easy to read? "Avoid that sizzling hot pink paper," says the Personnel Director of Commodore Cruise Line.
"Bright neons may get attention but are very difficult to read."
Use your zebra-stripe stationery and hot pink ink for another project. No photocopied resumes or cover letters! Poor quality copies look like you don't really care about where you're applying.
A conservative, simple resume is your best bet. Start with white 8 1/2 x 11, 20# bond paper or, if you prefer, a light color such as buff, grey, or light blue. Use black ink and choose a type size that is easy on the eye. Ten or twelve point is preferable. Leave a one-inch margin on all sides.

4.   Be specific.

Your qualifications and desired position must be understandable at a glance. Most personnel professionals initially spend less than ten seconds reviewing your resume. If they are interested, they will set your resume aside for further consideration. Like Celebrity and Royal Caribbean, personnel departments receive an avalanche of unsolicited resumes. Your mission: to get hired now; or be considered for the next job opening.

5.   Make your resume work for you!

The reverse chronological resume format is popular and easy to read. You present your qualifications and work experience beginning with your current position, most recently held job, or educational status. Divide your resume into these sections:

- ❒ **Identifying Information**
- ❒ **Job Objective (position desired)**
- ❒ **Employment Experience**
- ❒ **Education**
- ❒ **Talents and Skills**
- ❒ **Awards, Honors & Membership**
- ❒ **Professional References**

❒ *Identifying Information*

Identify yourself with your first name and surname; street address; city; state; postal code and nation. Include your complete telephone number with area code. You want the cruise line to notice and remember your name, so print your name in capital letters in a bold typeface, centered at the top of the page. Center your address and telephone number under your name.

Hot Tip: Once your resumes have been sent out, be prepared to respond to inquiries by mail and telephone. You may be contacted by telephone. Be prepared to answer your phone in a professional manner or record a professional, brief message for your answering machine. Always return telephone calls and any correspondence immediately.

❏ *Job Objective*

You must be specific about the position you desire. "It's easier to place you when we know what position you want," says a personnel director with Royal Caribbean. You may wish to state a specific position, example: youth counselor. Also state a department such as cruise staff. Your job objective must be broad enough so as to not exclude you from jobs, yet specific enough that the cruise line can match you with a job opening.

Be direct - describe briefly how you are qualified for the job, and how you can contribute to the company.

The National Association of Colleges and Employers NACE, suggests that you ask yourself this series of questions to help determine your job objective:

(a) Why am I the best person for this job?

(b) What do I have to offer the employer (cruise line)?

(c) How am I qualified for the position?

(d) Which of my skills and aptitudes are best suited for this job?

(e) With whom do I want to work?

❏ *Employment Experience*

Your employment history serves as your professional biography - it tells about you as an employee. The cruise line is interested in your dependability and commitment, and will compare the level of responsibility you've had at other jobs with the demands of a cruise position.

List your most recent job first. Include both paying and non-paying jobs or experience. List the company name, city, and state of each employer.

Include your job title along with a brief action-packed description of your duties. Tailor these descriptions to match the requirements of the job you're applying for.

❑ *Education*

Cruise lines hire people who have demonstrated commitment and stability, either in school or on the job. A college degree is preferred, but not always necessary for every position. Use your education to enhance your application by showing how it applies to your desired job. List education with school name, followed by city and state, degree earned or the degree you are pursuing. Example: Associate of Arts, Bachelor of Arts, Bachelor of Science. State your major field of study. List all computer skills. List any special interest courses in hospitality, recreation, business, dance, theatre or public speaking. Also mention clubs like Toastmasters or courses such as Dale Carnegie.

❑ *Talents and Skills*

Describe your skills as they apply to the new position. List them by category; for example: computer skills, languages, public speaking and entertainment talents. Explain briefly how your skills and talents can help the company.

❑ *Awards, Honors and Membership*

List awards, honors, and memberships by name. List offices held, committees you were involved in and major goals you achieved.

❑ *Professional References*

The standard procedure is to add this statement, *'references available upon request,'* at the end of your resume.

Hot Tip: Ask in advance for good referrals from instructors, employers and business associates. Supply these people with a copy of your resume. Prepare a list of references with contact name, title, company name, address and complete business telephone number with area code and extension.

6. Introduce yourself with a personal cover letter

Always attach a polite, brief cover letter to your resume. Make it short and sweet, personnel does not have the time to read a novel. Write as if the recipient is your business associate. Be friendly and professional.

Address your cover letter to the Director of Personnel, or the director of a department such as Marine Operations, Entertainment, Cruise Staff. Do not address your cover letter 'To whom it may concern, or 'Dear Sirs.' These may be appropriate formalities - but better to introduce yourself with a 'Dear Personnel Director' or 'Dear Mrs. Peterson'.

Be specific! Your qualifications and desired position must be understandable at a glance. Write your cover letter with this goal: to make it easy for personnel to hire you. State the specific position which interests you, for example: salon staff or youth counselor. Also state the department, for example; Entertainment or Cruise Staff. Briefly review how your employment experience, skills, education and talents can contribute to the passenger's cruise experience.

Hot Tip: Include your return address on both the cover letter and envelope: your name, street address, city, state, nation, postal code and complete telephone number.

7. Your photograph is worth a thousand words.

Include a simple, current photograph. The necessary photo is a 'head and shoulders' pose. You may wish to also enclose a full body photograph. Photos should be

113

current, with you as the only subject. No family members or pets, and no 'party' photographs. Dress as you would for a job interview. Dress the part - copy what cruise employees wear; a tailored dress, suit, jacket or blazer and tie. Appear professional, personable and happy!

Hot Tip: Type or write your full name, address, telephone number and position desired on a plain mailing label. Affix the label to the reverse side of your photograph. Attach photograph/s to resume and cover letter with a paper clip.

8. Special Delivery. Don't be lost in the 'in' basket with one thousand other plain white business size envelopes. Use an 8 x 10 or 9 x 12 envelope and your resume and cover letter will arrive neat and flat, not folded. You may develop a 'publicity package,' a colorful portfolio folder or file folder containing all your materials. If you are in the vicinity of the cruise line headquarters, consider delivering your resume and cover letter in person.

9. Follow Up - Do not give up. Accept the fact that you may not hear from personnel right away, and concentrate on what you can do to help personnel hire you. While you await a reply, continue to prepare yourself, complete your education, take a job in hospitality or tourism and practice public speaking.

You may not hear from a cruise line because:
   ✓ There are no jobs open at the time of your application.
   ✓ Personnel did not feel you were the precise person for the job with your current qualifications.
   ✓ Your resume was misplaced or misfiled.
   ✓ Your application is being held for future consideration.

Job opportunities and competition are two factors out of your control. Focus on preparing yourself and continue to promote yourself to the cruise lines. After you've sent your resume and made your first contact, send a thank you card. You may also resubmit your application or send an update on your resume. Draft a new cover   letter noting additional educational or employment accomplishments. Your goal: to keep your name, resume and photograph in front of the personnel director. Become a familiar face.

10. Follow up - Using the Phone Should you telephone to ask about your application? Do not telephone unless it is absolutely necessary. Most cruise line personnel departments strongly discourage phone inquiries. If you choose to follow-up by phone, do not appear impatient or inconsiderate.

These tips on friendly phone etiquette will help you make a good impression. When you telephone, announce your name clearly, in a friendly tone of voice and smile! State clearly with whom you wish to speak and the specific position you are interested in. Ask to be announced. 'Would you please tell Ms. Wilde that Nancy Johnson is calling about the gift shop staff position?' Show the receptionist respect, as he or she can be a valuable ally.

Use your voice to help make your best impression. Practice a friendly, alert and enthusiastic speaking voice. Telephoning a stranger can be intimidating, don't allow nervousness to get in your way. Do some vocal exercises to relax your voice before calling. Try this exercise: Open your mouth as wide as possible, yawn, and open wide again. This will open up your vocal passages and give your voice a fuller sound. Enunciate your words slowly and distinctly.

Smile when you speak and your voice will take on a warm and friendly tone. Many telemarketing firms place a mirror by the telephone of each employee, to remind them to smile. Good breathing also makes a big difference in the quality of your voice.

Try this exercise: breath in for three counts, hold your breath for three counts, and let the air out for five counts. Repeat five times. This is an easy way to relax before you make a phone call. This technique works to calm you before interviews or any stressful meeting. By relaxing your nerves and throat, your voice will become relaxed and more resonant.

Hot Tip: Take copies of your resume and list of references with you on all interviews. You'll save time completing applications.

GO GET THAT JOB!

6

CRUISE LINE PROFILES

**We've done your homework for you!
Use Cruise Line Profiles for quick answers
to important questions:**

- Which cruise lines should I apply to?
- Where can I go?
- When can I travel?
- Will there be people like me onboard?
- What type of guest travels with each line?
- What ships are in each fleet?
- What New ships are planned?
- How big are the ships? How many guests?
- What hallmark programs & facilities are there?

Plus:

✔ **Job Contacts**
✔ **Cruise Line Addresses**
✔ **Employment Hotline Telephone Numbers**
✔ **Employment agencies/Concessionaires**
✔ **Web Sites**
✔ **New Ships**
✔ **New Cruise Lines**

Key:

Size is noted by 'grt' or gross registered tons. Each grt equals 100 cubic feet of enclosed revenue-earning space (volume). It is not the ship's actual weight.

Capacity is noted as the ship's maximum number of berths, or beds, based upon two passengers per stateroom.

Cruise Line Profiles

We've done your homework for you.

Match your education, work experience, skills and talents to a specific cruise line and Go!

Cruise companies want to hire qualified people with an understanding of the cruise line's programs, future plans and 'personality.' The more you know about the cruise line - the better chance you have of being hired. Review these details on 40 major cruise lines, begin your job search and get paid to travel!

How to Use Cruise Line Profiles

The cruise line's 'personality' is expressed by its standards in accommodations, dining, itineraries and service. Personality is also determined by the size of the ship; type of guest; type of programs, facilities, shore excursions and entertainment.

Most major cruise lines offer these facilities and programs: boutiques, casinos, entertainment productions, medical office, front desk or purser's service, restaurant and bars, beauty salons-cosmetology and massage, photography services, shore excursions, swimming pools.

Here's an example of common job opportunities:

- ◆ *Boutiques:* sales & cashier staff
- ◆ *Casino:* dealer, slot technician, cashier
- ◆ *Show lounges & bars:* entertainer, dancer, singer, comedian, magician, lecturer, duos, bands, light & sound technicians.
- ◆ *Medical office:* - physician, nurse.
- ◆ *Front desk/purser's desk:* - Chief purser, asst. purser, guest services staff
- ◆ *Restaurants & bars*: food and beverage staff: chef, sous chef, pastry chef, baker, wait staff, bus boy, dishwasher, buffet staff, wine steward...
- ◆ *Salon & spa*: hair stylist, nail technician, cosmetologist, massage therapist
- ◆ *Photography service*: photographer

Cruise Line Profiles make it easy to match your experience and skills to a cruise line's job opportunities. Our review of each cruise line's exceptional or hallmark programs and facilities will help you identify additional job opportunities.

Cruise Line Classification

Four basic cruise market sectors are suggested by *Travel Agent Magazine Cruise Desk*. Cruise lines are identified by price and vacation type to help you understand the cruise line's 'personality' and primary market.

The four market sectors are:
Adventure/Specialty
Deluxe
Resort-style - popular price
Resort-style - upscale/premium price

Use these classifications to identify the lines which are most likely to hire you. As the industry grows, cruise lines will expand into new markets and add ships to their fleet. 63 new ships are expected to set sail by 2005. Several cruise lines qualify for multiple classification.

Cruise Areas & Seasons

Where do you want to go? Are you ready for world-wide travel? Use this guide to plan your travel opportunities. Once you are hired you may travel the world while working on different ships within one cruise line's fleet or transfer jobs between companies.

Use this destination listing to save time and money on your job search. If you're a watersports instructor, skip Alaska cruises and target the South Pacific or Caribbean. Lecturers - target lines destined for less common ports-of-call. See *Cruise Guide to Destinations.*

The Fleet

You'll learn what ships belong to each cruise line's fleet, plus details on new ships. More ships equals more job opportunities, and with 63 new ships in the works, your chance for employment continue to improve.
See Ships of the Future: New Ship Additions

Nationality of Crew/Staff

A cruise ship is an international city with primarily Greek, Italian, British and Norwegian officers and a multi-national crew and staff. Janitorial, restaurant and bar, deck and engineering crew originate primarily from Africa, Asia/Pacific, Caribbean, Eastern Europe, Europe, Indonesia, Central and South America. Cruise staff positions are often held by US, UK, Canadian and European citizens.

Your nationality does not ultimately define your job opportunities. Hiring decisions are based on demand for your talents, skills and work experience. Labor agreements and company operations goals also determine hiring. US-flagged cruise lines are required to hire US citizens for a majority of jobs.

Example: Due to labor agreements that Holland America Line is party to with unions in Holland, Indonesia and the Philippines; most crew positions are limited to members of these unions.

Guest Profile

Who will you find aboard? Job opportunities are often determined by the type of passenger. For example, if you want to travel as a youth counselor, look for lines that cater to families. Action-seekers love ships with casinos and large-scale Broadway productions. These ships need casino staff and entertainers. Lecturers and solo entertainers will find more opportunities on cruise lines favored by mature travelers and experienced cruisers.

Our definition of guest profile is from demographic and interest categories proposed by *Cruise & Vacation Views.*

Demographic and interests categories:

Families: Parents and/or grandparents traveling with children
20's: Young singles & couples, honeymooners
Boomers: Individuals and couples from age 30-60
Mature Travelers: Mature singles and couples
Active: Prefer exploration and adventure itineraries
Experienced: Sophisticated, frequent travelers
Action Seekers: Enjoy on-board activities, casino and entertainment

Insider's Information

It's the next best thing to having a relative in the business! You'll find Web sites, resume and application tips to help you succeed; special programs and facilities plus hiring policies particular to each cruise line.

Job Contact

Does the cruise line hire direct through its own personnel department - or via a concessionaire or employment agency? You'll save time and money by applying to the correct department or agency.

Web sites

Addresses

Job Hotline Telephone Numbers

CRUISE LINE PROFILES

AMERICAN CLASSIC VOYAGES CO.
[http://www.deltaqueen.com]

American Classic Voyages Co., AMCV, is the largest owner and operator of US-flag passenger vessels with several lines under its umbrella: the renewed United States Lines, American Hawaii Cruises, The Delta Queen Steamboat Co. and Delta Queen Coastal Cruises.

AMCV's 'Project America' promises a new age of American ship building. The two newbuilds of the United States Lines will be the largest US cruise ships ever built and the first large US-built cruise ships in more than 40 years. See American Hawaii Cruises, Delta Queen Steamboat Co., Delta Queen Coastal Cruise, United States Lines.

AMERICAN CRUISE LINES

American Cruise Lines' first ship, *American Eagle* sails from Maine to Florida's Gulf Coast on 7- and 14-day sailings.

Cruise Line Classification: Resort-style/popular

Cruise Areas & Seasons: US East Coast

The Fleet
American Eagle

Nationality of Crew/Staff: American, International

JOB CONTACT:
American Cruise Lines
c/o Delta Queen Steamboat Company
Human Resources
Robin Street Wharf
1380 Port of New Orleans Place
New Orleans, LA 70130-1890

AMERICAN HAWAII CRUISES

[http://www.cruisehawaii.com]

American Hawaii Cruises offers an authentic Hawaiian experience with year-round cruises aboard its ship, the ss *Independence*. Seven-night cruises depart from Honolulu to visit five ports on four islands. The line's shore excursions were recognized with *Travel Holiday's* 'Best of the Best' award. Experience Old Hawaii as the ship's 'kumu' (teacher) share stories of the fire goddess while you sail past active volcano Mt. Kilauea.

American Hawaii is popular with first-time Hawaii visitors, mature travelers, golfers, honeymooners and families with children.

Cruise Line Classification: Resort-style/popular

Cruise Areas & Seasons: Year-round: Hawaii

The Fleet	Size	Capacity
Independence	30,090 grt	867

Nationality of Crew/Staff: American, International

Insider's Information
(504) 586-0631 (Ask for Employment Hotline.)
Say Aloha to a more than 75% American crew.

The Passenger Services Act of 1896 prohibits the carriage of passengers or cargo between any ports within the United States other than by US built, maintained, and registered vessels. As an operator of American-flagged vessels, American Hawaii Cruises is required to hire a majority of American officers and crew. Operated by the Delta Queen Steamboat Co. No casino.

American Hawaii Employment Procedure

When you are first hired, you will be hired on an on-call basis until a permanent rotation becomes available (occasionally permanent on-call positions are available). American Hawaii also hires youth counselors seasonally.

During each tour of duty (rotation), all crew members live aboard ship. Crew cabins are generally shared between two to four persons (dormitory style). Officers and Staff have different living accommodations. While aboard ship you will be provided with meals, laundered uniforms (depending on the specific job), access to a crew weight room and TV lounge. Ample soap, washers and dryers are provided to do your laundry. Medical care for emergencies is also available. The Human Resources department plans a variety of sports and social activities for crew members in various ports.

American Hawaii promotes a safe, drug-free work environment. You will be subject to a pre-employment physical and a strict, zero-tolerance pre-employment drug-testing program. During your employment you will be subject to a strict, zero-tolerance random drug-testing program.

American Hawaii(AMCV, US Lines) Employment Requirements

US citizen, have the legal right to work in the US.

At least 18 years old (21 for our Bar or Pursers

department.)

Obtain a US Coast Guard Merchant Mariners

Document (MMD.)

Be friendly, outgoing, and have hospitality experience.

Have the stamina to work long hours.

Be able to pass a drug test & background investigation.
Work under pressure and be adaptable to vessel life.

JOB CONTACT:

Beauticians, Masseuse
        The Stylists, Inc.
        Attn.: Paul Grabb
        4644 Kolohala St.
        Honolulu, HI 96816
        Phone: 808-923-3855
        Fax: 808-735-6717
        email: Salons@aloha.net

Doctor, Nurse
        email strum@amcvhnl.com

Band Members
        The Weinstein Agency
        PO Box 37725
        Honolulu, HI 96837
        Contact: Abe Winston
        Phone: 808-941-9974
        Email: AEWjazfest@aol.com
Photo Manager, Photographers
        Trans Oceanic Photo
        Attn.: Rob Harrow, President
        New York Passenger Terminal, pier 88
        711 12th Ave. Suite 1
        New York, NY 10019
        Phone: 212-757-2707
        Fax: 212-265-6943
        email: transocean@aol.com

Showplace Entertainers
Kennedy Entertainment
Attn.: Bonnie Brown
244 S. Academy St.

Mooresville, NC 28115
Phone: 704-662-3501
Fax: 704-662-3668

The following licensed positions are hired directly through the American Maritime Officers: Deck Department: Master, First, Second, and Third Officers, Engine Department: Chief Engineer, First, Second, and Third Engineers

The following unlicensed positions are hired directly through the Seafarers' International Union (Honolulu Hall): Deck Department: Boatswain, Boatswain Mate, Carpenter, Ordinary Seamen, Able Bodied Seamen,

Hotel Department: Dishwashers, Food porters, Housekeeping porters, crew porters, etc. Engine Department: Chief of Refrigeration, Refrigeration Technicians, Wipers, Oilers, Firemen/Watertenders, Electricians, QMEDs, Machinist, Plumbers, Engine Storekeeper, Engine Utilities

Seafarers' International Union
606 Kalihi St.
Honolulu, HI 96819
808-845-5222

The following SIU represented hotel positions can be hired via American Hawaii's Web site: Cabin Attendants, BellPorters, Laundry Supervisor, Laundry Attendants, Bartenders, Cocktail Servers...

Bar Porter, Deck Attendants, Waiters, Bussers, First, Second and Third Cooks, Cook Trainees, Storekeepers, Assistant Storekeepers

All of the above positions are hired on an on-call basis until a permanent 12 week schedule is available (If you are locally available, you may apply to become a permanent on-call employee).

The following management and corporate hotel positions can be hired via American Hawaii's Web site: Hotel Director, Night Manager, Guest Relations Coordinator, Guest Relations Manager,

Chief Purser, Senior Purser, Junior Assistant Pursers, Cruise Director, Assistant Cruise Director, Stage Manager, Assistant Stage Manager, Host (ess), Kumu (teacher of Hawaiian traditions), Sports and Activities Coordinator, Youth Counselors, Disc Jockey, Maitre D'Hotel, Head Waiter, Assistant Head Waiter, Bar Manager, Executive Chef, Saucier, Sous Chef, Garde Manger, Gift Shop Manager, Gift Shop Sales Associate, Executive Housekeeper, Assistant Executive Housekeeper, Crew Services Manager, Human Resources Manager, Vessel Controller (accountant), Provisions Manager, Deck & Engine Yeoman, Shore Excursion Manager, Shore Excursion Sales Representatives.

Frequently Asked Questions (American Hawaii)

Will I have to relocate my home permanently? No.

What sort of schedule will I work? Crew members typically work 12 weeks aboard then have six weeks off to relax after they receive a permanent rotation schedule. Unlike many cruise lines, American Hawaii Cruises does not ask for (nor give) employment contracts. We do ask that you give us two weeks notice before you leave.

Will I have to join a union and pay dues? While a few crew members are non-union corporate employees, most crew members belong to either the Seafarers' International Union (SIU) or the American Maritime Officers (AMO).

Members of the SIU pay $270.00 for a physical and drug test; corporate employees pay between $75.00 - $150.00 for a physical and drug test.

The basic Coast Guard MMD cost is $150.00. Some positions require licenses, certificates of registry, or ratings from the Coast Guard, which may be an additional cost.

Can I get hired for just the summer? No, summertime employment is not available. However, Youth Counselors can work during the summer as well as school holidays.

What is the pay and benefit structure? Wages are calculated based on a daily rate, and some positions have added gratuities. SIU members have initiation fees and union dues taken out of their paycheck, and SIU union benefits go into effect after 75 days of employment. SIU employees will become dues paying members, and will receive benefits such as medical insurance through the union. All licensed marine employees will become members of the AMO.

Management and staff will be salaried, and receive corporate benefits. All employees are paid every two weeks, and direct deposit is available. Paychecks can either be sent to the vessel, or to your home.

What kind of uniforms will I need to buy? While some uniform pieces are provided at no cost, other pieces must be purchased aboard. Each position has different requirements that can be provided to you when you are hired.

AMERICAN WEST STEAMBOAT
[http://www.columbiarivercruise.com/]

Visit the historic routes of Lewis and Clark and the Oregon Trail aboard authentic stern- and paddlewheelers. Narrated shore excursions on 4- and 7-night riverboat cruises introduce guests to the history, culture and scenery of the Pacific Northwest. Learn the rich legacy and cultures of the early Native Americans, early explorers, fur traders and pioneer settlers. The captain of the sternwheeler *Queen of the West* can pull up to the river's edge, lower the 45 foot bow ramp, and allow the guests to experience the serendipity of an unscheduled stop. Enjoy live, showboat variety entertainment with musical themes including Country and Western, Riverboat Jazz, Golden Oldies and Big Band.

Cruise Line Classification: Adventure/Specialty

Cruise Areas & Seasons:
Columbia River, Snake River and Willamette River

The Fleet

Ship Name	Size	Capacity
Queen of the West	230-feet	163

Nationality of Crew/Staff: American

JOB CONTACT:
American West Steamboat
601 Union Street Suite 4343
Seattle, WA 98101

BERGEN LINE, INC. (Norwegian Coastal Voyages)
[http://www.bergenline.com]

Bergen Line, Inc. is the US marketing company for Norwegian Coastal Voyages; whose 11 ships sail the scenic west coast of Norway year-round; carrying cargo and passengers between Bergen and Kirkenes. Bergen Line is the US representative of Silja Line, Scandinavian Seaways and Color Line.

Norwegian Coastal Voyages appeals to passengers age 50+, and special interest groups in search of an in-depth cultural experience. Highlights include Norwegian art and culture theme cruises and whale safari excursions.

Cruise Line Classification: Adventure/Specialty, Resort-Style/popular price

Cruise Areas & Seasons:
Year-round: Norway

The Fleet

Ship Name	Size	Capacity
Harald Jarl	2,620 tons	164
Kong Harald:	11,200 tons	490
Lofoten	2,597 tons	213
Midnatsol	5,205 tons	328
Narvik	4,073 tons	312
Nordkapp	11,350 tons	490
Nordlys	11,200 tons	482
Nordnorge	11,384 tons	464
Polarlys	12,000 tons	479
Richard With	11,200 tons	490
Vesteralen:	4,073 tons	318

Nationality of Crew/Staff: European, International

Guest Profile: Boomers, Families, Mature Travelers

JOB CONTACT:
Norwegian Coastal Voyage Inc.
c/o Bergen Line Services/Human Resources
405 Park Avenue
New York, NY 10022

CAPE CANAVERAL CRUISE LINE
[http://www.capecanaveralcruise.com]

Cruise for 2-or 4-nights to the Bahamas and Key West aboard a sleek ocean liner, the venerable *Dolphin IV*. Cape Canaveral Cruise Line offers the perfect complement to an Orlando theme park vacation with comfortable staterooms and quality service at affordable rates.

Cruise Line Classification: Resort-Style/popular

131

The Fleet

Ship Name	Size	Capacity
Dolphin IV	13,650	718

Nationality of Crew: International

Guest Profile: singles, couples and families; 20's, boomers, mature travelers; action-seekers.

Insider's Information: See the company Web site for opportunities. [http://www.capecanaveralcruise.com] When a position is listed, FAX a letter of intent, resume and salary history. Please include Requisition Numbers on all job applications.

Fax: (321) 783-4120
email: dolphin4@capecanaveralcruise.com

Job Contact:
Cape Canaveral Cruise Line, Inc.
Human Resources Dept.
7099 N. Atlantic Avenue
Cape Canaveral, FL 32920

CARNIVAL CRUISE LINES
[http://www.carnival.com]

Known for its festive-yet-casual atmosphere, Carnival offers a variety of on-board dining, entertainment and activity options for all ages. The 'Most Popular Cruise Line,' is the largest in the world, based on number of passengers carried. One of the 'Big Four', Carnival's Fun Ships sail on voyages of three to 16 days.

Carnival breaks new ground with 28 different short cruise itineraries from nine different North American homeports - Miami, Tampa, Los Angeles, New York, Galveston, Boston, Charleston, Newport News and Port

Canaveral, FL. Highlights: Camp Carnival boasts one of the largest year-round youth counselor staffs; mega casinos; lavish Broadway-style entertainment.

Carnival Cruise Lines is a member of the World's Leading Cruise Lines alliance which also includes Holland America Line, Cunard, Seabourn Cruise Line, Costa Cruises and Windstar Cruises.

Cruise Line Classification: Resort Style/popular

Cruise Areas & Seasons:
Seasonal: Alaska, Hawaii, Panama Canal, Canadian Maritime Provinces, Bermuda
Year-round: Caribbean, Mexican Riviera, Bahamas

The Fleet

Ship Name	Size	Capacity
Carnival Victory	102,000 tons	2,758
Carnival Destiny	101,353 tons	2,642
Carnival Triumph;	102,000 tons	2,578
Celebration	47,262 tons	1,486
Ecstasy	70,367 tons	2,040
Elation	70,367 tons	2,040
Fantasy	70,367 tons	2,040
Fascination	70,367 tons	2,040
Holiday	46,052 tons	1,452
Imagination	70,367 tons	2,040
Inspiration	70,367 tons	2,040
Jubilee	47,262 tons	1,486
Paradise	70,367 tons	2,040
Sensation	70,367 tons	2,040
Tropicale	36,674 tons	1,022

Newbuilds

Name	Estimated Delivery Date	Size	Capacity
Carnival Spirit	early 2001	84,000 tons	2,112
Carnival Pride	late 2001	84,000 tons	2,112
Carnival Legend	2002	84,000 tons	2,112
Carnival Conquest	Fall 2002	102,000 tons	2,758
Carnival Glory	2003	102,000 tons	2,758

Nationality of Crew/Staff: International

Guest Profile: 20's, Boomers, Families, Action Seekers

Insider's Information: Job Hotline: (305) 599-2600 (press 2 for Employment Hotline)
Entertainers - Applicants for social host/hostess, cruise director/assistant, aerobics instructor, tour director must be professional entertainers: vocalists, dancers, musicians, comedians, ventriloquists, acrobats or magicians. For any entertainment position, including disc jockey, sound and mike technician, musician, duo, group, bands - send a demo tape: audio or VHS video with resume and photograph. No live auditions.

Carnival hires throughout the world. Person to person interviews are desirable, although in rare cases, a telephone interview is acceptable.

Food & Beverage positions are hired through:
Seachest Associates
3655 NW 87th Avenue
Miami, FL 33178-2428

Gift Shop staff hired through:
Greyhound Leisure: (305) 592-6460

JOB CONTACT:
Carnival Cruise Lines
Human Resources
3655 NW 87th Avenue
Miami, FL 33178-2428

CELEBRITY CRUISES
[http://wwwcelebrity-cruises.com]
Celebrity Cruises' port-intensive worldwide itineraries attract an international guest list of 85 percent American and 15 percent international travelers. Celebrity appeals to families, couples, honeymooners and singles. Guests range in age from 35-60, with a median of 48 years . Most hold professional/managerial positions, and have household incomes of $60,000 +.

The line is one of two cruise brands owned and operated by Royal Caribbean Cruises Ltd., which also operates Royal Caribbean International. Highlights: AquaSpa facilities are among the industry's most advanced. The *Millennium* and *Infinity* at 91,000 gross tons, are the first of four millennium-class newbuilds. They will be the largest liners to transit the Panama Canal and among the newest ships to sail the Hawaiian Islands.

Cruise Line Classification: Resort Style/premium

Cruise Areas & Seasons:
Seasonal: Alaska, Caribbean, Bermuda, Bahamas, Hawaii, Panama Canal, Mexico, Europe, Mediterranean, Western Canada, South America

135

The Fleet

Ship Name	Size	Capacity
Century	70,606 tons	1,750
Galaxy	77,713 tons	1,870
Horizon	46,811 tons	1,354
Mercury	77,713 tons	1,870
Zenith	47,255 tons	1,375
Millennium	91,000 tons,	1,950

Newbuilds

Name	Estimated Delivery Date	Size	Capacity
Infinity	February 2001	91,000 tons	1,950
Millennium class	2002	91,000 tons	1,950

Nationality of Crew/Staff: International

Guest Profile: Boomers, Families, Mature Travelers, Experienced

Insider's Information: Celebrity/RCI Job Hot Line: (305) 530-0471. Entertainers - include a brief 3-5 minute video cassette with resume. Direct your application to Entertainment Director/Production Department.

Ocean-based jobs:
[http://www.celebritycruises.com/celebrity_profile/car ccrops_obj.html] Please fax your resume with salary history to 305-539-6168.

Land-based jobs: [http://www.celebritycruises.com/ celebrity_profile/gocelebrityjobs.html]

JOB CONTACT:
Ocean-based jobs
Celebrity Cruises

Hotel Human Resources
1050 Caribbean Way
Miami, FL 33132

Land-based jobs
Celebrity Cruises
Human Resources
1050 Caribbean Way
Miami, FL 33132

CLIPPER CRUISE LINE
[http://www.clippercruise.com/]

Clipper Cruise Line's intimate ships bring travelers to secluded waterways and seldom-visited beaches. Zodiac landing craft allow for shoreside exploration of locales larger ships never see. Clipper combines a high level of comfort and unique itineraries including the Orinoco River, 'Yachtsman's Caribbean,' Far East and South Pacific.

Highlights: The captain and his officers maintain an open-bridge policy, allowing passengers to drop in anytime. The lifestyle onboard is casual and unregimented, with an intimate ambiance conducive to camaraderie. Naturalists, historians and other experts offer informal lectures, lead expeditions and invite questions.

Cruise Line Classification: Resort Style/premium

Cruise Areas & Seasons
Caribbean, Greenland, High Canadian Arctic, Central and South America, Antarctica, Far East, Pacific

The Fleet

Ship Name	Size
Yorktown Clipper	138
Clipper Adventurer	122
Nantucket Clipper	100
Clipper Odyssey	128

Nationality of Crew/Staff: American, International

Guest Profile: Boomers, Mature Travelers, Experienced

Insider's Information: Ship's Registry: US; no children's facilities; entertainers and lecturers are hired from ports of call. All positions hired direct through cruise line headquarters. New World Ship Management Company, LLC, provides employment opportunities with Clipper. Email contact: employment@nwship.com. Online employment applications: [http://www.clipper-cruise.com/]

Clipper Cruise Line requires onboard crew to begin their employment at Clipper in an entry-level position: house-keeper, server or deckhand.

Clipper Crew Member Qualifications

At least 21 years of age

US citizen with valid passport (or must be able to secure passport upon employment.)

Physically strong, with stamina to work long hours

Well-groomed (no visible tattoos or body piercings, etc.; men must have short hair) and drug-free.

Friendly and outgoing

Strong communication skills

Work experience in customer service, housekeeping, table service or other related area.

Ability to work under pressure
College experience preferred

JOB CONTACT:
New World Ship Management Co.
Human Resources Department
7711 Bonhomme Avenue, 2nd Floor
St. Louis, Missouri 63105
Fax: 314-721-1412
E-mail: ClipperHR@intrav.com

CLUB MED
[http://www.clubmed.com]

Club Med's worldwide network of resort villages now includes a floating resort; the *Club Med 2*. Club Med's floating playground for 392 guests sails jet-set style to popular ports and untouched, pristine beaches. Whether you choose a Caribbean, Mediterranean or Transatlantic itinerary, freedom of choice, intimacy and a relaxed yet " chic " European atmosphere are the trademarks of your Club Med cruise.

Club Med caters to fans of both the adventure of sailing and the comforts of luxury cruising. The ship is powered by fully computerized sails during 70% of the cruise.

Cruise Line Classification: Resort-style/premium

Cruise Areas:
Mediterranean, Caribbean, South Pacific, Pacific

The Fleet
Club Med 2

Nationality of Crew/Staff: International

Guest Profile: 20's, Boomers, Action Seekers

Insider's Information: Positions hired direct through cruise line headquarters. Club Med employs gentils organisateurs (G.O.s) as cruise staff, hosts, tour guides and entertainers. Staff Aboard each ship; 32 French officers and crew, 66 multinational G.O.s, 83 service personnel, 5 Casino employees, 2 photographers. The *Club Med 2* offers a watersports platform for SCUBA diving, water skiing, windsurfing and sailing.

JOB CONTACT:
Club Med Cruises
Human Resources
40 West 57th St.
New York, NY 10019

COMMODORE CRUISE LINE
[http://www.commodorecruise.com]
Commodore offers casual cruising to popular ports at affordable rates. Big Band, Singles, Jazz theme cruises appeal to travelers in their mid 30s to early 60s with middle to upper-middle incomes.

Cruise Line Classification: Resort-style/popular
Cruise Areas & Seasons
Year-round: Caribbean, Mexico
Select sailings: Maya Explorer Cruises (Honduras

and Mexico); Key West, Mexico
The Fleet

Ship Name	Size	Capacity
Enchanted Isle	23,395 tons	725
Enchanted Capri	15,410 tons	525
Universe Explorer		

Nationality of Crew/Staff: Officers: Norwegian and Filipino, Crew: European, American and Filipino
Guest Profile: 20's, Boomers, Mature Travelers, Experienced

Insider's Information: Job Hotline: (954) 967-2100 (follow instructions for Employment Line.)
FAX (954)-967-2135 attn.: Shipboard Manager Crew Personnel

JOB CONTACT:
Commodore Cruise Line, Ltd.
Human Resources
4000 Hollywood Blvd.
Suite 385, South Tower
Hollywood, FL 33021

COSTA CRUISE LINES
[http://wwwcostacruises.com]
Costa's international fleet of six ships spans the globe offering Italian-style cruises of seven-nights and longer. Costa was voted one of the top ten cruise lines by *Travel and Leisure* readers; and voted 'Head of the Class' and 'Top Value Index' by *Cruise Reports*.

Costa appeals to honeymooners, families and mature travelers. Caribbean cruisers are 35+ with a household income of $50,000+, European cruise travelers are 35+ with a household income of $75,000, college educated, well-traveled and destination oriented.

Highlights include the 'Golf Academy at Sea' program, hosted by a PGA-member golf instructor on Caribbean Cruises.

Cruise Line Classification: Resort-Style/popular

Cruise Areas & Seasons:
Caribbean, Canary Islands, Russia, Fjords, Baltic, North Cape, Mediterranean, Transatlantic

The Fleet

Ship Name	Size	Capacity
CostaAlegra	28,500 tons	820
CostaClassica	53,000 tons	1,308
CostaMarina	25,500 tons	776
CostaRiviera	30,400 tons	974
CostaRomantica	53,000 tons	1,356
CostaVictoria	76,000 tons	1,928
CostaAtlantica	84,000 tons	2,112

Nationality of Crew/Staff: Italian, International

Guest Profile: Boomers, couples and families, mature travelers, ship buffs.

Insider's Information: Job Hotline at (305) 358-7325 ext. 609.

JOB CONTACT:
Costa Cruise Lines
Human Resources
80 SW 8th Street

World Trade Center Bldg.
Suite 2700
Miami, FL 33130-3097

CROWN CRUISE LINE

Departures from Aruba, personal attention and moderate prices make the *Crown Dynasty* a great vacation value. Crown Cruise Line appeals to travelers in their mid 30s to early 60s with middle to upper-middle incomes. A full children's program is available summer and holidays.

Cruise Line Classification: Resort-style/premium

Cruise Areas
Caribbean
The Fleet

Ship Name	Size	Capacity
Crown Dynasty	20,000 tons	800

Nationality of Crew/Staff: Officers: Northern European, Scandinavian, Crew: Filipino, Staff: International

Guest Profile: Boomers, Mature Travelers, Action Seekers

JOB CONTACT:
Fax Resume and salary request to: Crown Cruise Line, Attn.: H.R. Manager 954-967-2147.

CRUISE WEST
[http://www.cruisewest.com/]

Cruise West provides 'casual, up-close cruising with a personal touch aboard their fleet of small ships. Transit the locks of the Columbia and Snake River dams that make inland voyages possible. Ask your captain to stop the ship to give you a closer look at bear ashore; he'll even shut down the engines so you can listen as eagles cry and glacial ice crackles.

Highlights: Shore excursions to Mt. St. Helens Volcanic National Monument; guest speakers including balladeer Linda Russell, who has performed at Carnegie Hall and for *A Prairie Home Companion*; and Phil George, a Nez Perce tribal elder.

Cruise Line Classification: Adventure/Specialty

Cruise Areas & Seasons:
Columbia & Snake Rivers, Coastal Canada, Alaska, Pacific Coast, Sea of Cortes, Mexico.

The Fleet	Capacity
Ship Name	
Spirit of '98	96
Spirit of Endeavor	102
Spirit of Glacier Bay	52
Spirit of Alaska	78
Spirit of Columbia	78
Spirit of Discovery	84
Sheltered Seas (day cruising only)	

Nationality of Crew/Staff: American

Guest Profile: Boomers, mature travelers, explorers

144

Insiders information: Apply online at [http://www.cruisewest.com/] Information on hours, scheduling, living accommodations, requirements. Fax (206) 441-4757 Attn: Human Resources.

JOB CONTACT:
Cruise West
Human Resources
2401 4th Ave, Suite 700
Seattle, WA 98121

CRYSTAL CRUISES
[http://www.crystalcruises.com]

Crystal Cruises received awards for 'World's Best Cruise Line,' and 'World's Best Cruise Ship' from *Travel & Leisure* readers survey and 'Best Large Ship Line' from *Conde Nast Traveler* readers survey. Crystal guests are primarily 35+ with a median age of 64. Most are married, upscale, discriminating travelers. Approximately 85 percent are from the US and Canada; 15 percent are international.

Highlights: Caesar's Palace at Sea casino, Italian and Asian alternative restaurants, Callaway Golf partnership. Theme cruises include: Crystal Wine & Food Festival, Health & Fitness/Alternative Medicine, Best of Broadway, Computer University @ Sea and Big Band.

Cruise Line Classification: Deluxe

Cruise Areas & Seasons
Spring: Panama Canal/Caribbean, Mexican Riviera, World Cruise, Mediterranean
Summer: Alaska/Canada, Western Europe, Baltic, North Cape, British Isles, Mediterranean

Fall: Panama Canal/Caribbean, Black Sea, Mediterranean, Red Sea, Asia, Australia, New Zealand
Winter: Panama Canal/Caribbean, South America, World Cruise
Holiday: South America, South Pacific

The Fleet

Ship Name	Size	Capacity
Crystal Harmony	49,400 tons	940
Crystal Symphony	51,044 tons	940

Nationality of Crew/Staff: Crew: International, Hotel Staff: European

Guest Profile: Boomers, Mature Travelers, Experienced

Insider's Information:
[http://www.crystalcruises.com/employmentinfo.html]
(310) 785-9300 (ask operator for job hotline)

JOB CONTACT:
Shore side employment:
Crystal Cruises
Human Resources
2049 Century Park East, Suite 1400
Los Angeles, CA 90067

Ship board employment:
Gift Shop
Crystal Cruises
Attn.: Gift Shop
2049 Century Park East, Suite 1400
Los Angeles, CA 90067

Casino
Caesars Palace at Sea
3570 Las Vegas Blvd. South
Las Vegas, NV 89109

Entertainment and Enrichment Programs
Crystal Cruises
Attn.: Entertainment Department
2049 Century Park East, Suite 1400
Los Angeles, CA 90067

Spa, Salon, Health & Fitness and Sports Director
Steiner TransOcean
1007 North American Way
Miami, FL 33132
FAX: 305-372-9310

Photographers
Ocean Images
7 Home Farm Business Center
Lockerley, Romsey
Hampshire S051 0JT
United Kingdom, FAX: 44-1794-341415

For all other shipboard positions
International Cruise Management Agency
Attn.: Svein Pedersen
P.O. Box 95
Sentrum
0101 Oslo, Norway

CUNARD
[http://www.cunardline.com]

With 160 years of classic British heritage, Cunard offers authentic British service and far-reaching itineraries. 'The Queen Mary Project' will introduce a new class of 'grand dame' ships in the tradition of the classic *Queen Mary, Queen Elizabeth* and *QEII*.

This newest 'World's Largest' will be longer than three football fields or four city blocks!

Cunard Line Limited operates Cunard and Seabourn Cruise Line; members of the exclusive World's Leading Cruise Lines alliance, which includes Carnival Cruise Lines, Holland America Line, Costa Cruises and Windstar Cruises.

Cruise Line Classification: Resort-style/premium

Cruise Areas & Seasons:
Summer: Mediterranean, New England, Bermuda, Northern Europe, Ireland/Scotland, Transatlantic.
Spring: South Pacific, Panama Canal, Caribbean, Orient, Colonial South, Transatlantic, World Cruise.
Winter: Caribbean, Asia, Australia, World Cruises, Panama Canal, South Pacific.
Fall: Africa, Mediterranean, New England, Caribbean, Adriatic, South America, Arabia, Transatlantic
Christmas Holiday: Panama Canal, Arabia, Caribbean

The Fleet

Ship Name	Size	Capacity
Queen Elizabeth 2:	70,327 tons	1,715
Caronia (fka Vistafjord)	24,492 tons	665

Newbuilds
Name   Est.   Size
                              Delivery Date
The Queen Mary Project   2002   110,000 tons

Nationality of Crew/Staff: Officers-British,
Crew/Staff British & International

Guest Profile: Boomers, Mature Travelers,
Experienced

Insider's Information: Job Hotline: (305) 463-3000
(ask operator for Human Resources)
An online employment section will be available in the
near future.

JOB CONTACT:
Cunard Cruise Line
6100 Blue Lagoon Drive
Suite 400
Miami, FL 33126

Cunard & Seabourn Cruise Line represent nearly
50 percent of the world's luxury cruise market.

DELTA QUEEN COASTAL CRUISES
[http://www.deltaqueen.com]
Beginning in 2001, Delta Queen Coastal Cruises will
offer cruise vacations on specially designed 226-passen-
ger ships along the East and West Coasts of the United
States, the Caribbean and Mexico. Parent company is
American Classic Voyages Co.

Cruise Line Classification: Adventure/Specialty

Cruise Areas:
US East and West Coastal cruises, Caribbean, Mexico

The Fleet

Name	Estimated Delivery Date	Size	Capacity
Unnamed	2001	TBA	226
Unnamed	2001	TBA	226

Nationality of Crew/Staff: American, International
Guest Profile: Mature Travelers, Experienced.

Insider's Information:
The Delta Queen Coastal Cruises' fleet is registered in the US. A majority of the crew/staff are American. Parent company is American Classic Voyages Co.

JOB CONTACT:
Delta Queen Steamboat Company
Human Resources
Robin Street Wharf
1380 Port of New Orleans Place
New Orleans, LA 70130-1890

DELTA QUEEN STEAMBOAT COMPANY
[http://www.deltaqueen.com]
The Delta Queen Steamboat Company provides overnight paddlewheel steamboat vacations with an old-fashioned, American theme. The *Delta Queen, Mississippi Queen,* and the *American Queen,* cruise the US inland waterways on 3- to 16-night excursions.

The *Columbia Queen* offers eight-night Pacific Northwest cruise vacations. Parent company is American Classic Voyages Co.

Cruise Line Classification: Explorer

Cruise Areas
US inland waterways, Pacific Northwest

The Fleet
Ship Name
American Queen
Delta Queen
Mississippi Queen
Columbia Queen

Nationality of Crew/Staff: American, International

Guest Profile: Mature Travelers, Experienced.

Insider's Information: (504) 586-0631 (Ask   operator for Employment Hotline.) The Delta Queen Steamboat Company's fleet is registered in the US. A majority of the crew/staff are American.   Parent company is American Classic Voyages Co.

JOB CONTACT:
Delta Queen Steamboat Company
Human Resources
Robin Street Wharf
1380 Port of New Orleans Place
New Orleans, LA 70130-1890

DISNEY CRUISE LINE
[http://www.disneycruise.com]

The land vacation experts; Disney; offer an exciting cruise vacation experience for all ages with original Broadway-style entertainment and extensive children's programming. 'Rotation dining' gives guests an opportunity to experience a different dining atmosphere nightly - while receiving continuing personal attention from the same waiter.

Disney caters to adults *and* kids; with an entire deck for children's activities, a year-round youth counselor staff and an adults-only restaurant. Disney now offers three-, four- and seven-day cruises aboard the *Disney Magic* and *Wonder.*

Cruise Line Classification: Resort-style/premium

Cruise Areas & Seasons
Year-round: Nassau and Castaway Cay (Disney's private Bahamian island).

The Fleet

Ship Name	Size	Capacity
Disney Magic	83,000 tons,	875
Disney Wonder	83,000 tons	875

Nationality of Crew/Staff: International, American

Guest Profile: 20's, couples, families, boomers, mature travelers.

Insider's Information: [http://disney.go.com/disney cruise/jobs/] Job Hotline: 407-566-7447. Entertainers telephone 407-566-7577.

JOB CONTACT:
Disney Cruise Line
Casting
PO Box 10165
Lake Buena Vista, FL 32830-0165

FIRST EUROPEAN CRUISES (Festival Cruises)
[http://www.first-european.com]
First European's new flagship, *Mistral*, attracts a cosmopolitan guest list: her inaugural hosted cruisers from more than 25 nations, including France, Austria, Belgium, Germany, Italy, Spain, Switzerland, UK, Australia, Brazil, China, Peru and the US.

First European Cruises' departures from Guadeloupe and port-intensive European cruises appeal to upper-middle and middle-class experienced cruisers, age 30 to 70.

Cruise Line Classification: Resort-Style/popular

Cruise Areas & Seasons
Winter: Canary Islands, Caribbean
Spring & Fall: Egypt/Israel, Turkey/Black Sea, Italy, Spain, Western Mediterranean, Morocco, Tunisia , West Africa,
Summer: Greek Islands, Turkey, Scandinavian Fjords, Baltic Sea

The Fleet

Ship Name	Size	Capacity
Azur	14,717 tons	720
Bolero	16,107 tons	802
Flamenco	17,042 tons	784
Mistral	47,900 tons	1,200

Newbuilds

Name	Estimated Delivery Date
Unnamed	2001
Unnamed	2002

Nationality of Crew/Staff: International

Guest Profile: couples, boomers, mature travelers, ship buffs

JOB CONTACT:
FAX your resume and cover letter listing specific job, skills, experience and dates of availability.
Piraeus, Greece Fax # 011-301-429-0170.

HOLLAND AMERICA LINE
[http://www.hollandamerica.com]

Holland America Line offers premium cruises to more than 250 destinations worldwide including popular Alaskan voyages and new Hawaiian itineraries. Now in its 53rd year in Alaska, Holland America's voyages feature an on-board naturalist to help guests better understand and appreciate the geography, geology, biology and ecology of the 'Last Frontier.' HAL's seven-day Glacier Bay Inside Passage cruises feature 30 hours of port time during visits to Juneau, Skagway and Ketchikan, in addition to a nine-hour cruise the full length of Glacier Bay National Park.

HAL's "Great Land Tour" of Alaska was designated an official American Pathways 2000 itinerary, part of the White House Millennium Trails initiative. The tour includes meetings with the Haida people of Ketchikan's rain forest and the Inupiat Eskimo of Kotzebue.

154

Highlights: Club HAL children's activity program, exclusive children's shore excursions, Passport to Fitness activity program, 'Flagship Forum' cultural lecture series, gentleman social hosts on all sailings of 14 days and longer.

Cruise Line Classification: Deluxe, Resort-style/premium

Cruise Areas & Seasons
Spring: Mexico, Hawaii, Trans-Atlantic, Pacific Coast, Panama Canal, Caribbean, Far East/Orient, Southeast Asia
Summer: Alaska, Europe, Mediterranean, Scandinavia, Russia, New England, Canada, Caribbean
Fall: Mexico, Hawaii, Trans-Atlantic, Pacific Coast, Panama Canal, South America, New England/Canada, Caribbean
Winter: Southeast Asia, Africa, Far East/Orient, Australia, Grand World Voyage, Panama Canal, Caribbean
Winter: Spring & Fall: Panama Canal

The Fleet

Ship Name	Size	Capacity
Maasdam	55,451 tons	1,266
Noordam	33,930 tons	1,214
Rotterdam	59,652 tons	1,316
Ryndam	55,451 tons	1,266
Statendam	55,451 tons	1,266
Veendam	55,451 tons	1,266
Westerdam	53,872 tons	1,494
Volendam	65,000 tons	1,440
Zaandam	65,000 tons	1,440

Newbuilds

Name	Estimated Delivery Date	Size	Capacity
Amsterdam	Fall 2000	61,000	1,380

Nationality of Crew/Staff: Officers - Dutch, Crew - Filipino/Indonesian/International

Guest Profile: Families, Mature Travelers, Experienced, Action Seekers

Insider's Information: Job Hotline: (206) 286-3496 [http://www.hollandamericapreview.com/aboutus/jobs /jobs.htm]
Nurses
Requires ER/ICU/CCU experience, *ACLS Certification, 4 yrs ER/CC Experience
Apply to Attn. Medical Dept., 300 Elliott Avenue West, Seattle, WA 98119 E-mail to: ssuver@halw.com.

Gift shop
Greyhound Leisure Services
151 SE 17th Street
Suite 200
Ft. Lauderdale, FL 33316
phone: (954) 763-8551, fax: (954) 764-3505.

Photographers
Image
300 Biscayne Blvd. Way
Suite 1111, Miami, FL 33131
Phone: (305) 371-3303, fax: (305) 358-6768.

Casino:
Carnival Casinos
5225 NW 87th Avenue
Miami, FL 33178-2193
phone: (305) 522-7466, fax: (305) 599-1967.

Hair salon, masseur/masseuse:
Steiner of London
57 The Broadway,
Stanmore, Middlesex, England HA7 4DU
phone: 44 81 954 6121,
fax: 44 81 954 7980.

Fitness
Steiner Group, Ltd.
1007 North America Way
4th Floor
Miami, FL 33132
Phone: (305) 358 9002
Fax: (305) 372 9310.
Enclose a passport size photo with your resume.

Professional entertainers:
Holland America Line
300 Elliott Ave West
Seattle, WA 98119
Attn: Entertainment Department.

Other Passenger Program/Entertainment positions (including chaplains), please call the Entertainment Job Line at (206) 286 3499.

JOB CONTACT:
Holland America Line
Human Resources
300 Elliot Avenue West
Seattle, WA 98119

MEDITERRANEAN SHIPPING CRUISES
[http://www.msc.cruisesusa.com]
Mediterranean Shipping Cruises offers unique European itineraries on smaller ships appealing to couples, families and honeymooners from their mid-40's to 70's.

Mediterranean Shipping Cruises ' varied fleet carries from 100 guests to more than 1,000. Set sail on cruise ships, sail-assisted cruise vessels, or a paddle-wheel riverboat.

Cruise Areas & Seasons
Winter: Caribbean, South America, South Africa
Spring, Summer & Fall: Sicily, Tunisia, Spain, France, Greek Islands, Egypt, Israel, Portugal, Malta, Black Sea, Lebanon, Syria, Italy

The Fleet

Ship Name	Size	Capacity
Melody	36,500 tons	1,072
Monterey	20,040 tons	550
Rhapsody	16,495 tons	760
Symphony	16,852 tons	760

Nationality of Crew/Staff: Greek, Italian, International

Guest Profile: Couples, Families, Mature Travelers, Experienced, Action Seekers

JOB CONTACT:
Mediterranean Shipping Cruises
Human Resources
420 Fifth Avenue
New York, NY 10016

NORWEGIAN CRUISE LINE
[http://www.ncl.com]

As one of the world's largest lines, NCL offers more than 100 cruise itineraries, ranging from three to 23 days, and calls at over 200 destinations. NCL attracts families, active singles and young professionals 25-49, and special interest groups. Cruise the Norwegian Way with Broadway shows, Sports Afloat®, Dive In™ snorkeling, and a great Kid's Crew™ program.

NCL Holding ASA is the parent company of Norwegian Cruise Line, Orient Lines and Norwegian Capricorn Line an Australia-based line catering to the Spanish cruise market. Star Cruises holds a controlling interest in NCL.

Cruise Line Classification: Resort-style/popular

Cruise Areas & Seasons
Fall: Canada/New England
Winter: South America
Summer & Fall: Mediterranean
Spring, Summer & Fall: Alaska, Europe, Bermuda, Hawaii
Year-round: Bahamas, Caribbean, Mexico
Repositioning: Panama Canal, Transatlantic

The Fleet

Ship Name	Size	Capacity
Norway	76,049 tons	2,032
Norwegian Dream	50,760 tons	1,748
Norwegian Majesty	38,000 tons	1,460
Norwegian Sea	42,000 tons	1,510
Norwegian Sky	80,000 tons	2,002
Norwegian Wind	50,760 tons	1,748

Newbuilds

Name	Estimated Delivery Date	Size	Capacity
Unnamed	June, 2001	80,000 tons	2,000
Unnamed	April, 2002	80,000 tons	2,000

Nationality of Crew/Staff: Officers - Norwegian, Crew - International

Guest Profile: 20's, Boomers, Families, Action Seekers

Insider's Information: Employment opportunities posted online at Career Mosaic. [http://www.careermosaic.com/] Entertainers/Lecturers in demand for theme cruises (Country, Jazz, Big Band, 1950's Nostalgia.) Dancers, vocalists, orchestra musicians, soloists, comedians, magicians. Sponsored sports cruises: golf, tennis, auto racing, skiing, tennis, NFL football, baseball, basketball, hockey. Fitness and beauty cruises.

JOB CONTACT:

Norwegian Cruise Line
Human Resources
7665 Corporate Center Drive
Miami, Florida 33126

ORIENT LINES
[http://www.orientlines.com]

A specialist in destinational cruising, Orient Lines has been awarded 'Best Itineraries' and 'Best Value' by the World Ocean & Cruise Liner Society. Cruises are five to 27 days with guest lecturers and gentlemen hosts featured on long voyages.

Orient Lines appeals to travelers 35+ seeking value-oriented cruise vacations with a destinational/educational focus, four-star comforts and excellent service. Exotic itineraries attract passengers 55+. Orient Lines is owned and operated by Norwegian Cruise Lines.

Cruise Line Classification: Resort-Style/premium

Cruise Areas & Seasons
Spring: India/Egypt, Southeast Asia
Fall: Egypt/Africa
Winter: Australia, New Zealand, Java Sea, Antarctica
Spring, Summer & Fall: Mediterranean/Greek Isles

The Fleet

Ship Name	Size	Capacity
Marco Polo	22,080 tons,	850
Crown Odyssey	34,250 tons	1,050

Nationality of Crew/Staff: Filipino Crew, International staff

Guest Profile: Boomers, Mature Travelers, Active, Experienced

JOB CONTACT:
Orient Lines
138 Park Street
London, England W1Y 3PF

PREMIER CRUISE LINES
[http://wwwpremiercruises.com]
Premier Cruise Lines sails its fleet of 'Big Red Boats' from the four corners of the US. In addition to Port Canaveral, new embarkation points for the line's family-focused itineraries will include New York for New England/Canada cruises, Houston for Mexico cruises, and Los Angeles for Southern California and Mexico cruises.

Premier Cruise Lines provides guests with an intimate and affordable cruise experience with unique itineraries on its fleet of smaller ships. 'The Cruise Line of NASCAR' appeals to honeymooners, families, mature travelers, Eco-tourists and adventure seekers.

Cruise Line Classification: Resort-style/Popular

Cruise Areas & Seasons
Fall & Winter: Mexico, Roatan, Belize, Honduras, Key West, Canary Islands
Summer & Fall: North Atlantic, Mediterranean
Year-round: Bahamas, Salt Cay

The Fleet

Ship Name	Size	Capacity
IslandBreeze	38,175 tons	1,146
OceanBreeze	21,486 tons	776
Oceanic	38,772 tons	1,180
Rembrandt	39,674 tons	1,061

| SeaBreeze | 21,000 tons | 840 |
| Seawind Crown | 24,000 tons | 742 |

Nationality of Crew/Staff: Crew- Filipino, Staff - International

Guest Profile: Boomers, Mature Travelers, Active, Experienced

JOB CONTACT:
Premier Cruises
Human Resources
400 Challenger Road
Cape Canaveral, FL 32920

PRINCESS CRUISES
[http://www.princesscruises.com]

One of the 'Big Four,' Princess Cruises, the popular 'Love Boats' visit 220 ports worldwide on voyages of seven to 65 days. Princess Cruises appeals to first-timers and experienced travelers including young couples, families and mature cruisers. The line currently carries 620,000 passengers annually; and with its newest ships will cater to cater to more than one million guests by 2001.

Sail away on award-winning vacations: Princess' Alaska Cruisetours; 10-day Northern European voyages or the 72-day world cruise, which visits 26 ports on six continents. Highlights: Hearts & Minds wedding chapel, *Love Boat* Kids children's program.

Cruise Line Classification: Resort-style/upscale, premium price

Cruise Areas & Seasons

Spring: Bermuda, Caribbean, Hawaii/Tahiti, Holy Land, Mexico, Orient/Asia, Panama Canal, South America, South Pacific
Summer: Alaska, Europe
Fall: Australia/New Zealand, Caribbean, Hawaii/Tahiti, Holy Land, Mexico, Orient/Asia, Panama Canal, South America
Winter: Africa/India, Australia/New Zealand, Caribbean, Mexico, Panama Canal, South America
also: World Cruise

The Fleet

Ship Name	Size	Capacity
Crown Princess	70,000 tons	1,590
Dawn Princess	77,000 tons	1,950
Grand Princess	109,000 tons	2,600
Pacific Princess	20,000 tons	640
Regal Princess	70,000 tons	1,590
Royal Princess	45,000 tons	1,200
Sea Princess	77,000 tons	1,950
Sky Princess	46,000 tons	1,200
Sun Princess	77,000 tons	1,950
Ocean Princess	77,000 tons	1,950

Newbuilds

Name	Est. Delivery	Size	Capacity
Unnamed	4/2001	109,000	2,600
Unnamed	1/2002	109,000	2,600
Unnamed	2002	88,000	1,950
Unnamed	2003	110,000	2,600
Unnamed	2003	88,000	1,950
Unnamed	2004	110,000	2,600

Nationality of Crew/Staff: Officers - Italian, Crew - British, International

Guest Profile: 20's, Boomers, Mature Travelers, Families, Experienced

Insider's Information: Job Hotline: (310) 553-6330 Shipboard positions apply to: Hotel Personnel. Corporate positions apply to: Human Resources.

JOB CONTACT:
Princess Cruises
10100 Santa Monica Blvd.
Suite 1800
Los Angeles, CA 90067

P & O
[http://www.pocruises/]

Traveling to more than 180 destinations in 75 countries, P & O draws on its heritage as a pioneer of cruising to offer delightful British-style holidays. The parent company of Princess Cruises, P & O (Peninsular and Oriental Steamship Company) began in 1840 with routes to Egypt and India and by 1845, P & O's regular steamer service reached Malay and China.

The line's world-class superliner *Aurora* will make her maiden voyage in January 2001. She'll sport a 30-foot high waterfall, wrap-around promenade deck and three pools; one with a terraced design, one with a sliding glass roof and another just for families.

Cruise Line Classification: Resort-style/popular

Cruise Areas:
World Cruise, Panama Canal, Mexican Riviera, South Pacific, Asia, Egypt, India

The Fleet
Arcadia
Oriana
Victoria

Newbuilds
Name
Aurora
Unnamed

Nationality of Crew/Staff: Officers - Italian, Crew - British, International

Guest Profile: Boomers, Mature Travelers, Experienced

JOB CONTACT:
P&O Cruises
Human Resources
77, New Oxford Street
London WC1A 1PP

RADISSON SEVEN SEAS CRUISES
[http://www.rssc.com]
This fleet of distinctive luxury ships; including the catamaran styled *Radisson Diamond*; travels to 500 destinations worldwide. Radisson Seven Seas Cruises attracts experienced cruisers, age 45 to 50+, well-educated, with household incomes of $100,000+.

Highlights: Aboard the trend-setting *Seven Seas Navigator*, every stateroom is a suite with its own private balcony. Royal Music Festival, PGA Golf cruises in Europe, Asia and the Caribbean.

Cruise Line Classification: Resort-style/upscale premium price

Cruise Areas & Seasons
Winter: Antarctica, Australia, New Zealand, Caribbean, Indonesia, Panama Canal & Costa Rica, Vietnam, China, Hong Kong, Singapore
Spring: Arabia, Baltic, Caribbean, Europe, India, Mediterranean, North Cape, Panama Canal, Costa Rica
Summer: Alaska, Baltic, Europe
Fall: Antarctica, Arabia, Caribbean, Central and South America, India, Mediterranean, Panama Canal, Costa Rica, Vietnam, Singapore, Hong Kong
Year-round: Tahiti, French Polynesia

The Fleet

Name	Size	Capacity
Hanseatic	9,000 tons	184
Paul Gauguin	18,800 tons	320
Radisson Diamond	20,295 tons	350
Seven Seas Navigator	30,000 tons	490
Song of Flower	8,282 tons	180

New Builds

Name	Estimated Delivery Date	Size	Capacity
Seven Seas Mariner	2/2001	146,000 tons	720

Nationality of Crew/Staff: Officers - Norwegian,

Crew - Norwegian, Dutch, Japanese, British, International

Guest Profile: Experienced, Mature Traveler

JOB CONTACT:
Radisson Seven Seas Cruises
600 Corporate Drive, Suite 410
Fort Lauderdale, Florida, 33334

Seven Seas Cruises
K-Line Canada
2300-555 West Hastings St.
Vancouver, B.C.. V6B 4N5.

REGAL CRUISES
[http://www.regalcruises.com]
Affordable vacations aboard the classic *Regal Empress* range in length from one-to three-night Sunspree Party cruises to 12 night voyages through the Canadian Fjords. The *Regal Empress* sails seasonally from Port Manatee, FL (Tampa Bay), Philadelphia, Mobile, New York, and Savannah. Theme cruises include Country & Western, Big Band, and Oldies. 'Sail the ship where everybody knows your name.'

Cruise Areas & Seasons
Winter & Spring:(from Port Manatee, FL,
Philadelphia & Mobile, AL)
Caribbean, Costa Rica, Colombia, Mexico, Panama,
Grand Cayman, Key West, New Orleans
Summer & Fall: (from New York & Savannah),
Bahamas, Caribbean, Canada, New England,
Newfoundland, South America

168

Nationality of Crew/Staff: International

Guest Profile: Boomers, Mature Travelers, Active, Experienced

Insider's Information: regalcruises1@aol.com

JOB CONTACT:
Regal Cruises
Attn: Human Resources
P.O. Box 1329
Palmetto, FL 34220

RENAISSANCE CRUISES
[http://www.RenaissanceCruises.com]
Renaissance offers destination intensive itineraries, open seating in every dining room, and an all-adult, smoke-free environment. The Renaissance fleet consists of two distinct product lines. Four nearly identical 'R-Class' ships, the *R1, R2, R3* and *R4* each carry 684 guests on 11-16 day vacations. The all-suite *Renaissance VII* and *Renaissance VIII* accommodate 114 passengers. Highlights: retractable sports platforms support Zodiac landing craft, sailboats and snorkeling instruction.

Cruise Line Classification: Resort-style/premium

Cruising Areas
Asia, Africa, Greek Isles, Mediterranean, South Pacific

The Fleet

Ship Name	Capacity
R1	684
R2	684
R3	684
R4	684
R5	684
Renaissance VII	114
Renaissance VIII	114

Newbuilds

Ship Name	Estimated Delivery Date	Capacity
R6	2000	684
R7	2000	684
R8	2001	684

Nationality of Crew/Staff: European, International

Guest Profile: Upscale, Mature Travelers, Experienced

Insider's Information: On-board enrichment lectures feature guest experts. Entertainers: trios, soloists, entertainers from ports-of-call. No concessionaires. Send resume and cover letter to Renaissance Cruises. Comprehensive employment questions & answers Web site. [http://www.RenaissanceCruises.com]

JOB CONTACT:
Corporate opportunities:
Renaissance Cruises, Inc. Attn: Human Resources
P.O. Box 29009
Fort Lauderdale, FL 33302-9009
fax to: 954-759-7727

Shipboard opportunities:
Renaissance Cruises, Inc.
Attn: Fleet Operations
Recruiter/Scheduler
P.O. Box 20307
Fort Lauderdale, FL 33335-0307

ROYAL CARIBBEAN INTERNATIONAL
[http://www.royalcaribbean.com]

One of the 'Big Four,' Royal Caribbean International appeals to couples and singles age 30-50, and families. With worldwide itineraries and an expanding fleet of profitable ships, Royal Caribbean affordable cruise vacations give active travelers high value and variety.

Highlights: RCI's Royal Journeys program offers Explore Overnight excursion where guests may leave the vessel, spend one to three nights at an alternative destination and then rejoin the ship in another port-of-call. The *Voyager of the Seas* boasts a 900-seat arena with broadcast facilities and recreational facilities that include a rock climbing wall, in-line skating rink, golf course and regulation-sized sports court; a wedding chapel and the cruise industry's largest conference area.

Royal Caribbean Cruises Ltd.,operates Royal Caribbean International and Celebrity Cruises.

Cruise Line Classification: Resort-style/popular

Cruise Areas & Seasons
Summer: Mediterranean, Scandinavia, Russia, Norwegian Fjords, Europe
Fall: Mexican Riviera, New England
Summer & Fall: Alaska, Bermuda, Transatlantic, Hawaii

171

Fall/Winter: Europe, Middle East, Australia,New Zealand
Winter, Fall & Spring: Panama Canal
Year-round: Bahamas, Caribbean, Baja Mexico

The Fleet

Name	Size	Capacity
Enchantment of the Seas	74,140 tons	1,950
Grandeur of the Seas	74,140 tons	1,950
Legend of the Seas	69,130 tons	1,800
Majesty of the Seas	73,941 tons	2,350
Monarch of the Seas	73,941 tons	2,350
Nordic Empress	48,563 tons	1,600
Rhapsody of the Seas	78,491 tons	2,600
Sovereign of the Seas	73,192 tons	2,250
Splendour of the Seas	69,130 tons	1,800
Viking Serenade	40,132 tons	1,500
Vision of the Seas	78,491 tons	2,000
Voyager of the Seas	102,000 tons	3,114

Newbuilds

Name	Estimated Delivery Date
Radiance of the Seas	2001
Brilliance of the Seas	2002
Explorer of the Seas	2000
Adventure of the Seas	2002

Nationality of Crew/Staff: Officers - Scandinavian, Crew - International

Guest Profile: Families, 20's, Boomers, Mature Travelers, Experienced, Action Seekers

Insider's Information: RCI/Celebrity Job Hot Line: (305) 530-0471 Entertainers - include brief 3-5 minute video cassettes with resume. Direct your application to Entertainment Director/Production

Ocean-based jobs
[http://extranet.rccl.com/apptrackroot/ webclassapptrack7.asp]
Land-based jobs
[http://www.goroyaljobs.com/]

JOB CONTACT:
Ocean-based jobs
Royal Caribbean International
Hotel Human Resources
1050 Caribbean Way
Miami, FL 33132

Land-based jobs
Royal Carlbbean International
Human Resources
1050 Caribbean Way
Miami, FL 33132

ROYAL OLYMPIC CRUISES
[http://www.royalolympiccruises.com]
Royal Olympic Cruises upholds the traditions of predecessors Sun Line and Epirotiki; and is the largest cruise line in the Greek Isles. Specializing in a more personal, culturally-enriching vacation experience, the line features destination-oriented itineraries with an extensive 'World Affairs' ambassador lecturer series including winter soft-adventure cruises to South America and the 'Land of the Maya.'

Royal Olympic appeals to experienced travelers, ages 40-70, affluent and college-educated, who prefer cultural, destination-focused itineraries.

Cruise Line Classification: Resort-style/popular

Cruise Areas & Seasons
Spring, Summer & Fall: Greek Isles, Turkey, Holy Land, Egypt and Black Sea
Winter: Amazon River/Carnival in Rio, Land of the Maya, Panama Canal, circumnavigation of South America, Orninoco River.

The Fleet

Name	Size	Capacity
Odysseus	12,000 tons	400
Olympic Countess	18,000 tons	840
Orpheus	6,000 tons	280
Stella Oceanis	5,500 tons	300
Stella Solaris	18,000 tons	620
Triton	14,000 tons	620
World Renaissance	12,000 tons	457
Olympic Voyager	25,000 tons	840

Newbuilds

Name	Estimated Delivery Date	Size	Capacity
Unnamed	2001	25,000 tons	840

Nationality of Crew/Staff: International

Guest Profile: Families, 20's, Boomers, Mature Travelers, Experienced, Action Seekers

JOB CONTACT:
Royal Olympic Cruises, Inc.
Human Resources
805 Third Avenue
New York, NY 10022-7513. USA

Royal Olympic Cruises
Human Resources
Akti Miaouli 87
18538 Piraeus, Greece

ST. LAWRENCE CRUISE LINES
[http://www.stlawrencecruiselines.com/]
Enjoy early 1900's decor, private shore excursions, afternoon tea and nightly entertainment as you cruise the sheltered waters of canals and locks. All-inclusive calm water cruises include tours, entertainment, accommodations and generous home-quality meals. More than 95 percent of Canadian Empress passengers are 55 and older, some retired with married couples in the majority. (50 percent American, 34 percent Canadian, 16 percent British and European.)

Cruise Line Classification: Adventure/Specialty

Cruise Areas
Canadian Coast and Rivers

The Fleet
Canadian Empress

Nationality of Crew/Staff: American

Guest Profile: Boomers, Mature Travelers, Experienced, Explorers, Ship Buffs

JOB CONTACT:
St. Lawrence Cruise Lines
253 Ontario St.
Kingston, Ontario K7l 2Z4
Canada

SEABOURN CRUISE LINE
[http://www.seabourn.com]

Seabourn appeals to affluent cruisers 45+ who are accustomed to top-grade hotels and resorts, First Class air travel and fine dining. The line also appeals to first-time cruisers. With voyages ranging from 4 to 99 days, Seabourn's itineraries and exceptional shore excursions take you worldwide. Cruise up the Chang Jiang River and explore ancient palaces or take a moonlit Amazon River safari in a dugout canoe! Enjoy gourmet single-seating dining, elegant restaurants and casual dining. Seabourn is operated by Cunard Line Ltd., and is a member of the Carnival family of cruise lines.

Seabourn is dedicated to the highest level of personal service, equal to that found in celebrated hotels, resorts and restaurants on shore. Spaciousness and elegance is the rule, with an ambiance that allows pampered guests to establish their own pace befitting their own lifestyles. All gratuities are included in your cruise fare.

Cruise Line Classification: Deluxe

Cruise Areas
Asia, Arabia, India, Europe, European Rivers, Mediterranean, North America, Russia, Scandinavia, South America, Trans-Oceanic cruises, including transatlantic and transpacific voyages; and World Cruise.

The Fleet

Name	Size	Capacity
Seabourn Sun (fka Royal Viking Sun)	37,845 tons	758
Seabourn Goddess I (fka Sea Goddess I)	4,250 tons	116
Seabourn Goddess II (fka Sea Goddess II)	4,250 tons	116
Seabourn Pride	10,000 tons	208
Seabourn Legend	10,000 tons	208
Seabourn Spirit	10,000 tons	208

Nationality of Crew/Staff: European and American

Guest Profile: Upscale, Mature Traveler

Insider's Information: Upscale musicians and duos; retractable watersports platform aboard *Seabourn Goddess I & II*: possible watersports opportunities.

JOB CONTACT:
Seabourn Cruise Line
Human Resources
6100 Blue Lagoon Drive
Miami, FL 33126

SEA CLOUD CRUISES
[http://www.seacloud.com]
Enjoy smooth passage aboard the carefully restored classic 1931 sailing yacht, *Sea Cloud*. Four masts, brilliant white sails, rich mahogany and gleaming brass promise an authentic cruise experience. River vessel *River Cloud*, offers cruises through heart of Europe: the Rhine, Main, Moselle, and Danube.

Sea Cloud's newest tall ship, the 96-passenger *Sea Cloud II* will cruise in Northern Europe, taking her five-star service to the Mediterranean and South America.

Cruise Line Classification:
Adventure/Specialty/premium

Cruise Areas
Europe, The Rivers Rhine, Main, Moselle, Danube; Mediterranean, South America.

The Fleet
Sea Cloud
River Cloud

New Builds

Name	Estimated Delivery Date
Sea Cloud II	2000
River Cloud II	2000

Nationality of Crew/Staff: International

Guest Profile: Boomers, Mature Travelers, Experienced, Ship Buffs

JOB CONTACT:
Sea Cloud Cruises GmbH
D-20095 Hamburg, Ballindamm 17
Germany

Sea Cloud Cruises GmbH
32-40 North Dean Street
Englewood, New Jersey 07631   USA

SILVERSEA CRUISES
[http://www.silversea.com]
Silversea's yacht-like vessels cater to only 296 guests with spacious surroundings, all-suite accommodations and all-inclusive rates. The line attracts discriminating guests accustomed to plush accommodations and individual service. Highlights: The 'Silver Links Golf Series' gives guests an opportunity to play as many as seven full rounds of golf in five countries within 12 days.
Conde Nast Traveler Reader's Choice Awards named Silversea the 'World's #1 vacation choice' 1996, and 'World's Best Small Cruise Line' *Travel & Leisure's* Reader's Choice Awards 'World's Best Small Cruise Line'

Cruise Line Classification: Deluxe

Cruise Areas
Mediterranean, Northern Europe, Baltic, Far East, Canada, Colonial America, Australia, New Zealand, South Pacific, Africa, India, Panama Canal, Mexican Riviera, Amazon, South America.

The Fleet

Name	Size	Capacity
Silver Cloud	16,800 tons	296
Silver Wind	16,800 tons	296
Silver Shadow	25,000 tons	388

New Builds

Name	Estimated Delivery Date	Size	Capacity
Silver Mirage	2001	25,000 tons	388

Nationality of Crew/Staff: International

Guest Profile: Boomers, Mature Travelers, Experienced, Action Seekers

Insider's Information: FAX 954-522-4499 (attn.: Human Resources)

JOB CONTACT:
Silversea Cruises
110 East Broward Blvd.
Fort Lauderdale, FL 33301

SOCIETY EXPEDITIONS
[http://www.societyexpeditions.com/]

The remote, the untamed, the exotic! Society Expeditions offers cruises for the adventuresome traveler. Originally established as a cruise line for educational archaeological tours, Society Expedition's itinerary has expanded to include zoological, anthropological, and fascinating itineraries for nature lovers.

Society's shallow draft expedition ships and inflatable Zodiac boats take passengers on authentic expeditions;

led by naturalists, biologists, zoologists, and other experts.

Cruise Line Classification: Specialty/Adventure

Cruise Areas: England, Ireland, Scotland, New World-Canadian Arctic, Hudson Bay, Newfoundland, Iceland, Greenland, South Pacific, New Guinea, Australia, Amazon, Antarctica and the Sub Antarctic islands, the Galapagos Islands, Indonesia, Easter Island, Madagascar, Seychelles, and East Africa.

The Fleet:
Society Explorer
World Discoverer
Society Adventurer

Nationality of Crew/Staff: International

Guest Profile: Mature Travelers, Experienced, Active

Insider's Information: Officers, hostess, hotel staff, cabin stewards, salon, photographers and gift shop staff are hired by Society Expeditions' parent company, Discover Rederei of German. You must speak both English and German.

JOB CONTACT:
Society Expeditions/Human Resources
2001 Western Avenue, Suite 300,
Seattle, Washington 98121

Society Expeditions/Human Resources
Marcusallee 9, 28359 Bremen, Germany

Sven-Olof Lindblad's SPECIAL EXPEDITIONS
[http://www.expeditions.com]

Lindblad's Special Expeditions' shallow-draft ships and flexible itineraries bring you up close to wildlife and cultural sites. Hop a Zodiac landing craft and explore anywhere, anytime - on a moment's notice. 30 to 110 guests receive personal attention and expert answers from highly qualified naturalists and historians. Highlights: All-inclusive rates, informal talks about destinations and unassigned dining, high staff to guest ratio.

Cruise Line Classification: Specialty/Adventure

Cruising Areas:
Africa, Alaska, Antarctica, Baja California, Caribbean; Central, North and South America; Egypt, Galapagos, Middle East, Pacific Northwest, Transatlantic

The Fleet

Ship Name	Capacity
Sea Lion	70
Sea Bird	70
Polaris	70
Caledonian Star	70
Swedish Islander	70
Hapi	70

Nationality of Crew/Staff: Officers: Swedish, Crew: Filipino
Guest Profile: Mature Travelers, Experienced, Explorers

182

Insider's Information:
[http://www.coolworks.com/specialexpeditions/]
Onboard there is a small gift shop, no photographer, casino nor nightly entertainment; and no salon. Special Expeditions offers a work experience where you can learn about the environment, ecology, and natural history of a region. Applicants must enjoy hiking and spending time outdoors.

JOB CONTACT:
Special Expeditions Marine- CW
1415 Western Avenue Suite 700
Seattle, Washington 98101

STAR CLIPPERS
[http://www.starclippers.com/]
Named for the 19th Century tall ships whose high masts could clip the stars, all three ships in the Star Clippers fleet are sail-powered and fitted out luxuriously in mega-yacht fashion. Casual elegance is the style with open-seating dining, and a high staff to guest ratio. .

Explore the Caribbean, Mediterranean, Aegean and Asia up-close. Sail the French & Italian Riviera in high style;.aboard the *Royal Clipper;* the world's largest true sail ship.

Cruise Line Classification:
Deluxe/Specialty/Adventure

Cruise Areas
Year-round: Caribbean, Mediterranean
Summer: Greek Islands
Winter: Indonesia

The Fleet

Ship Name	Capacity
Star Flyer	174
Star Clipper	174
Royal Clipper	228

Nationality of Crew/Staff: German/ International

Guest Profile: Boomers, Mature Travelers, Experienced, Action Seekers, Ship Buffs

Insider's Information:

Highlights: no casino, no dedicated children's facilities; watersports platform and equipment, Scuba diving program (PADI Resort Certified) Submit your Curriculum Vitae (CV or Resume) online at: [http://www.starclippers.com/job.htm] email: info@star-clippers-ltd.mc

JOB CONTACT:

Star Clippers
Human Resources
Ermanno Palace
27, Boulevard Albert 1er
98000 Monaco

Star Clippers
Human Resources
4101 Salzedo Avenue
Coral Gables, Florida, 33146

STAR CRUISES
[http://www.starcruises.com]

'The Leading Cruise Line in Asia-Pacific' appeals to international travelers with fly/cruise packages from Australia, Japan, Europe, Korea, Taiwan, China and South East Asia.

Star Cruises is one of the four largest cruise lines in the world; and by year 2005, will have a fleet of 12 vessels sailing from Singapore, Port Klang, Phuket, Bangkok, Hong Kong, Taipei and Osaka/Kobe.

Star Cruises made its debut in September, 1993, and has captured 70% of the cruise market in Asia-Pacific, carrying more than 1 million passengers during in the first 5 years. The company plans to market its new vessels more to Europe, the Middle East and the US.

Star Cruises holds a controlling interest in Norwegian Cruise Line.

Cruise Line Classification: Resort-style/popular

Cruise Areas
South Korea, Taiwan, Hong Kong, Singapore, Vietnam, Thailand, China, Malaysia.

The Fleet
Star Aquarius
Star Pisces
SuperStar Aries
SuperStar Gemini
SuperStar Leo
SuperStar Virgo
MegaStar Aries
MegaStar Taurus
SuperStar Taurus

New Builds

Name	Estimated Delivery Date	Size
SuperStar Libra	2001	91,000 grt
SuperStar Scorpio	2002	91,000 grt
Sagittarius-Class vessel 2003		112,000 grt
Sagittarius-Class vessel 2005		112,000 grt

Nationality of Crew/Staff: Japanese, British, International

Guest Profile: Families, 20's, Boomers, Mature Travelers, Experienced, Action Seekers

Insider's Information:
Visit [http://www.starcruises.com] for information on corporate and shipboard employment including positions in: Hotel, Finance, Club, Information Technology, and Marine Operation. For complete Corporate Addresses Worldwide go to [http://www.starcruises.com/start6.html.]

JOB CONTACT:
Star Cruises/Human Resources
Level 3, Shijuku Mitsui 2nd Bldg,
3-2-11 Nishi-shinjuku Shinjyuku-Ku
Tokyo, Japan 160-23

Star Cruises/Human Resources
Port Terminal 2F, 4-5
Shinko-Cho, Chuo-ku,
Kobe-city, Hyogo, Japan

Star Cruises Terminal/Human Resources
Pulau Indah, Pelabuhan Barat,
42009 Pelabuhan Klang,
Selangor Darul Ehsan. 1, Shenton Way #01-02
Singapore 068803

UNITED STATES LINES
[http://www.unitedstateslines.com]
"American-owned, American-built & American-crewed."

A new fleet cruise ships is now being developed under the American Classic Voyages Company's Project America initiative. The original United States Lines' ships, such as the *ss America, ss Manhattan, ss Leviathan and ss George Washington*, were the favorites of a glamorous passenger list that included the Duke and Duchess of Windsor, 'Tennessee' Williams, Cary Grant and Salvador Dali. In 1969, United States Lines' last remaining passenger vessel, the fabled *ss United States* withdrawn from service.

Three vessels will form the new United States Lines fleet. American Classic Voyages Co. has contracted with Holland America Line to acquire the 1,214-passenger *Nieuw Amsterdam*. The ship is scheduled to be delivered to AMCV October, 2000 and will begin year-round 7-night Hawaiian Island cruises in December 2000.

The company has also contracted for two 1,900-passenger, 72,000 grt cruise ships - the first major, ocean-going passenger ships to be built in the US in more than 40 years.

Cruise Line Classification: Resort Style/popular

Cruise Areas
Hawaiian Islands

The Fleet
Patriot (fka Nieuw Amsterdam)

New Builds

Name	Estimated Delivery Date	size	capacity
TBA	2003	72,000	1,900
TBA	2004	72,000	1,900

Nationality of Crew/Staff: American/International

Guest Profile: Families, 20's, Boomers, Mature Travelers, Action Seekers, Ship Buffs

JOB CONTACT:
United States Lines
c/o American Classic Voyages
Human Resources
Robin Street Wharf
1380 Port of New Orleans Place
New Orleans, LA 70130-1890

VICTORIA CRUISES
[http://www.victoriacruises.com]
The only cruise line sailing the entire navigable length of the majestic Yangtze River. Experience ancient wonders on 3-10 day cruises aboard comfortable modern ships. Victoria's western cruise directors introduce you to Chinese heritage and culture with lectures, demonstrations, shore excursions and entertainment.

Interesting lectures on history and culture, Tai Chi lessons, painting and calligraphy demonstrations

Cruise Line Classification: Resort-style/popular

Cruise Areas & Seasons
Yangtze River, China

The Fleet
Victoria I
Victoria II
Victoria II
Victoria IV
Victoria Princess
Victoria Pearl
Victoria Blue Whale
Victoria Angel

Nationality of Crew/Staff: Japanese, American, British, International

Guest Profile: Boomers, Mature Travelers, Experienced, Explorers

JOB CONTACT:
Victoria Cruises
#3 Xin Hua Road 3F
 Chongqing, China

Victoria Cruises Taipei Office
Room 620 Orient BLDG. No. 121 Chung Ching South Road Sec. 1,
Taipei, Taiwan R.O.C.

WINDJAMMER CRUISES
[http://www.windjammer.com]

Welcome aboard, kick off your shoes and get ready for an adventure you'll never forget.

"Were' 'barefootin'" aboard this fun fleet of classic ships- named for their sail power - the "wind-jammers." Each Tall Ship boasts a distinctive nautical heritage: they've been the personal vessels of the world's most legendary financial moguls; carried members of European royalty; and several were commissioned for oceanographic and meteorological research

Informality and a relaxed itinerary take guests where big ships cannot reach. An easy camaraderie develops between guests and staff aboard these authentic one-of-a-kind vessels as they sail the "yachtsman's Caribbean" and beyond. Highlights: Winner of *Travel and Leisure* Best Award, *Conde Nast Traveler* Best Adventure Cruise.

Cruise Line Classification: Adventure/Specialty

Cruise Areas
Caribbean

The Fleet
Amazing Grace
Flying Cloud
Legacy
Mandalay
Polynesia
Yankee Clipper

Nationality of Crew/Staff: American, British, International

Guest Profile: 20's, Couples, Boomers, Active, Explorers, Ship Buffs

Insider's Information: FAX 305-674-1219
Take a virtual tour of the fleet:
[http://www.realestateipix.com/clients/stepaboard/tours.html]

JOB CONTACT:
Windjammer Barefoot Cruises, Ltd.
Human Resources
1759 Bay Road
Box 190120
Miami Beach, FL 33119-0120

WINDSTAR CRUISES
[http://www.windstarcruises.com]

Known for its upscale cruise experience, superb cuisine and casual dress code, Windstar Cruises operates three identical 148-passenger sail cruise ships and one 312-passenger sail cruiser. The four masted-sail yachts cruise to over 65 worldwide ports of call and offer an affordably priced, luxury vacation.

Windstar passengers range in age from 20 to 70, with an average age of 52; and an average income of $75,000 to $200,000. They are mostly professionals, experienced travelers and first-time cruises

Windstar finished in the top two for small ship cruising in both *Travel and Leisure's* World's Best Awards and *Condé Nast Traveler UK* Readers' Choice Awards for 1999, and was recently named to the *Condé Nast Traveler* 2000 Gold List of Best Places to Stay in the World.

Cruise Line Classification: Resort-style/premium

Cruise Areas & Seasons:
Fall, Winter & Spring: Caribbean, Costa Rica, Virgin Islands, Panama Canal, Belize
Spring, Summer & Fall: Caribbean, Mediterranean (Greek Isles, Amalfi Coast, Dalmatian Coast, French and Italian Rivieras, Rome, Venice, Spain, Portugal, Provence and Andalusia)

The Fleet	Size	Capacity
Wind Song	5,350 tons	148
Wind Spirit	5,350 tons	148
Wind Star	5,350 tons	148
Wind Surf	14,745 tons	312

Nationality of Crew/Staff: International

Guest Profile: Couples, Boomers, Mature Travelers, Experienced, Ship Buffs

Insider's Information: Job Hotline: (206) 286-3496 Take a 'virtual cruise' via streaming video clips at Windstar Cruises' Web site.
[http://www.windstarcruises.com]

JOB CONTACT:
Windstar Cruises/ Human Resources
300 Elliott Avenue West
Seattle, WA 98119

7
TRENDS IN CRUISING

A. Growth & Expansion
- New Ships through 2005
- 'One-Upsman-Ship'
- What's new: the newest ships.

B. Accommodations
- Public Areas
- Facilities
- Technology

C. Activities
- Programs
- Entertainment

D. Dining
- New Restaurant Styles

E. Itineraries
- Ports of Departure
- Destinations
- Shore Excursions
- Cruising and the Environment

A. Trends in Growth and Expansion Cruising's Future is Full Speed Ahead!

"If it works, we'll grow it. We're going for the gold,"
Michael Eisner, Chairman, Walt Disney Co., commenting on
Disney Cruise Line's debut.

The Cruise Industry is Booming!

With 63 newbuilds on order through 2005, cruise fans have a lot to look forward to: new ships, exotic itineraries and super savings. Cruise companies will have 43 percent more beds to fill; more than double the increase over the previous five-year period. Executives and investors are betting that demand will soon catch up with supply, since passenger boardings increased by 73 percent between 1995 - 2000.

Multi-million-dollar investments.

$2.9 billion is the total newbuilding order placed by Carnival Corporation, parent company of the World's Leading Cruise Lines, an alliance of Carnival Cruise Lines, Holland America Line, Cunard Line, Seabourn Cruise Line, Costa Cruises and Windstar Cruises.
Carnival Cruise Lines has five new ships on order: Three 102,000-ton "Destiny-class" ships scheduled to enter service over the next four years: the *Carnival Victory*, expected to enter service August, 2000, *Carnival Conquest* and *Carnival Glory*, slated to debut in 2002 and 2003, respectively. Carnival Cruise Lines' Destiny class of newbuilds will cost a minimum of **$450 million each**. Two new 'Spirit-class' vessels, the *Carnival Spirit* and *Carnival Pride* are expected to cost **$375 million each**.

194

Carnival's sister company, Holland America Line, has two **$400 million** dollar ships on order: the 1,440-passenger *Zaandam*, due spring 2000 and the 1,380-passenger *Amsterdam*, scheduled to be delivered in fall 2000. Collectively, these seven vessels have an estimated value of more than **$2.9 billion.** Also on order for Costa Cruises, another Carnival-affiliated cruise line, is the 2,112-passenger *CostaAtlantica*, which is scheduled to debut in late spring 2000.

Norwegian Cruise Line has ordered two new Sky-class vessels with pre-construction prices of **$351 million** and **$334 million.**

Royal Caribbean International plans to build four new Millennium-class ships (85,000-ton,1,950 -passenger) for Celebrity Cruises: minimum price tag **$350 million each.**

All amounts in US dollars.

SEE THE COMPLETE GUIDE TO 63 NEWBUILDS; New Ships set to launch 2000-2005, at the end of this book.

Maiden Voyage Opportunities
◆One thing you can be sure of, the best employees promote upwards to the newest ship, it's an honor and a reward. Service should be top-notch!
◆Be dazzled! Cruise lines pull out all the stops to celebrate a maiden voyage!

Virtual Reality Tours

Visit these sites for a virtual tour of these ships.
Royal Caribbean International's *Voyager of the Seas*
[http://www.rccl.com/voyageroftheseas/]
Holland America Line's *Veendam*
[http://www.hollandamerica.com/vr/veendam_vr_index.html]

Princess Cruises' *Grand Princess*
[http://www.princesscruises.com/fleet/grand/index.html]

Visit this site to view a video.
Radisson *Seven Seas Navigator*
[http://www.streamingtravel.com/]

Highlights of the
Cruise Line International Association's
Cruise Industry General Overview.

The cruise industry is the fastest growing segment of the travel industry and has achieved **more than 1,000 percent growth since 1970**, when an estimated 500,000 people took a cruise. In 1998, 5.4 million people took a cruise. By 2000, CLIA estimates that as many as 7 million people will cruise each year.

The North American cruise industry's growth is also reflected by a big jump in capacity. During the 1980's some 40 new ships were built. Global capacity has also increased by almost 50 percent. **63 new vessels are on order for delivery by 2005.**

Over the past six years, **cruise vessel embarkations** from North American ports **have increased by almost 50 percent.** 3 million plus passengers sailed from the Floridian ports of Miami,

Port Everglades,   Port Canaveral   and Port Tampa. A significant number of passengers also embarked from ports in Alaska, California, Louisiana, New York, Texas and Massachusetts. 3.5 million passengers boarded cruise vessels from ports outside North America.

- ✓ North American Passengers :**5.5 million**
- ✓ Total Worldwide Passengers : **9.0 million**
- ✓ Vessels Embarking from North America: **131**

The top cruise destination markets are the Caribbean, Alaska, Mediterranean, Europe, Trans-Canal (Panama), Mexico, and Bermuda.

source: Cruise Lines International Association, CLIA [http://www.cruising.org]

Size and 'One-upsman-ship'

Mega VS Boutique	Size	# of PAX
Mega-ships	60,000 to 109,000 grt	1,500 to 3,100
Midsize ships	20,000-60,000 grt	500 to 1,500
Small/Boutique	20,000 grt	100 to 500

The next generation of newbuilds will be mega-ships and small boutique ships, with little in-between. Expect the game of 'one-upsman-ship' to continue as 2000+ passenger ships compete for the title of *'world's largest.'* Another strong trend shows small or 'boutique' ships with 100-400 passengers capturing the soft adventure and ultra-luxe vacation market.

Is bigger better? Is less more?

Larger ships usually offer more activities, entertainment, children's programs and choice of discos, nightclubs and restaurants. Wide-open spaces and ships of 10 passenger decks or more do wonders for the resort vacation fan. There's sure to be something for all ages aboard these floating resorts.

Smaller ships have their own cache and offer a range of cruise experiences; unusual itineraries and specialty programs aboard ships catering to 100 to 500 guests. These smaller ships provide two types of cruise vacations: exclusive, ultra-deluxe cruise vacations and hands-on, up-close soft adventure.

Economies of Scale

For chief financial officers and shareholders, nothing could be finer than the profitable economies of scale achieved by building 2000-3100 passenger mega-ships. Beginning with the super-liners of the 1980's, a majority of newbuilds have steadily increased in size, speed, and facilities. The fleet of the future boasts entire decks dedicated to children's activities, alternative a-la-carte restaurants and ice skating rinks.

Carnival Cruise Lines' 102,000-ton *Carnival Triumph* outdid her sistership *Carnival Destiny's* record for the **most passengers on a single voyage: 3,315.** *Destiny's* listing in *The Guinness Book of World Records* will be replaced by *Carnival Triumph's* August 22nd, 1999 voyage which carried 3,413 passengers.

198

One foot too wide.

PANAMAX dimension standards enable Panama and Suez canal transits for worldwide deployment. Carnival's *Destiny* is one foot too wide for passage through the Panama Canal. Carnival Corporation's new Destiny-class ships carry 2,578-pax each and are "fabulously profitable."

At 159 feet wide, Princess Cruises' *Grand Princess* is also *too 'beamy' for Panamax standards.* Look for more 2,600 passenger Grand-class ships from Princess.

At 951 feet, Holland America Line's Rotterdam-class vessels will be among the *longest passenger vessels in the world,* but will still transit the Panama Canal.

Made In the USA?

US law prohibits any ship not built in the US from flying a US flag. If your ship flies a Liberian or Panamanian flag, it's one of the majority: 80 percent of vessels calling on US ports are foreign-flagged. In the past 20 years, the US shipbuilding industry has produced defense vessels rather than cruise ships.

The winds are changing: a shipbuilding contract for two cruise vessels has been announced by American Classic Voyages and Ingalls Shipyard (Miss.), a subsidiary of Litton Industries. Delta Queen Steamboat has contracted with Nichols Bros. Boat Builders, Inc. for the *Columbia Queen* and Atlantic Marine for two new-builds for subsidiary Delta Queen Coastal Cruises. World City also plans to build at US shipyards.

The Phoenix World City Also Rises

[http://www.developmentchannel.com/content/ppho9712.htm]

Phoenix World City, Knut Kloster's dream of a 6,200-passenger floating city has a new lease on life, a new management partnership and a new name. Westin Hotels and Resorts has teamed up with Kloster to market and manage *America World City*: The Westin Flagship. Westin would manage the $1.2 billion 'floating hotel'.

World City has already secured $100 million in equity from strategic partners and is pursuing a US Department of Transportation Title 11 loan guarantee for 87 percent of the cost of the ship. An initial public offering in commercial stock has also been proposed, along with strategic equity agreements with partners like Westin.

Highlights of America World City

◆   US built and staffed, the ship would be slightly larger than the biggest aircraft carrier afloat and two-and-a-half times bigger than any ship currently in development.

◆   Size? Nearly a quarter of a mile in length.

◆   The ship will accommodate 6,200 guests in 2,800 rooms and suites.

◆   15 international restaurants.

◆   Most staterooms would be in one of three hotel towers on the ship's deck.

◆ The *America World City* would have its own marina and fleet of four 400- passenger daycruisers.

◆ The vessel will become a meeting Mecca. Plans call for 100,000 square feet of function space. As the only major cruise ship sailing under the US flag, *America World City* would have a unique tax-deductible status.

◆ The vessel would deploy in the Caribbean.

The project also includes a 90-acre development at Port Canaveral, Florida, as well as development of a Northeast cruise port at the 452-acre now defunct Military Ocean Terminal site in Bayonne, N.J.. At least two more floating cities are planned, one to cruise the West Coast and Hawaii, the other to sail in Asia.

Home away from home

Surely the 50 room beach cottage and the mountain-side estate will shortly become passé. Soon you can purchase your own private getaway that really 'gets-away': a residence at sea aboard a luxury ship.

The newest concept in cruising, *World of ResidenSea* is expected to enter service in April 2001, at which time she will embark on a three year fixed itinerary of world cruises.

It's no surprise that Knut Kloster, Jr. is the pioneer behind this project, along with other recognized cruise industry pros. The Kloster family started Norwegian Cruise Lines (NCL) and Knut Kloster, Jr. has served as chairman and CEO of both Royal Cruise Lines and NCL.

The *World of ResidenSea* also inherits the vision of the marine architects who designed the *Seabourn Pride* and *Spirit, Silver Cloud, Silver Wind, Seabourn Goddess I* and *II* and the *Royal Viking Queen*. The ship will be managed by Silversea Cruises Ltd. and will be built in Rissa, Norway by Fosen Mek. Verksteder A/S at an estimated cost of USD 262.5 million.

This 40,000-ton ship is expected to carry an average of 285 guests plus a crew of 252. ResidenSea expects guest/owners to be 40% Americans, 40% Europeans and 20% from other nations.

Money Talks

Choose from 110 'apartments' ranging from 1,100 square feet to 3,200 square feet in size. Prospective residents will have a choice of six floor plans including penthouses and bi-level residences. Each unit will feature two or three bedrooms, each with its own complete bathroom fully equipped kitchen; private terrace with whirlpool; walk-in closets; audio system; television and VCR; mobile phone; fax and a personal computer; built-in safe; and 24-hour security.

In addition, there will be 88 guest suites ranging in size from 220 to 500 square feet. Your new home will come stylishly decorated and furnished; complete with linen, china, cutlery and crystal.

Daily housekeeping service, repairs and replacement of appliances, fixtures and fittings supplied by the builder will be covered by an annual maintenance charge of between USD $60,000 to $240,000.

Two entire decks will be dedicated to a combination resort and village. You'll find dining, entertainment, sports, shopping, business and leisure activities. There will be several restaurants and a number of lounges and bars, a casino, night club, and theater, as well as a library, museum, and business center. Your home at sea also sports a retractable marina, so bring the toys.

Oh - one mustn't forget: guests can take advantage of the "market room" with a licensed stock and bond broker and of course, the helicopter landing pad.

By Invitation Only.

Prices for *World of ResidenSea* homes range from USD $2,000,000 to $6,840,000 and they are being sold by invitation only.

Amenities and Services offered by the ResidenSea Club:

◆ Reciprocal privileges at private clubs around the world.

◆ Full-size indoor tennis court.

◆ Golf Academy with professional instructor; driving range and putting green.

◆ Swimming pools, whirlpools, deck sports and water sports.

◆ Spa and Health and Fitness Center.

◆ 5 restaurants and a gallery of lounges, bars, and shops.

◆ Casino, nightclub, dancing, and cabaret.

◆ 150-seat theater/cinema.

◆ Wind-shielded outdoor garden.

◆ Rooms for private functions.

◆ Library, museum, art exhibitions, business center.

World of ResidenSea Itinerary 2001

April - US, East Coast
May - US, East Coast, Channel Islands, England, North France
June - North France, North Spain, Holland, Belgium
July - Holland, Svalbard, Norway, North Cape
August - Baltic, Estonia, Sweden, Finland, Russia, Scotland
September - Scotland, Iceland, Greenland, England
October - Mediterranean, Spain, Sicily
November - Mediterranean, West Coast Africa, South Africa
December - South Africa, East Africa

World's Largest?

Cunard's Project Queen Mary is expected to be *the largest passenger vessel ever built*. The new liner is scheduled to make her debut in 2003, sporting a classic design reminiscent of the grand dames of the past. Look for a dramatic raked prow, similar to *QE2*, a matte black-painted hull and a giant single stack, painted historic "Cunard Red" with black bands.

At more than 1100 feet long, her hull will be longer than three football fields-as long, in fact, as four city blocks-making her the longest passenger vessel ever built. Her power plant will produce sufficient electricity to light a city the size of Southampton, England. Her engines will produce a mighty 140,000 horsepower and you'll hear her great whistle from 10 miles away.

"The true nature of an ocean liner is that of a majestic thoroughbred roaming the oceans of the world. They are conceived with a long, streamlined hull, a proportionally long bow section and a stepped stern, giving them a sleek profile that is distinctive and pleasing to the eye. They are capable of very high speeds. The speed of Project Queen Mary will probably not exceed that of Queen Elizabeth 2, Cunard's current flagship, which is the fastest deep sea passenger ship in the world. However, she will certainly be built to operate at speeds in the vicinity of 30 knots. She must therefore possess an inherent strength and stability necessary for high-speed passage through open ocean conditions, and a deep, narrow draft to cut the water for a comfortable and stable ride.

Modern cruise ships stick more closely to ports of call which they visit on an almost daily basis. The seagoing experiences are uniquely different. Certainly, there is a vast public for the cruise experience. We believe, similarly, there is an eager and growing audience for the drama, elegance and shipboard ambiance exemplified by sailing aboard a true Atlantic ocean liner.

We know that details of our liner are eagerly awaited but no one has built a true ocean liner in more than 30 years. It is nearly a lost art. Shipbuilders can't simply go into their plans files and pull out a convenient blueprint. *We are recreating history."*

Larry Pimental, President, Cunard

The liner will carry 2500 guests in dramatic palatial interior spaces, reminiscent of the White Star liner *Titanic.* Guests can meet and mingle their way through expansive promenades, elegant grand restaurants, gracious public rooms and grand staircases. Highlights include an onboard Maritime Museum of liner history; a pub with its own onboard micro-brewery; an advanced Computer Learning Center.

Royal Caribbean International's Eagle-Class sisterships to the popular *Voyager of the Seas* will also vie for the title of "**World's Largest**." RCI's 136,000 grt Eagle-class ships carry 3,114 passengers.

"World's Largest True Sail Ship,"

Royal Clipper, "World's Largest True Sail Ship," will join the Star Clipper fleet Spring, 2000 for its inaugural season in the Mediterranean. You can cross the ocean under sail, twice yearly, as the ship repositions from the Far East to the Eastern Mediterranean and on to the Eastern Caribbean.

At 439 feet, *Royal Clipper* is only the second sailing ship in history to be built fully-rigged with 5 masts and square sails on all 5 masts. The first was the Preussen, the 1902 flagship of Flying P lines. Nearly a century later, the modern *Royal Clipper* offers suites with whirlpools and private verandahs, a retractable watersports platform and three on-deck swimming pools.

Hoist, Mateys!

Strap on a safety harness and climb the 'ratlines' to a lookout area mid-way up your choice of five masts. *Royal Clipper* bar staff can deliver champagne or other beverages to your perch. Your selection will be hoisted up to you by a block and tackle rig.

Go, Go Speed Racer!

What dogs were the fastest oceanliners compared to? The Greyhound. Speedy Blue Riband winners were often referred to as the *"greyhounds of the sea."*

Highlights of the Small & Boutique Experience

Soft Adventure:
Ecuador and Galapagos Island Cruises

Cruise 600 miles west of Ecuador in the Pacific, aboard the *Tropic Sun* or another small ship, and you'll find the 48 islands and rocks of the Galapagos archipelago. Only 5 of the islands are populated. The animals and birds on these islands have no fear of man. You will never forget the many strange and familiar creatures you will be able to observe in their natural and totally undisturbed habitat.

The *Tropic Sun;* a converted research vessel; is a favorite of adventure travelers, vacationers, scuba divers, and snorkelers. The vessel accommodates 40 passengers in 20 double occupancy cabins. All cabins are outside, have private bathrooms with showers, 3 x 4 ft picture windows and are air-conditioned. Two suites have private balconies. A special swim and dive platform allows easy access to the water and small boats.

Alaska's Glacier Bay Tours & Cruises

Alaska's Glacier Bay Tours & Cruises is a Native-owned Alaska cruise line specializing in adventure cruises and wilderness tours. These exclusive small ship cruises allow adventurers the unique opportunity to explore up close by sea kayaking and hiking on shore.

The line's Alaska's Inside Passage aboard the Wilderness Discoverer features guided shore excursions, Mendenhall River rafting tours and visits to the Alaskan Raptor Rehabilitation Center and American Bald Eagle Foundation.

The *Executive Explorer's* streamlined catamaran design allows for faster cruising and more time in port. Visit a traditional Tlingit Indian village, watch for whales in Frederick Sound, and search for grizzlies along Admiralty Island. Guests sailing with the *Wilderness Explorer* have an opportunity to spend up to two days kayaking and hiking in spectacular Glacier Bay.

After the exhilaration of kayaking, hiking, wildlife observation and nature photography, return to your cruise ship 'base camp' to relax, share experiences, enjoy delicious meals, and sleep in comfort while the vessel positions you for the next day's adventure.

Because this unique charter vessel accommodates a mere 34 passengers, you travel with a small group of fellow adventurers, who, like you, are looking for an active and intimate experience in Alaska's pristine wilderness. Kayak and shore expeditions are limited to groups of 12 to minimize tourist impact on the environment. Each voyage is different because the itinerary can be adjusted to suit the interest of passengers, and to accommodate wildlife and glacier viewing opportunities.

Old Money

Heiress Marjorie Merriweather Post and financier E. F. Hutton spared no expense when they commissioned the largest private sailing ship ever built. In the 30s and 40s, the *Sea Cloud* hosted the Duke and Duchess of Windsor, Franklin D. Roosevelt and Sweden's King Gustavus V.. Fitted with 30 sails and staffed with 60 crew, the *Sea Cloud* caters to only 69 passengers on Mediterranean, Caribbean and Atlantic voyages.

Snorkel, windsurf or water-ski from untrammeled beaches or take Zodiacs and tender boats ashore. The dining room accommodates all guests at one sitting; and beverages are complimentary with lunch and dinner. All cabins are air-conditioned and offer a safe, telephone, hair-dryer and bathrobes.

Sea Cloud has placed an order for two 100-passenger newbuilds: *Sea Cloud II* and *River Cloud II.*

Live the Luxe Life
Seabourn Goddess I & II

The 'yacht-like' casual luxury experience found aboard Seabourn Goddess vessels was created to serve an affluent and discriminating travelers. The line's well-earned reputation for offering one of the most exclusive vacations in the world is built on a refined blend of personal attention, yacht-like elegance and a variety of amenities and services usually reserved for grand ocean liners. At just 4,250-tons, the ships accommodate 116 guests in 58 outside "suite-rooms."

Travel & Leisure rated the Dining Salon to a two-star Michelin restaurant, featuring international cuisine and offering leisurely dinners prepared to individual order during one sitting. All beverages are complimentary wine and tipping is discouraged. Sail in splendor to the Caribbean, Mediterranean or Transatlantic.

Silversea gets the Gold

Winner of "World's Best Small Cruise Line" in *Travel & Leisure* Magazine's World's Best Awards. Aboard Silversea, the tangibles of ultra-luxury travel - Christofle silverware, Frette bed linens monogrammed with the Silversea logo, soft down pillows and Bvlgari bath amenities - are subtly blended with an intangible at-your-service atmosphere to satisfy your every desire, 24-hours a day.

Whether you crave champagne and caviar on their private verandah, or an elegant dinner served course-by-course in your suite, you'll appreciate the impeccable service and attention to detail that have earned the line the industry's highest accolades.

At just 16,800-tons, *Silver Cloud* and *Silver Wind* cater to 296 guests on journeys to the world's intimate waterways and exotic destinations with voyages to the Mediterranean, Northern Europe, Africa and India, South America, the Far East, Australia and New Zealand, and Canada and New England.

Silversea's all-inclusive fares feature all ocean-view suite accommodations (most with private verandah); round-trip air transportation with complimentary or reduced rate upgrades to Business Class airfare available on select itineraries; deluxe pre-cruise hotel accommodations; all beverages, including select wines and spirits; all gratuities; all port charges; transfers and portage and 'The Silversea Experience,' a special shore event offered on select itineraries.

B. Trends in Accommodations, Public Areas, Facilities, Technology

What's stands out aboard the newest ships? What are the latest trends in accommodations, public areas, facilities and technology? You'll be delighted.

Balconies, verandahs & suites galore.
Be sure to pack extra sunscreen - you'll need it for sunny afternoons on your private balcony. For a majority

of newbuilds, balconies or verandahs come standard with an outside stateroom. In keeping with this trend, a premium cruise line may convert existing picture windows to sliding glass French doors.

'all-suite, all-balcony'
Radisson Seven Seas Cruises has signed an agreement to build a new, all-suite, all-balcony, 720-guest luxury cruise ship scheduled for delivery in February 2001. The new ship will feature 280 standard ocean view suites of 28 square meters including balconies. An additional 80 suites will range from 35 to 100 square meters. Sistership *Seven Seas Navigator's* suites range from 301 to 1,173 square feet (including balcony), and offer walk-in closets and full bathrooms. While the *Seven Seas Navigator* is the cruise line's first all-suite ship (90 percent with private balconies), the newbuild will be its first all-balcony, all-suite vessel.

Reserve a suite aboard Celebrity Cruises *Millennium* and enjoy these services and amenities: Welcome Aboard champagne, personalized stationery, a private portrait sitting, Celebrity tote bag, 100% cotton oversized bath towels, priority check-in and debarkation, express luggage delivery at embarkation, dining room seating preference, invitation to private art preview, opportunity to book in-suite massages.

Millennium suites also provide butler service, which includes: Full breakfast, lunch and dinner service in suites, evening hors d'oeuvres daily, complimentary espresso, and cappuccino, daily news delivery, in-suite afternoon tea service, assistance with packing and unpacking, shoeshine service, and delivery of requested board games.

Wow! No Waiting!

Outside staterooms on Disney Cruise Lines' *Wonder* have two bathrooms! One with a sink and a second with sink, toilet and shower. Aboard Carnival's *Destiny* you can lounge in a steaming Jacuzzi - on your own private verandah. Quite a leap from cruising's humble beginnings, when there was no running water in cabins - only public bathing rooms.

9-10 and 11-deck-high atria, 2-story restaurants and promenades...

See and be seen in cruising's first horizontal atrium aboard Royal Caribbean International's *Voyager of the Seas*. The Royal Promenade is the length of two football fields and four decks high with two 11 deck-high atria (The Centrums.) The Promenade is fashioned after London's Burlington Arcade with a wide selection of shops, restaurants and entertainment areas fronting on a winding street. Highlights include the world's largest interactive roulette wheel, activated by a four-deck-high roulette ball tower; and street festivities and performers.

The *Voyager of the Seas* also features **inside staterooms with a view - a cruise ship first.** These atrium-view staterooms have bay windows overlooking the Royal Promenade with great people-watching views of boutiques and restaurants.

Carnival Cruise Lines' *Carnival Triumph* features a towering nine-deck-high glass-enclosed atrium. The *Carnival Pride* boasts a two-level main restaurant for all guests, and two consecutive decks of bars, lounges and nightspots, one with an outdoor wrap-around promenade.

212

Meet me at the Spa.
Celebrity Cruises AquaSpas.
An oasis for both body and mind awaits you in Celebrity Cruises' AquaSpas. Schedule your appointments the first day of your voyage and enjoy the revitalizing powers of the sea with hydro-based treatments. Onboard the *Century, Galaxy* and *Mercury*, guests may experience a 10,000-square-foot spa environment that includes a 115,000-gallon Thalassotherapy pool with a choice of stimulating water therapies guaranteed to ensure complete relaxation.

You'll be transported body and soul: enjoy the best of Eastern and Western meditation and spa therapies in at atmosphere reminiscent of traditional Japanese bathouses and opulent Moorish architecture.
Various modalities of massage and personal fitness training sessions are also available. The spa treatment programs are custom-designed by Steiner Leisure Ltd. of London.

Ship Shape
Every Royal Caribbean ship has its own custom designed solarium and spa facilities. Invigorate yourself in state-of-the-art fitness centers, take an exercise class or renew your spirit in the spa. Pamper yourself with a facial massage or mudbath. Get set for an evening of glamour with complete salon services: hair styling, manicure and pedicure and makeovers.

Holland America Line's 1440-passenger *Volendam* has increased its spa treatment rooms from four to six. All treatment rooms have private showers and toilets; two of the six spa treatment rooms will accommodate wet treatments such as hydrotherapy baths, seaweed wraps and mud treatments.

Holland America's Steiner-operated spas offer stress relief treatments and fitness consultations including aromatherapy massage, reflexology, facials, back stress relief programs, Ionithermie slimming treatments, personal training, fitness analysis and hair and manicure services.

Fun Design Features

Mirror, Mirror
The spa entryway mirrors aboard the *Grand Princess* make you look 10 pounds lighter!

Water, Water Everywhere: Pools
Guests aboard today's newbuilds may share the sense of novelty experienced by cruisers aboard the maiden voyage of Cunard's *Aquitania*. In 1914, the first shipboard indoor pool opened. This new millennium will treat passengers to a variety of water slides, lap pools, wading pools, solarium pools, whirlpools; even a glass-bottomed pool.

Freestyle on the *Royal Clipper*
Three decks above the atrium and lounge; the ceiling is a **glass-bottomed pool**! Watch the swimmers above you burn calories while you order an apertif.

Pack extra swimsuits for the *Carnival Triumph's* seven whirlpools and four swimming pools -   one with a **214-foot-long twisting, turning water slide!**

Kids big and small might find themselves taking an few extra rides on Holland America Line *Zaandam's* 'exterior elevators.' The outside elevators on both port and starboard decks offer 10 decks worth of panoramic views.

Fans of Route 66 can get their kicks aboard Disney Cruise Line's *Wonder*. 1950's-era billboards, road map carpeting and highway light poles guide guests along Route 66 from nightclub to lounge to comedy club.

Technology at your fingertips.
Technology fans, computer users and Internet junkies are the winners in the cruise industry's 'techno-battle of the seas.' Here are some of the developments in shipboard high-tech:

Stay in touch with friends and family from your in-stateroom Internet/e-mail data ports aboard Holland America Line's new Rotterdam-class vessels.

Princess Cruises' *Grand Princess* offers a 'motion-based' virtual reality theater and a 'blue screen' backdrop where guests can star in their own video.

Carnival Cruise Lines' virtual-reality machines allow players to compete in virtual combat. Movement is tracked by video headsets to determine the scenery and challenges.

RCI's *Voyager of the Seas*' Conference Center seats up to 400 guests, and converts into six large breakout rooms. Other features include a multi-media screening room, wireless control of audio-visual equipment, sound, light, and room temperature; and tele-video conferencing facilities. The state-of-the-art La Scala Theater brings hi-tech Broadway style productions to sea with a hydraulic-powered rising orchestra pit.

C. Trends in Activities, Programs & Entertainment

Take advantage of fun activities and programs as cruise lines outdo each other with new theme cruises, celebrity guests, expert lecturers, fun gimmicks and phenomenal facilities.

There's plenty to do onboard whether you lounge poolside or practice your golf game on the putting green. Sports facilities on today's ships have expanded way beyond ping pong and shuffleboard. New you can play tennis, basketball and volleyball. Days at sea are filled with a range of activities, from traditional cruise pastimes such as bingo and passenger talent shows to ice skating and rock climbing.

Rock-climbing *in the middle of the Caribbean?* Royal Caribbean International's *Voyager of the Seas* has a thirty-foot rock wall mounted on the ship's funnel - two hundred feet above sea level. Climbing equipment and novice lessons are provided. The *Voyager of the Seas* also offers full-court basketball, an in-line skating track, a golf simulator and a 9-hole putting green.

It's your turn!

Now that World Champion Figure Skating legends Katarina Witt, Robin Cousins, Brian Orser, and Todd Eldredge have sliced the ice of the world's first permanent floating ice rink, its your turn. Skate your heart out aboard the *Voyager of the Seas*, that's what Brian Boitano would do!

Located in the 900-seat Studio B, the ice rink is part of a multi-purpose entertainment complex that will feature open skating, spectacular ice shows by professional skaters year-around and celebrity skaters on select sailings. (Yes, they have a Zamboni.)

Ice carving too...

Holland America's hostess demonstrations introduce the art of ice carving, vegetable and melon carving, origami, napkin folding and scarf tying and 'how to' workshops for making marzipan and famous Dutch cheese fondue.

Get in a workout

Royal Caribbean International's ShipShape fitness activities include low and high impact aerobics, an on-deck jogging track, basketball hoops, step and stretch classes, free weights, Lifecycle, treadmill and other cardio machines.

Sample Lectures and Workshops

Join Holland America Line's hosts for an art and history tour of your ship's art and antiques collection, worth approximately $2 million per ship.

National Geographic journalists and photographers will share their personal travel experiences with Silversea Cruises passengers during "*National Geographic Traveler*" voyages. See the world through their eyes with lectures, slide presentations and discussions.

Attend wine-themed seminars and tastings as you visit some of Europe's most famous wine regions. Norwegian Cruise Line's Wine and Romance voyages aboard the *Norway* has brought aboard experts such as Joseph Ward, wine editor at *Conde Nast Traveler*, Malcolm Gluck, wine correspondent for The *Guardian*, and Jilly Goolden, host of the BBC program "Food and

Drink." Visit Barcelona, Southampton, Florence, Pisa, Palma de Mejorca, Malaga, Lisbon, Bordeaux, Le Havre.

Even at sea, "Men are from Mars, Women are from Venus," and Carnival Cruise Lines has invited certified facilitators to present Mars-Venus Workshops aboard select sailings. Based on Dr. John Gray's best-selling series of books, *Men are from Mars, Women are from Venus*; these entertaining workshops feature Gray's video seminars, exercises and discussion. Prices for scheduled sailings include the workshop, champagne & chocolates!

Royal Olympic Cruises' Maya Equinox cruise features a complimentary full day tour to Chichen Itza, timed to coincide with the vernal equinox. The yearly *'return of the sun serpent'* is just one of the fascinating aspects of Maya culture presented in lectures, round-table discussions and casual conversations with renowned archaeologists, historians, and astronomers.
Previous on-board specialists include Dr. Anthony Aveni, Dr. Edwin C. Krupp, Dr. Tom Bopp, Tim W. Kuzniar, M. Scott Carpenter, Phyllis Burton Pitluga, Darien D. Gould, Dr. Rebecca Storey, George T. Keene and Dr. Randolph Widmer. The Maya itinerary features fascinating ports-of-call: Isla de Roatan, Honduras; Cozumel, Mexico; Puerto Cortes, Honduras; Playa del Carmen, Mexico; Belize City, Belize.

Broaden your vocabulary aboard a Holland America Line cruise. Spanish language instruction is available on all Caribbean cruises, and introductory Dutch language classes on most cruises.
Join Bridge lecturers as they tip their hand and share winning strategies on Holland America 10+ day voyages.

D. Trends in Dining

Anything you'd like - anyway you like it - anytime!
A majority of today's floating resorts are supplementing the formal, *Titanic*-style dining experience, with a variety of menu choices, dining times and themed settings. With more than 63 new ships joining the worldwide fleet, you'll find satisfying menu choices for children, vegetarians, gourmets, meat-and-potato lovers and health-conscious diners.

You'll also have your choice of dining times and restaurant themes. Feel like lingering over sushi and steak at a Japanese restaurant? Want a quick-n-easy pizza? (Open 24-hours) You'll find more ships are offering new dining options, plus the traditional 5-course feast served promptly at 6 and 8 p.m..

Trendsetters in dining options

Disney Cruise Line's unique 'rotation dining' gives guests an opportunity to experience a new restaurant nightly, while receiving continuing personal attention from the same waiter. You and your tablemates 'rotate' to a different restaurant each evening - and your waiter comes with you. Enjoy French, California-contemporary and Caribbean cuisine. Disney also offers a Northern Italian restaurant for adults-only.

Crystal Cruises *Crystal Harmony* and *Crystal Symphony* feature specialty restaurant experiences including traditional Japanese cuisine at Kyoto on *Crystal Harmony*, and innovative Asian cuisine prepared with a contemporary flair at Jade Garden on *Crystal Symphony*. Both ships offer Old World charm and authentic regional Italian cuisine at Prego. There is no additional charge.

219

Visit Crystal Cruises' Web site for a Virtual Reality tour of the Crystal Dining Room, Kyoto, Jade Garden and Prego. [http//:www.crystalcruises.com]

Royal Caribbean's Eagle-class ships offer a variety of dining options. The spectacular *Voyager of the Seas* three-level main dining room has separate themed dining areas; Carmen, La Boheme and Magic Flute; interconnected by a dramatic three-deck grand staircase. The adjoining Seville and Granada dining rooms are available for smaller parties.

Other dining opportunities include: Café Promenade, for continental breakfast, all-day pizzas and specialty coffees; Island Grill, for casual dinner, without reservations, featuring freshly grilled entrees and a display kitchen; Portofino, an upscale Euro-Italian restaurant, for dinner with reservations and SeaSide Diner, a 1950s 24-hour eatery featuring jukebox hits and indoor/outdoor seating.

What next, waitresses on roller-skates?
Royal Caribbean has teamed up with Johnny Rockets restaurant to offer its popular 40s - 50s style hamburger-malt shop onboard the first Eagle-class vessel, *Voyager of the Seas*. Johnny Rockets' features a retro-styled burger-malt shop environment complete with vintage memorabilia, singing and dancing waiters and tabletop jukeboxes that still cost only a nickel.

Casual dining is the goal at Carnival Cruise Lines' Seaview Bistros, which feature flexible evening dining from 6-9:30 p.m. on the Lido deck - no reservations required. Guests can enjoy a light fare of soups, salads, pastas as well as steaks cooked to order and desserts. This cafe-like dining choice also offers a daily chef's special; and a wide selection of wines by the glass, bottle or carafe.

Carnival's fleetwide 24-hour pizzerias serve seven different kinds of pizza and calzone, along with garlic bread and Caesar salad.

Carnival's casual dining options complement full-service meals available in the main dining rooms. Don't pass up the late night buffet - tempting hot and cold appetizers, salads, meats carved to order, nightly specialty items and scrumptious desserts.

Decisions! Decisions!
Meat, Fowl or Fish? Red or White? Steamed or Poached? Au jus or chutney? Too many choices!? Ask the Maitre d'!

When the mind-boggling array of delicious cuisine begins to puzzle you - Ask the Maitre d' - with an average of 20 years of experience with cruise cuisine, he's sure to recommend a few favorites. Maitre d's often begin their careers as waiters, buffet stewards or assistant bartenders.

Working closely with a multicultured staff, the Maitre d's masterpiece is a seamless dining room experience. The Maitre d's goal? Guests will talk about this cruise for a lifetime.

Princess Cruises' Maitre d's recommend:

✦ Italian native Balbiani Anbelo adores the Princess Love Boat Dream, a lovely dessert created by Giovanni, the chief baker on *Regal Princess.*

✦ Tinonin Elia's favorites are Beef Wellington, Rack of Lamb, Crepes Suzette and Tiramisu.

✦ Pasta Arrabiata hits the spot for Giorgio Pisano, 24 year Princess veteran.

✦ Top choices for Rui G.R. Pereira, of Lisbon, Portugal; are Rack of Lamb and Grand Marinier Soufflé.

Princess Cruises galleys are staffed with as many as 150 hardworking folks working round-the-clock throughout the fleet, preparing approximately 15,000 meals and snacks daily.

Aboard Holland America Line's ships, the ratio of dining room stewards to guests is 1:10. Two dining room stewards work in a team with an assistant dining room steward and a head steward to assure the highest quality service.

E. Trends in Itineraries, Ports of Departure, Destinations, Shore Excursions

Caribbean Winters, Alaskan Summers...and so much more.
63 new ships, plus efforts to satisfy and retain experienced repeat passengers, prompt cruise lines to develop more " exotic" itineraries and new ports of departure. Watch for sailings to Africa, Southeast Asia, South America, the South Pacific and India; plus new 'home ports' of departure. You'll also find more 'soft adventure,' voyages and specialty or age-specific shore excursions.

How are ports-of-call chosen?
Prime considerations for including a destination on an itinerary include passenger demand, ship design and tourism infrastructure.
Itinerary planners must consider the following:

◆Can the ship travel fast enough to offer a port-per-day or more time in port? ◆Is the ship small enough, or does it have a shallow draft allowing visits to less developed destinations? ◆How will the itinerary appeal to passengers? Is it salable?◆Is there a supporting tourism infrastructure, such as dockage facilities, passenger terminals, ground transportation, air service and shore excursion companies?◆Can the port handle larger ships and greater numbers of passengers?◆Are there appropriate "home" ports of departure from which to begin the voyage?

Developing and Enhancing "Home" Ports

Competition for cruise line business intensifies as port authorities worldwide invest in infrastructure and promotion. Here are some examples of what it takes to get in the game.

Seattle's Bell Street Pier Vs Vancouver.

After 10 years of negotiations, Seattle's port commission voted to build a $12.7-million passenger ship terminal near the popular waterfront Pier 66 shopping and entertainment area. Bell Street Pier is positioned as an alternative homeport for the Alaska cruise market - heretofore dominated by Vancouver. Obstacles to development range from federal restrictions on foreign-flag passenger ships, to funding for facilities and marketing.

Currently 32 cruise ships call at Bell Street Pier, and the port is expected to handle at least 116,000 passengers compared with 7,000 in 1999. Bell Street was chosen as the homeport for Royal Caribbean International's *Vision of the Seas* summer cruises in the Pacific Northwest and Norwegian Cruise Line's first summer Alaskan sailings.

Port Canaveral, Disney Style

Disney Cruise Lines' Art Deco cruise ship terminal in Port Canaveral, Florida welcomes a dedicated fleet of buses transporting passengers from Walt Disney World resorts or the Orlando International Airport.

Long Beach

Carnival Corporation plans to construct and operate a new cruise ship terminal in the city of Long Beach, Calif. The new terminal will be built adjacent to the *Queen Mary* attraction and hotel, and is slated for completion in 2001.

As the new homeport for the West Coast- based ships of the company's Carnival Cruise Lines division, the facility will include a single cruise berth large enough to accommodate vessels the size of Carnival Cruise Lines' 102,000-ton "Destiny-class" series; and a 1,200 vehicle parking garage.

Port of Tampa

Tampa's proximity to the Western Caribbean and Mexico, plus nearby popular attractions (Walt Disney World, the Gulf beaches, Busch Gardens, Florida Aquarium, and Tampa Bay Devil Rays and Buccaneers) continues to draw cruise business. The Port hosted five lines in 1994: Carnival Cruise Lines, Holland America, Regency Cruises, Premier Cruises and OdessAmerica Cruise Lines.

Currently two lines operate from Tampa, Carnival Cruise Lines and Holland America. Carnival has replaced the *Tropicale* with a larger, higher capacity   vessel: The 1,4856 passenger *Jubilee* will operate one four-day and two five-day cruises over every two-week period. Ports of call include Key West, Playa del Carmen/Cozumel and Grand Cayman.

"Our cruise operations from Tampa have grown more dramatically since we began service there in 1994 than in any other homeport we sail from," said Carnival president, Bob Dickinson. "The local community has been particularly supportive and there are a large number of dedicated cruisers and loyal travel agents in the greater Tampa Bay area who are eager to support another, larger 'Fun Ship' there," he added.

The Garrison Seaport Center's Cruise Terminal 2 underwent a $6.5 million renovation that doubled its size. Included are a 5 lane passenger embarkation / disembarkation area, multi-deck parking garage, improved customs and baggage handling facilities and many other state of the art amenities designed with passenger comfort, security and convenience in mind.

Tampa stands ready to take advantage of three positive trends:

(1) Fleet expansion (63 new ships by 2005 will need new home ports.)

(2) Repeat cruisers drive demand for new itineraries.

(3) The potential re-opening of Cuba to US travelers.

Popular Puerto Rico

Could Puerto Rico's Ricky Martin campaign be paying off in more port calls?

'Shake it Ricky! You're so fine!' squealed travel agents as they watched Ricky's promotional commercial for Puerto Rico. Consumer demand for more port-intensive Caribbean itineraries coupled with the island's strategic location attracted more than one dozen lines in 1999.

Singapore

Singapore's $28 million cruise terminal complex and massive promotional efforts are spearheading Pacific Asia's entry into the global leisure cruise market. See the *Cruise Guide to Destinations* for Pacific - Asian itineraries.

Will the Pacific Asia region grow into a strong cruise market?

Itineraries showcasing Asian destinations are gaining in popularity, as US travelers move from tried-and-true Alaskan and Caribbean voyages to test unfamiliar waters. Asian travelers are also cruising more and investments by cruise companies and port authorities are higher than ever.

Star Cruises is one of the four largest cruise lines in the world and by year 2005, will have a fleet of 12 vessels sailing from Singapore, Port Klang, Phuket, Bangkok, Hong Kong, Taipei and Osaka/Kobe.

During its first five years, Star Cruises carried more than 1 million passengers. Star will relocate Norwegian Cruise Line's *Norwegian Wind* to Asia with seven-night sailings between Hong Kong and Singapore; and longer voyages to Australia and New Zealand, all designed for the North American market.

Port of Miami

The Port of Miami's latest addition is a new multi-million-dollar, 250,000-square-foot terminal was constructed specially to accommodate Royal Caribbean's *Voyager of the Seas*. The terminal is designed to expedite the boarding and disembarking process for up to 8,400 guests with spacious check-in areas and hospitality suites for relaxation or last-minute business conferences.

Cruisers will appreciate state-of-the-art security and baggage handling systems, plus secured covered parking for 733 cars in a four-story garage. The terminal features a series of sail-like structures that rise high above the two-story roofline and is crowned by a replica of Royal Caribbean's Viking Crown Lounge.

Trends in Shore excursions

Look for more active, interest-specific and age-specific shore excursions in addition to shopping excursions and popular sightseeing tours.

Black diamond or bunny slope?

Many cruise lines rate their shore excursions according to level of aerobic difficulty or physical exertion required. Carnival Cruise Lines rates their Alaskan shore excursions in three activity levels--"easy," "moderate," and "adventure/considerable" -- to help guests determine which tour best suits their physical condition.

In Search of "soft" adventure.

Explore your world - conveniently! Soft-adventure cruises are catering to the experienced traveler who wants to visit new and exotic locales from the comfort and safety of a home-base cruise ship. See the Yangtze without the hassle of local hotels, get closer to the Galapagos aboard your ship's fleet of Zodiacs. Cross the Amazon rainforest by rope hanging bridges. All this and more - it's adventure made easy by the increasing number of 'expedition' cruise companies. Look to Lindblad's Special Expeditions, and Society Expeditions for the newest itineraries and unique programs in soft-adventure cruising.

Radisson Seven Seas Cruises' 170-passenger *Hanseatic's* "Indian Ocean Odyssey" joins up with Lifelong Learning to offer lectures and workshops with naturalists, and other experts from scientific organizations. Guests explore exotic mammals, birds and plants on their voyage from Capetown, South Africa to Madagascar.

Shore excursions created 'Just for Kids'

"Step right up, see the largest gold nugget in the world," is just one popular feature of Holland America Line's educational adventures geared to "Tween" cruisers on Alaskan voyages.

Tweens (ages 6-12) and teens (13-18) have their own kind of fun, accompanied by a Holland America Line youth coordinator or naturalist. Extreme Sports Fans will enjoy the Dyea Mountain Bike and Float Adventure: a mountain-bike ride to historic Dyea and raft trip on the gentle Taiya River. Included are bikes, helmets, raingear, boots, lifejackets and a light snack, as well as round-trip transportation from the dock.

Teens suitup in rainwear and lifejackets for the Sitka Sea Kayaking adventure. Knowledgeable instructors coach them on safety and steering and they're off - in search of brown bear, Sitka black-tailed deer, harbor seals or sea otters. The 3-hour tour includes a hot beverage, snack and transfer back to town.

Local flavor

Bangkok: Sign up for a Theravada Buddhist meditation class at the World Fellowship of Buddhists. Classes are offered every Sunday. *Hong Kong*: Gaze into your future at Fortune Teller's Alley

Trends in Destinations

Look for more diverse itineraries as cruise lines add new destinations to satisfy sophisticated cruisers.

Now Open for Business: Saudi Arabia.

The once off-limits Kingdom can now be toured via Lindblads Special Expeditions 15-day "Journey to Saudi Arabia" travel program. Get to know the history and culture of Saudi Arabia, beginning with a tour of the capital of Riyadh. Highlights include visits to the oil-producing region of Dhahran, the ancient city of Sakaka and the northern oasis of Domat Al-Jandal. A knowledgeable historian, regional expert and expedition leader will accompany guests throughout the journey.

Can't decide where to go? Try a World Cruise!

Holland America Line's, Year 2000 Grand World Voyage fulfills the ultimate wish list for Century Club Members seeking more stamps for their passports. This 96-day odyssey aboard the *Rotterdam* includes new ports and ports not visited in ten years by Holland America Line. The *Rotterdam* will visit 40 locations on five continents as it circumnavigates the globe.

The Grand World Voyage visits these ports: Georgetown, Grand Cayman; Manta, Ecuador; General San Martin (Pisco), Peru; Coquimbo (La Serena), Chile; Puerto Montt, Chile; Ushuaia Tierra del Fuego, Argentina; Buenos Aires, Argentina; Durban, South Africa; Zanzibar, Tanzania; Victoria, Seychelles; Male, Maldives; Madras, India; Singapore; Hong Kong; Xingang, PRC; Cheju City Cheju Island, South Korea; Kagoshima, Japan; Tokyo; Honolulu; Oahu; Kona;

Hawaii; Balboa, Panama; Callao Per Arica, Chile; Valparaiso, Chile; Experanza Station, Antarctic Peninsula; Cape Town, South Africa; Nosy B, Madagascar; Mombassa, Kenya La Digue and Praslin, Seychelles; Cochin, India; Phuket, Thailand; Vung Tau, Vietnam; Shanghai, PRC; Dalian, PRC; Nagasaki; Osaka; Midway Island; Lahaina, Maui; Los Angeles.

Is cruising environmentally sound?
Then and Now.

Then: 1992 Princess Cruises' ships caught tossing plastic trash bags overboard, fined $500,000.

Now: Planet Princess

Princess Cruises has been awarded the US Coast Guard's William M. Benkert Award for excellence in marine environmental protection. The line's Planet Princess program was honored as the most comprehensive environmental program designed to reduce waste, conserve resources and educate employees.

The Benkert Award recognizes vessels and facility operators with marine environmental programs that exceed mere compliance with regulatory standards. The Coast Guard award recognizes Princess Cruises' superior level of environmental commitment and well-defined, dynamic environmental policy, which involves the participation of all employees.

In addition to the Benkert Award, Princess Cruises also recently received the ASTA/Smithsonian Magazine Environmental Award for environmental excellence, the British Airways Environmental Award for sustainable tourism and the Pacific Asia Tourist Association (PATA) Green Leaf Award.

Then: 1999, Royal Caribbean International, (RCI) fined for improper disposal of bilge water and 'gray-water.' The US Department of Justice concluded a five-year investigation into Royal Caribbean International's past environmental practices and RCI agreed to pay $18 million in fines, in addition to a recently paid $9 million penalty. RCI will also undergo five years of probation. Most of the violations occurred in 1994 and 1995.

Now: RCI strengthens its zero- tolerance policy toward environmental violations. Many of the company's own initiatives were incorporated into an Environmental Compliance Program (ECP), which was part of the settlement agreement reached with the Justice Department. Here's an example of what RCI has achieved:

◆ Developed and installed a state-of-the art filtering system that cleans bilge water three times more effectively than required by law.

◆ Assigned each ship an environmental officer, who monitors shipboard environmental procedures.

◆ Hired a new senior vice president of safety and environment, who oversees overall environmental compliance and reports directly to the president assembled a new management team in marine operations, the division accountable for onboard environmental practices.

◆ Initiated comprehensive environmental audits conducted by outside consultants.

◆ All RCI Millennium-class vessels, along with their Vantage-class ships; will be among the first cruise ships to incorporate gas turbine propulsion. This technology minimizes environmental impact by reducing air emissions, sludge and oil waste.

MARPOL

The International Convention for the Prevention of Pollution from Ships (MARPOL) sets strict regulatory standards to prevent ship-generated waste. This legislation regulates water discharge, air quality, onboard solid waste management and recycling on all vessels.

Burn it or compact and stow it? Let's hope the cruise industry doesn't 'waste' any opportunities to be enviro-friendly. Ships worldwide face the challenge of balancing bottom lines and environmental responsibilities. The Eco-violence committed on our oceans is not limited to the above-mentioned incidents or companies. Cruise company leaders promise it won't happen again and perhaps their enhanced environmental programs will lead the way to a litter-free Gulf Stream.

Now you see it -- now you don't.

"These are sites that define the history and the humanity of the peoples of the world. Once these sites are lost, they are gone forever," Bonnie Burnham, president, World Monuments Fund.

On your next cruise, visit one of the 100 Most Endangered Sites on the World Monument's Watch. This list identifies cultural heritage sites that are urgently at risk and seeks funds for their rescue. A panel of nine experts identify additional sites yearly. Sites on the 2000 List of 100 Most Endangered Sites include Machu Picchu in Peru, Teotihuacán in Mexico, and an 8000-year-old rock art site in Niger.

For the Current Cumulative List of 100 Most Endangered Sites visit [http://www.worldmonuments.org]

For more information on the World Monuments Watch, please contact the World Monuments Fund, 949 Park Avenue New York, NY 10028.

From Afghanistan to Zimbabwe - sites to see: A Sample of Endangered Sites

San Geronimo Fort, Portobelo circa 1653--1760; and San Lorenzo Castle, Colon, Panama circa 1595--1779

San Lorenzo Castle and Fort San Geronimo remain to testify to British and Spanish competition for domination over Caribbean basin colonies. The evolving architecture of these shoreline forts reveal Italian, French and Spanish influences.

Teotihuacán Archaeological Site, San Juan Teotihuacán, Mexico.

Once one of the world's largest cities; renamed Teotihuacán by the Aztecs, meaning "where the gods were born." Previous inappropriate conservation techniques along with inadequate monitoring and main-tenance have left unique mural paintings at risk.

Morgan Lewis Sugar Mill, St. Andrew, Barbados

The last surviving wind-powered sugar-cane crushing mill in the Caribbean; all original working parts intact. The Morgan Lewis Sugar Mill symbolizes the huge fortunes built by the one-time slave labor-powered Caribbean sugar industry.

Valley of the Kings, Thebes, Luxor, Egypt.

Where nearly all of Egypt's New Kingdom pharaohs including Tutankhamen, Seti I and Rameses II are buried. The greatest threat is posed by a total failure to control rapidly increasing numbers of tourists who inflict considerable damage to the decorated tomb walls.

Machu Picchu, Urubamba, Cusco, Peru.

The 15th-century ancient Inca city is threatened by a government-endorsed plan that seeks to build a cable-car lift from Aguas Calientes below the site to Machu Picchu which could destroy the serene, isolated quality of the site and lead to a quadrupling of visitors.

Old Bridge, Spanish Town, St. Catherine, Jamaica

'She waited for her lover to cross from Kingston to Spanish Town.' Recently closed for preservation, this circa 1800, cast-iron footbridge is considered the first of its kind in the Americas. Built of prefabricated iron structure made in England, and assembled on-site, it spans nearly 82 feet across the Rio Cobre.

Tanah Lot Temple, Tabanan, Bali, Indonesia.

The Gods of the Sea are honored in the Tanah Lot Temple. One hundred concrete tetrapods were installed along the shoreline as a way to protect some structures from the rise of the sea, however, this greatly compromises the aesthetic integrity of the temple and site.

National Art Schools, Cubanacán, Havana, Cuba.

Chronic poor maintenance and ill-conceived additions have greatly compromised the schools for modern dance, plastic arts, dramatic arts, music and ballet.

234

San Juan De Ulua Fort, Veracruz, Mexico 1535–1786

San Juan de Ulua marks the site of the beginning of Spanish domination in Mexico. Juan de Grijalva discovered the island for Spain, in 1518, and construction of the fort began in 1535. Fort San Juan de Ulua protected the first port in the Americas; and by the eighteenth century, held the greatest concentration of riches in the Americas

Bermuda-invitation only.

This island of pink sand beaches is one of the most closely controlled and expensive (for the cruise lines,) ports-of-call in cruising. Bermuda's proximity to the US east coast and her popularity with New Yorkers allows the island bargaining powers Caribbean islands only dream of. A limited number of ships are issued landing permits during the prime summer season, between May and October. While many Caribbean ports eagerly court cruise business, the cruise lines must compete for Bermuda's five-year contracts.

Will Cuba reopen to US travelers in your lifetime?

If the US re-instates American travel to Cuba, the cruise lines could capitalize on a whole new central Caribbean itinerary, with calls at Cuba, Jamaica, the Dominican Republic and Haiti.

Cuban cruises are already popular with Canadians and Europeans. Costa Crociere's Costa Playa has attracted cruisers from Britain, Italy, Germany, Spain, France, South America and Switzerland on sailings around the island's southern end. Departing from Cienfuegos, the Costa Playa called at Santiago de Cuba, Cayo Largo del Sur, Grand Cayman and Montego Bay.

235

Costa Crociere owns a 50% stake of Silares Terminales Caribe, a joint venture with the Cuban government, which operates three cruise terminals in Cuba. Silares Terminales Caribe invested $5.8 million in building a passenger terminal in Havana with two large vessel berths. The venture has an option to renovate four other Cuban berths: two in Havana, one in Mariel and one in Santiago de Cuba.

'I AM CUBA'

Politics aside; mouth-watering segments of this film are not to be missed. *Soy Cuba/Ya Kuba (I am Cuba,* 1964) is a calculated propaganda vehicle for the Soviet/Castro regime. Directed by Mikhail Kalatozov, the film promotes Castro as hero in the post-Batista, revolutionary days.
Whatever your heritage or political leanings, you'll appreciate this film's spectacular portrayal of Cuba's natural beauty. Unforgettable sequences of silvery sugar cane fields are sure to make exiles and travelers wish they were there. Runtime: 141 minutes, Russian and Spanish with English subtitles.

resources: Internet

Virtual Cities [http://www.virtualcities.com]

Lonelyplanet [http://www.lonelyplanet.com/]

Adventurous Traveler Bookstore
[http://www.adventuroustraveler.com]

Great Outdoors Recreation Pages
[http://www.gorp.com]

There's a hot new zip code for a ship -it belongs to Royal Caribbean International's *Voyager of the Seas*: **'33132-2028' - another cruise industry first!**

8
YOUTH COUNSELORS
CHILD CARE AT SEA

Children's Programs & Job Opportunities.

WANTED: Youth Counselors to coordinate children's activities. Childcare, teaching, or coaching experience helpful. Holiday & summer jobs available.

Cruises Keep the Whole Family Entertained.

Families are cruising's fastest-growing market segment and cruise executives are already banking on young cruisers for future business. Watch the cruise lines expand their children's programs - and their youth counselor staffs, to accomodate a new generation of cruisers. Most ships offer supervised children's programming during the summer and on holiday sailings. Several cruise lines have beefed up their youth counselor staffs to offer year-round, fleet-wide youth counselors and baby-sitting services.

Savvy cruise line executives have two goals in mind: to provide junior cruisers with the first of many unforgettable cruise vacations and secondly, to ensure that youthful exuberance doesn't disrupt the vacations of fellow passengers. Children's programs are designed so parents and grandparents can enjoy an activity on their own, knowing their children are also having fun in a safe environment. That's where you come in! With childcare, teaching and coaching skills; you can travel as a youth counselor aboard today's finest ships.

Cruising, Family Style!

▲Junior cruisers are welcomed aboard with special children's menus, age-oriented shore excursions and their own daily activity schedule.

▲Disney Cruise Line's new ships are 'purpose built' with kids in mind - they have a whole deck to themselves.

▲Royal Caribbean offers teens their own private disco (18 and under only!)

▲Look forward to more ships with family-size state-rooms that sleep six; plus teen discos, kids-only pools, virtual-reality gamerooms and activity centers.

▲In 2001, Carnival Cruise Lines expects to carry a record 250,000 children aboard its ships.

Sample Baby-Sitting Services

Carnival Cruise Lines: Baby-sitting services conducted by the youth staff in "Children's World" from 10 p.m. to 3 a.m., as well as from 8 a.m. to noon on port days for children under 2. The charge is $5 per hour for the first child and $3 for each additional child in the same family.

Holland America Line: Baby sitting is available on a staff volunteer basis.

NCL offers baby-sitting (individual or group) for a fee. Sitters are available between noon and 2 a.m.

Princess Cruises recently added in-port baby-sitting and extended day care hours past midnight on all ships. $4.00 per hour per child. It also lowered the minimum age to sail from 18 months to 12 months.

HIGHLIGHTS OF OUTSTANDING CHILDREN'S FACILITIES & PROGRAMS

The following highlights will give you a sense of what cruises offer children; including special menus, activities, facilities and age-specific shore excursions. This is a partial listing of cruise lines and their children's programs.

CARNIVAL CRUISE LINES

"Camp Carnival" features a wide variety of age-appropriate activities from 9 a.m. to 10 p.m., conducted by the lines' 100-member fleet-wide youth staff. Sample activities include puppet shows, sing-a-longs and face painting for the younger cruisers, while older kids enjoy talent shows, jewelry-making sessions, dance classes and scavenger hunts.

Teen-oriented activities include late-night movies, pool parties, Ping-Pong and video game tournaments and parties. The Carnival *Paradise* offers "Children's World," a 2,500-square-foot playroom overlooks the main pool area.

Carnival's famous pool-side slides make it hard to return home to a plain-old-pool. There's a 114-foot -long cascading water slide aboard the *Paradise*, plus a children's wading pool.

There's fun for all ages with a computer lab, 16-monitor video wall, arts-and-crafts center, activity center with toys, puzzles, games and a climbing maze.

The outdoor play area offers playground equipment such as jungle gyms and mini-basketball hoops, along with a schooner-shaped playhouse. Children of all ages flock to "Virtual World," a high-tech gaming and entertainment center with the latest in video and arcade games, including virtual reality games. Parents will appreciate the complete children's menu at all meals, as well as a 24-hour pizzeria serving up seven different kinds of pizza and calzone. Complimentary self-serve ice cream and frozen yogurt are available throughout the day, as well. "Fountain Fun Cards" are available for purchase, and are good for unlimited soft drinks.

DISNEY CRUISE LINE

Especially for Kids
With almost an entire deck devoted to age-specific children's programs, your kids will want to join the fun at Disney's Oceaneer Club or Disney's Oceaneer Lab. Wanna' dress up like the Little Mermaid? Play a part in a Bahamian legend? Dig for treasure on Castaway Cay, Disney's private island? There's enough fun for everyone from making a batch of "Flubber," to learning the sailor's craft of scrimshaw or playing a part in a 'Walt Disney Theatre production'.
Sample activities:
Ages 3-5: Do Si Do with Snow White, Flounder's Fish Tales interactive puppet show.
Ages 6-8: Animation Antics: Introduction to simple animation techniques, Pirate Story-teller.
Ages 9-10: Making TV commercials, Villainous Ventures Mysteries.
Ages 11-12: Marblemania: design the ultimate marble racetrack; Goofin' Around with Animation: create your own flipbook to take home!
Especially for Teens
Imagine a New York-style coffeehouse with music, games, large-screen TV, a lounge area, a coffee bar, and shipboard programs like photography, movie making,

and improvisational acting. Teens will appreciate the teens-only areas of Disney's Castaway Cay, where they can snorkel, bike, and kayak with their friends.

HOLLAND AMERICA LINE

Holland America's Club HAL recognizes young cruisers from the first night of their cruise - with a special welcome aboard from the Club HAL director. Club HAL's daily program is slipped under your cabin door each night along with the ship's daily activity guide. Each sea day is planned with at least one age-appropriate activity in the morning, afternoon and evening. There's an activity for three age groups: ages 5-8, 'tweens' ages 9-12 and teens, ages 13-17.

Club HAL activities include games and sports contests, scavenger or autograph hunts, candy bar bingo, disco parties, movie nights, a pizza party, a "coke-tail" party, coloring contests and show-and-tell time. Youngsters who participate receive a Club HAL T-shirt.

Kids-Only!

Holland America Line now offers Kids-only shore excursions. On HAL's 'Float Plane Adventure,' teens get to see Alaska's marvelous wilderness through the eyes of an eagle! A flight aboard an authentic Alaska bush plane allows spectacular views of scenic boat harbors, snow capped peaks and waterfalls in and around Ketchikan, Deer Mountain and Tongass National Forest.

'Giant Totems' helps 6-12 year olds immerse them-selves in the stories carved in 100-year-old totem poles; learn about Native Alaskan culture and try their hand at traditional crafts. (That'll give em something to report on in their next "What I did last summer" assignment...)

On Caribbean voyages, HAL offers kids-and teens-only shore excursion at private island Half Moon Cay. 'X'

241

marks the spot for Kids 6-12 - young treasure hunters gear up as pirates and use a marked map with clues to find the mother lode. Teens can dance and swoon under the moon at the beach party with snacks, music, beach volleyball and games.

NORWEGIAN CRUISE LINE

Kids Crew® offers year-round youth coordinators for kids 6-12, and teen coordinators for teenagers 13-17. During the summer months, winter break, Easter, Thanksgiving, Christmas and New Year's, NCL has coordinators for children 3-5.

NCL offers baby-sitting (individual or group) for a fee. Sitters are available between noon and 2 a.m..

PREMIER CRUISES

Premier offers children's program lead by trained youth counselors aboard all ships. The Big Red Boat Kid's Program features activities geared to five different age levels.

PRINCESS CRUISES

Love Boat Kids
On *Sky, Sun, Dawn, Sea, Ocean* and *Grand Princess*, you'll find complete Youth and Teen Centers with arts and crafts, board games, movies, discos and video games.

Sun, Dawn, Sea, Ocean and *Grand Princess* even offer a toddler's play area and theater, a dolls' house, a castle, computers and ice-cream kiosk. Aboard the *Grand Princess*, kids have their own deck space with a whale's tail slide and splash pool. Teens will enjoy their own Jacuzzi and sunning area.

Other children's programs include "Save Our Seas" which involves kids in activities and special shore excursions based on ecology and stewardship of the oceans.

Princess Cay, the line's private Bahamian island features Pelican's Perch, a supervised play area with a pirate ship playground and sandbox. Teens can swim and snorkel, ride a banana boat or play beach volleyball.

Junior passengers, AKA "mermaids" and "sailors," can now enjoy their favorite foods 24-hours-a-day. The special evening bistro menu just for children is offered as an alternative to the ship's formal dining room and other alternative dining venues. Kids will appreciate the Buccaneer Burger, High Seas Hot Dog, Spaghetti Snakes, Fish Sticks, Chick-Chick-Chicken Fingers, and even "PB & J" Sandwiches. Kid-friendly fare is also available at many of Princess' other dining areas, including the main dining room, pizzeria, poolside hamburger grill, and ice cream bar.

ROYAL CARIBBEAN INTERNATIONAL

Settle in with the whole family in special suites that sleep six. Royal Caribbean offers separate children's playrooms, a teens-only disco and special menus suited to a kid's taste. Children and teens receive "Compass" itineraries, highlighting the day's events and special activities.

"Adventure Ocean" is a specially designed program for kids from 3 to 12 and teens from 13 to 17. Children will find on-board pals in their age group: Aquanauts 3 - 5; Explorers 6 - 8; Voyagers 9 - 12; and Navigators 13 - 17. Children are always supervised by a professional certified youth staff member.

Aquanauts is for toilet-trained children *ages 3 to 5.* Activities include: Story time, face painting, dress-up days, building blocks, ring toss, art sculptures, Bingo, obstacle races, sing-alongs and more.

Explorers 6-8 years old and *Voyagers 9-12* activities include Scattergories, Movies, Pizza Parties, Trashcan Art and Crazy T-Shirt Graffiti, Shuffleboard, Ping Pong, Basketball, Ring Toss, Obstacle Courses, Golf Putting and Wacky Races. Pre-teen Voyagers also enjoy Tattoo Time & Cheek Art and scavenger hunts.

Navigators 13 to 17 can pursue their own agenda in the teen disco (restricted to those under 18.) They'll enjoy Prom Night, Sailaway Socials, Karaoke, Volleyball Beach Parties and Video Game Tournaments. Sporting events include Basketball Tournaments, Fun Fitness Walk-a-thons, Golf Putting and more.

For complete information on working as a youth counselor, see *Job Descriptions from People on the Job* Also see *Cruise Guide for Children.*

9
WANTED:
LECTURERS, INSTRUCTORS
AND GENTLEMEN HOSTS
To travel the world
aboard luxury cruise ships.

Registered nutritionist Jane Doty thought it was 'too good to be true,' when she found she could trade her skills as a lecturer for a two week luxury South Seas cruise. Jane sailed from Los Angeles to Hawaii, Bora Bora and Tahiti. Her working vacation consisted of presenting four one-hour lectures on general nutrition and the role of diet in the prevention of cancer and heart disease.

Jane shared her ocean view stateroom with an exercise physiologist and they both enjoyed the cruise. "She worked harder than I did," says Jane, "...because she taught two classes a day. But most fitness people like to exercise anyway. My impression is that the cruise line simply wants to make a lot of activity available to passengers. Our role is real minor."

Jane sailed the South Pacific for a song: the 14 day cruise could have cost a minimum of $3,400 - Jane only paid a small placement fee and her air fare of $275 to the port of departure, Los Angeles. What fun! And what a bargain! How did she do it? Through the hard work and connections of Lauretta T. Blake, President of Lauretta Blake The Working Vacation ™ .

Presenters, Lecturers, Instructors

Lauretta Blake The Working Vacation ™
Ms. Blake, has been actively involved in the cruise industry for the past twelve years. Her company specializes in bringing forth professionals from all fields who wish to trade speaking or specialty skills for travel. The bureau receives a small fee from the speaker or specialist for arranging the cruise booking.

Presenting one's area of expertise in this unique format is an unusual way to visit favorite places in the world, relax, and make new friends. Speakers, Activity Leaders in Arts & Crafts and Fitness, Dance Instructors, Classical Musicians, Celebrities, and Gentlemen Host™ volunteers all contribute to the enhancement, fun and community life of a vacation get-away for guests and cruise travelers.

Lauretta Blake matches 'presenters,' which include professional speakers and experienced instructors for cruise ship vacations. 'Speakers,' give five different presentations in 45 minute segments. The topic areas currently most applicable include health, self-development, humor, genealogy, image and beauty. 'Instructors' (i.e. crafts, bridge, fitness, golf, line dancing) must lead a variety of 45 minute classes in their area of expertise. Presentations should be fun, interactive and informative. The passengers are generally 50 years and older, may be retired and travel frequently.

In exchange for their presentation services, presenters receive their cruise, cabin and meals for free. Presenters cover their own air fare to and from the port cities. Presenters who are willing to share a cabin with another presenter are usually offered a wider variety of cruises.

246

The cruise companies do not pay presenters nor does the bureau receive any compensation from the cruise lines. A placement fee is paid to Lauretta Blake The Working Vacation™ by the presenter. The fee is determined by the length of the cruise and the cruise line.

Incidental costs, such as shore excursions and gratuities are the responsibility of the presenter. No fees are charges to applicants, nor are there any requirements to commit to a specific number of cruises. If selected, you will be called as cruises become available.

Speaker Categories
General
Beauty
Fashion
Accessories
Image Consultant
Color Consultant
Shopping Strategist
Etiquette
Communication
Memory Management
Time Management
Speed Reading
Culture
Art History
Port Enrichment
Wine
Computers
Photography
Celebrities
 Musician
 Writers
Entertainment
 Caricaturist
 Musician
 Comics
 Theme Cruise staff
 Humorist
Gerontology
 Community Care
 Retirement
 Leisure Activities
 Volunteerism
Health
 Chiropractor
 Pharmacist
 Exercise
 Physiologist
 RD/Nutritionist
 RN/General Health
 Herbalist
 Stress Mgmt.
 Massage Therapist
Medical Doctors
 Back Doctor
 Plastic Surgeon

Cardiologist
Podiatrist
Dentist
Rheumatologist
Dermatologist

Parapsychology
Astrology
Psychics
Graphology
Tarot Reading
Numerology

Psychology
Motivation
Self Awareness
Personal
Development
Self Esteem
Relationships
Self Improvement

Regional Specialist
Africa
Alaska
Orient
Australia
Panama Canal
Caribbean
Scandinavia
Europe
South America
Mediterranean
Mexico
South Pacific

Sciences
Anthropology
Geography

Archeology
Marine Biology
Astronomy
Mineralogy
Botany
Naturalist
Environmental
Oceanography
Gemology
Ornithology

Instructor Categories

Arts & Crafts
Calligraphy
Needlepoint
Ceramics
Drawing/Sketching

Fitness
Folk Dancing
Polynesian
Line Dancing
Social Dancing
Aerobics
Tai-Chi
Yoga

Languages
French
Italian
German
Spanish
Greek

Sports
Golf
Tennis
Youth Activities

The Gentlemen Host™ Program

WANTED: Charming, distinguished gentleman to provide gallant partnership for unescorted lady guests. Must enjoy dancing, dining, shore excursions, parties, card games, and musical shows aboard a luxury cruise. (Officers and Gentlemen are encouraged to apply.)

If you're ready to travel, and possess talents for conversation, dancing and socializing - this may be your ticket to adventure.

The cruise ship 'host program' was pioneered by the late Richard Revnes, past president of Royal Cruise Line. "My wife, Christa, used to point out the disproportion of single, mature women to single men aboard ships," said Revnes. "When we traveled on many cruises, my wife would have me dance with all the single, older women and it just plain wore me out. But we also saw how many of them never had a chance to dance. Dancing is a very enjoyable and important part of the cruise for women." Royal Cruise Line's 'Host Program' has been adopted by many companies wishing to enhance the cruise experience for solo women travelers. (source: *The Insider's Guide to Cruise Discounts*, Capt. Bill Miller.)

The Working Vacation ® Inc. is a cruise consulting company that places dance hosts on cruise ships. The company is the exclusive provider of Gentlemen Hosts™ for the following cruise lines:

Cunard Lines
Delta Queen Steamboat Co.
Holland America
Orient Lines
Premier Cruises
Radisson Seven Seas Cruises

Seabourn
Silversea Cruises
World Explorer Cruises

Perhaps you know someone who meets these general guidelines:

✓   **A single gentleman**
✓   **40+ years and very young at heart!**
✓   **Physically fit**
✓   **Social, a good conversationalist**
who enjoys dinner parties, card and deck games, other ship-board activities and touring ashore with both single and   married passengers.
✓   **Moderate or non-drinker**
✓   **A good listener**
✓   **A good dancer!**

The Gentlemen Host™ volunteer can expect varying benefits from each individual cruise line. Typical provisions offered by cruise lines are:

1. Round-trip economy air transportation to the designated embarkation and disembarkation ports from major airline gateway cities (i.e. Dallas, Portland, Miami, Boston, Chicago.)
2. Shared and/or single passenger accommodations.
3. Entitlement of services, meals, entertainment and receptions provided to paying passengers. (The exception: Hosts are strongly encouraged to avoid Bingo, Lottery, Horse-racing or Casino gambling.)

250

4. Gratuities to cabin and dining room stewards.

5. A bar and wine allowance to entertain passengers in lounges.

6. Laundry service.

7. Enjoyment of shore excursions, when space is available, at no charge.

If you are interested in becoming a Gentlemen Host™ volunteer, contact [http://www.theworkingvacation.com/]

Lauretta Blake The Working Vacation ® Inc.
The Gentlemen Host ® Program
345-A West Maple, Suite 1020
New Lenox, Illinios 60451-1611
Phone: 815-485-8307 - Fax: 815-485-7142
info@theworkingvacation.com

When you write or telephone, please request a Lauretta Blake The Working Vacation™ information packet and application. Be prepared to submit a complete application listing:

◆ the amount of time you are willing to travel
◆ special achievements and awards
◆ club or organization membership
◆ marital status
◆ card and indoor gaming experience
◆ cruise experience
◆ specific dancing abilities.

You will also complete a brief biographical summary and a 'dance review form'.

If you are selected as a Gentlemen Host™ volunteer by Lauretta Blake The Working Vacation™, you will be well prepared: Ms. Blake provides hosts with 'ship-shape' recommendations, from what to wear to shipboard protocol.

Hot Tip : Can you dance, dance and dance some more? Are you proficient in leading a dance partner in these styles: Fox Trot, Waltz, Cha Cha, Swing, Polka, Tango, Rhumba, Samba, Mambo, Salsa, Merinque, Free Style, Country Western, Line Dancing, Folk Dancing? Be prepared to show your stuff at the dance review, polish up your moves along with your dancing shoes.

For more savvy ways to sail for free or at a big discount; you need this handy book:

Cruise Chooser
Buyer's Guide to Cruise Bargains, Discounts & Deals.
How to Get the Best for Less by Mary Fallon Miller, Ticket to Adventure Publishing,   ISBN 0-9624019-2-7, $18.95.

AVAILABLE NOW!

This practical money-saving guide is available at fine bookstores or from the publisher, Ticket to Adventure, Inc. To order or request a brochure, telephone 1.800.929.7447 or visit our Web site: www.cruisechooser.com

BON VOYAGE!

10

TRAVEL AND TOURISM TRAINING PROGRAMS

If your heart is set on hitting the high seas in search of travel, adventure and romance; you might consider enrolling in a travel or tourism educational program. Cruise lines prefer employees with a hospitality or travel and tourism background. Completing a curriculum in these areas will help you gain employment.

Travel schools, universities, community colleges and vocational schools are great places to start your career. A school nearby may offer courses in travel, tourism, recreation or hospitality.

If you are already employed in the travel industry and would like to sharpen your skills and advance your career, the Institute of Certified Travel Agents (ICTA) can help. See ICTA, below.

Three easy steps to help you choose the right travel and tourism training program for you:

Choosing the Right Travel School

(1) Before you enroll at a university, community college, vocational school, or proprietary school; (travel schools independent of universities, colleges or vocational/technical schools,) ask these questions as suggested by the American Society of Travel Agents.

Make an appointment with an admissions or specific department counselor to discuss how their program can help you prepare for employment.

Questions to ask:
a. Is the school licensed within that state's Postsecondary Education Bureau or a recognized accreditation association? If there is no indication of such approval registration or license contact your State Department of Education for more information.

b. Who teaches on the faculty? What type of travel industry experience do the instructors have? Are instructors familiar with the cruise industry?

c. Is there hands-on computer training with airline reservations systems?

d. How long has the school been in operation?

e. What type of placement assistance is available through the school?

f. What type of facilities, equipment and materials are available?

g. What is the curriculum? The travel industry is complex, does this school offer courses in all aspects of travel including cruises?

ASTA affiliated travel schools are committed to excellent training in all aspects of the travel industry. ASTA recommends contacting your State Board of Education for information on community colleges, universities and proprietary schools. ASTA affiliated travel schools, both proprietary and university or college, are located worldwide.

254

For the ASTA affiliated travel school in your community, contact the American Society of Travel Agents, 1101 King Street, Alexandria, VA 22314 or PO Box 23992, Washington.

(2) Join the American Society of Travel Agents, (ASTA.) ASTA is the largest and most influential travel trade association, with over 20,000 members in 125 countries. If you are majoring in travel or tourism either in proprietary travel schools, community colleges or universities, consider joining ASTA as a student member. ASTA provides numerous financial, professional and social benefits to its membership, which consists of travel agencies, suppliers, tour operator and travel schools.

ASTA's Annual Internship Program Award to four deserving students. The Internship allows the student to attend ASTA's World Travel Congress, a convention comprised of over 6,000 delegates who have assembled to learn more about the travel and tourism industry.

ASTA
Membership/Internship Program
1101 King Street
Alexandria, VA 22314

or
PO Box 23992
Washington, DC 20026-3992

ASTA's US West Coast office address is:
4420 Hotel Circle Court.
Suite 230
San Diego, CA 92108

(3) Sign up with the Institute of Certified Travel Agents (ICTA.) ICTA is an international, nonprofit organization that educates travel industry members at all career stages. Founded in 1964 to enhance the quality of professional practice in the travel industry, its goal is to encourage the pursuit of excellence through continuing education.

Educational Programs

ICTA's primary programs are the Certified Travel Counselor (CTC) program, the Destination Specialist programs, and the Sales Skills Development video/workbook program. ICTA also offers an entry-level Travel Career development textbook and an Education on Location program for active CTC members.

Institute of Certified Travel Agents, 148 Linden Street, PO Box 812059, Wellesley, MA 02181-0012 617.237.0280.

Hot Tip: Those travel agents who have earned the title 'CTC' are leaders in the industry. Seek out CTC's and ask for their advice. They may help you get started or advance in your career.

(4) Meet your instructors.
Contact the International Society of Travel and Tourism Educators (ISTTE.)

You'll find most instructors share a passion about travel and a commitment to your success within the industry. Look for instructors with personal experience in the cruise industry. Contact the International Society of Travel and Tourism Educators ISTTE. This progressive organization promotes high standards for educators and curriculum.

256

The International Society of Travel and Tourism Educators is an international organization of over 300 educators in travel, tourism and related fields representing all levels of educational institutions, ranging from professional schools and high schools to four-year colleges and graduate-degree granting institutions. ISTTE members benefit from educational seminars and conferences which help keep these instructors at the top of their class.

International Society of Travel and Tourism Educators ISTTE, 19364 Woodcrest, Harper Woods, MI 48225

Beverley Citron, Cruise Employment Instructor

'Persistence breaks resistance!'

Beverley remembers the Super-8 movies her uncle would show of his adventures in the Royal Navy.

"That is where I first felt a desire to travel by ship, but I didn't want to join the Navy. I had a dream of traveling to exotic places by ship, but it seemed like a difficult career to get into.

"After three years of persistence, sending my resume to cruise lines and preparing myself by working at a resort, I was eventually successful!"

In two years, Beverley promoted from youth counselor to cruise staff exercise instructor and developed the first onboard aqua aerobics program. She now teaches a course on needed cruise line employment skills.

An instructor's experience within the cruise industry can be your most valuable asset. Instructors may have connections with cruise lines, know when jobs become available and know specifically what qualifications each cruise line desires.

Beverley's personal insight into the cruise industry helps her to match the person to the cruise line.

"Personnel directors are each looking for different types of employees to match their lines clientele," say Beverley.

"Up-market or deluxe lines may require more sophistication, college degrees and several foreign languages. On some lines an employee must also be an entertainer, or have a degree in communications, secondary education, psychology or art.

"Choose your school and instructor carefully, study hard and you will open the door to a world of travel, adventure and romance."

Guide to Travel Industry Associations

American Society of Travel Agents (ASTA)
      800-275-2782   [http://www.astanet.com]
Association of Retail Travel Agents (ARTA)
      888-ARTA-NOW   [http://www.artahdq.com]
Cruise Lines International Association (CLIA)
      212-921-0066   [http://www.ten-io.com/clia]
Institute of Certified Travel Agents (ICTA)
      800-542-4282   [http://www.icta.com]
National Association of Cruise Oriented Agents (NACOA)
      305-663-5626   [http://www.nacoa.com]
International Society of Travel & Tourism Educators (ISTTE)
      313-526-0710   [http://www.istte.org/index.htm]

INTERNATIONAL DIRECTORY OF CRUISE LINES

50 CRUISE LINES WEB SITES, ADDRESSES, JOB HOTLINES PHONE & FAX NUMBERS

For updated addresses visit [http://www.cruisechooser.com] Click on Cruise Line Address Update and log on with password: "voyage."

NOTE:
SEE CRUISE LINE PROFILE for exact address & contact for the position which interests you. To apply for employment: Send or Fax your resume or CV.

*** DO NOT TELEPHONE TO APPLY. Want to know the status of your application? Follow up first by mail - see Chapters 4 & 5.

All cruise lines require a written application: resume, cover letter and photo. Address your application: Attn.: Human Resources or Attn.: _____ (specific department, i.e. Entertainment.)

Telephone numbers are for general information only - the operator will not know the status of your application. JOB HOTLINES provide recorded employment information. Follow the instructions for corporate/shore-side or shipboard employment information. When available, FAX numbers are listed. *Bon voyage!*

ALASKA'S GLACIER BAY CRUISES
[http://www.glacierbaytours.com]
The following employment application must be printed, filled out completely, signed & mailed or faxed to:
Glacier Bay Park Concessions, Inc.,
Attention Human Resources Dept.,
226 2nd Avenue West, Seattle, WA 98119
Fax (206) 623-7809

AMERICAN CANADIAN CARIBBEAN LINE
[http://www.accl-smallships.com]
P.O. Box 368, Warren, RI 02885
(401) 247-0955 fax (401) 247-2350

AMERICAN CRUISE LINES
[http://www.americancruiselines.com]
One Marine Park, Haddam, CT 06438
(800) 814-6880
fax (860) 345-4265 email@americancruiselines.com

AMERICAN HAWAII CRUISES
[http://www.cruisehawaii.com]
(also Delta Queen Steamboat Company, Delta Queen Coastal Cruises, United States Lines)
Robin Street Wharf
1380 Port of New Orleans Place
New Orleans, LA 70130-1890

AMERICAN WEST STEAMBOAT CO.
[http://www.columbiarivercruise.com]
601 Union Street
Suite 4343
Seattle, WA 98101

BERGEN LINE
[http://www.bergenline.com]
Norwegian Coastal Voyage Inc.
Human Resources
405 Park Avenue
New York, NY 10022

CAPE CANAVERAL CRUISE LINE
[http://www.capecanaveralcruise.com]
Human Resources Dept.
7099 N. Atlantic Avenue
Cape Canaveral, FL 32920
email dolphin4@capecanaveralcruise.com
Fax (321) 783-4120

CARNIVAL CRUISE LINES
[http://www.carnival.com]
(apply by email)
Human Resources
3655 NW 87th Avenue
Miami, FL 33178
Job Hotline (305) 599-2600

CELEBRITY CRUISES
[http://wwwcelebrity-cruises.com]
5201 Blue Lagoon Drive
Miami, FL 33126
(305) 262-3526

CLASSICAL CRUISES
[http://classicalcruises.com]
132 East 70th Street
New York, NY 10021

CLIPPER CRUISE LINE
[http://www.clippercruise.com]
7711 Bonhomme Ave.
St. Louis, MO 63105
(314) 727-2929 (ask operator for Human Resources)

CLUB MED
[http://www.clubmed.com]
see online worldwide recruitment addresses
Club Med II
Recruitment Department
115 Hammersmith Road
London W14 0QH
United Kingdom

Club Med II
Recruitment Department
75 Valencia Avenue
Coral Gables, FL 33134

COMMODORE CRUISE LINES
[http://www.commodorecruise.com]
FAX resume & salary requirement:
Attn: HR Manager
FAX (954) 967-2147

COSTA CRUISE LINES
[http://www.costacruises.com]
Personnel
PO Box 019614
Miami, FL 33101-9835
(305) 358-7325 at prompt, press 9; ext. 609.

Costa Cruise Lines
CSCS
73 Ruix du Gabin
Gildo Pastor Center
mc98000
Monaco
tel. 011-377-92050248

CRUISE WEST
[http://www.cruisewest.com]
4th & Battery Building, Suite 700
Seattle, WA 98121
(800) 888-9378
Fax: (206) 441-4757

CRYSTAL CRUISES
[http://www.crystalcruises.com]
Attn: Human Resources
2049 Century Park East, Suite 1400
Los Angeles, CA 90067

International Cruise Management Agency
Attn: Svein Pedersen
P.O. Box 95
Sentrum
0101 Oslo
Norway

COPYRIGHT 2001 TICKET TO ADVENTURE

CUNARD
[http://www.cunardline.com]
Fleet Personnel Department
Mountbatten House
Grosvenor Square
Southampton S015 2BF UK
Corporate Employment
6100 Blue Lagoon Drive
Miami, Florida 33126
(305) 463-3000

DELTA QUEEN STEAMBOAT COMPANY
[http://www.deltaqueen.com]
(also American Hawaii Cruises, Delta Queen Coastal
Cruises, United States Lines)
Robin Street Wharf
1380 Port of New Orleans Place
New Orleans, LA 70130-1890

DISNEY CRUISE LINE
[http://www.disneycruise.com]
PO Box 10165
Lake Buena Vista, FL 32830-0165
(407) 566-7447
Note: Entertainers telephone (407) 566-7577

FIRST EUROPEAN CRUISES
[http://www.first-european.com]

HOLLAND AMERICA LINE
[http://www.hollandamerica.com]
300 Elliott Avenue W
Seattle, WA 98119
Phone: (206) 281-3535
Fax: (206) 285 1168

IMPERIAL MAJESTY CRUISE LINE
[http://www.imperialmajesty.com]

LINDBLAD SPECIAL EXPEDITIONS
[http://www.specialexpeditions.com]
Special Expeditions Marine- CW
1415 Western Avenue Suite 700
Seattle, Washington 98101
(206) 382-9593 (ask operator for Human Resources)

NORWEGIAN CRUISE LINE
[http://www.ncl.com]
7665 Corporate Center Drive
Bldg. 11, Floor 2
Miami, FL 33132
(305) 436-4000 (ask for ship personnel job line)
FAX (305) 436-4138
(ship personnel only - no corporate positions)

MEDITERRANEAN SHIPPING CRUISES
[http://www.msccruisesusa.com]
Human Resources
420 Fifth Avenue
New York, NY 10018-2702

COPYRIGHT 2001 TICKET TO ADVENTURE

OCEANIC CRUISES
Human Resources
5757 West Century Blvd.
Suite 390
Los Angeles, CA 90045

ORIENT LINES
[http://www.orientlines.com]
Human Resources
Orient Lines
138 Park Street
London, W1Y 3PF
United Kingdom

Human Resources
7665 Corporate Center Drive

Bldg. 11, Floor 2
Miami, FL 33132

P & O CRUISES
[http://www.pocruises.com]
Human Resources
77 New Oxford Street
London WC1A 1PP

PAQUET CRUISES
Human Resources
5, Boulevard Malesherves
75008, Paris, France

PREMIER CRUISES
[http://www.premiercruises.com]
Human Resources
400 Challenger Road
Cape Canaveral, FL 32920

PRINCESS CRUISES
[http://www.princesscruises.com]
Human Resources
10100 Santa Monica Blvd
Suite 1800
Los Angeles, CA 90067

RADISSON SEVEN SEAS CRUISE LINE
[http://www.rssc.com]
Human Resources
600 Corporate Drive Suite 410
Fort Lauderdale, FL 33334
Seven Seas Cruises
K-Line Canada
2300-555 West Hastings Street
Vancouver, BC. V6B 4N5

COPYRIGHT 2001 TICKET TO ADVENTURE

REGAL CRUISES
[http://www.regalcruises.com]
Human Resources
PO Box 1329
Palmetto, FL 34220

RENAISSANCE CRUISES
[http://www.renaissancecruises.com]
Corporate
Human Resources
PO Box 29009
Fort Lauderdale, FL 33302-9009
Fax to: (954) 759-7727

Shipboard
Attn: Fleet Operations
Recruiter/Scheduler
PO Box 20307
Fort Lauderdale, FL 33335-0307

COPYRIGHT 2001 TICKET TO ADVENTURE

ROYAL CARIBBEAN INTERNATIONAL
[http://www.royalcaribbean.com]
Human Resources
1050 Caribbean Way
Miami, FL 33132
(305) 262-6677 (Choose Shipboard or Corporate)
FAX (305) 539-3938
attn.: Shipboard Human Resources
(Important: FAX after 5 p.m. Eastern Standard Time)

COPYRIGHT 2001 TICKET TO ADVENTURE

ROYAL OLYMPIC CRUISES
[http://www.royalolympiccruises.com]
Human Resources
87 Akti Miaouli
Piraeus, 185 38, Greece
tel. 011-30-14291000
Fax: 011-30-14290639 or 0646

also
Human Resources
805 3rd Avenue
18th floor
New York, NY 10022
(212) 688-7555
(ask operator for Human Resources)

ST. LAWRENCE CRUISE LINES
[http://www.stlawrencecruiselines.com]
Human Resources
253 Ontario St.
Kingston, Ontario K71 2Z4
Canada

SCANDINAVIAN SEAWAYS
Human Resources
30 Samkt Annae Plads 1295
Copenhagen K, Denmark

SEABOURN CRUISE LINE
[http://www.seabourn.com]
Human Resources
6100 Blue Lagoon Drive
Miami, FL 33126
(305) 463-3000 (ask operator for Human Resources)

SEA CLOUD CRUISES
[http://www.seacloud.com]
Human Resources
32-40 North Dean Street
Englewood, NJ 07631

SILVERSEA CRUISES
[http://www.silversea.com]
Human Resources
110 East Broward Blvd.
Fort Lauderdale, FL 33301
(954) 522-4477 (ask operator for Human Resources)
FAX (954) 522-4499 (attn.: Human Resources)

270

SOCIETY EXPEDITIONS
[http://www.societyexpeditions.com]
Human Resources
2001 Western Avenue, Suite 300
Seattle, WA 98121

Human Resources
Marcusallee 9, 28359
Bremen, Germany

SPICE ISLAND CRUISES
[http://www.indo.com/cruises]

COPYRIGHT 2001 TICKET TO ADVENTURE

STAR CLIPPERS
[http://www.starclippers.com]
4101 Salzedo Street
Coral Gables, FL 33146
(305) 442-0550 (ask operator for Human Resources)
FAX (305) 442-1611

Human Resources
Ermanno Palace
27, Boulevard Albert 1er, 98000 Monaco

STAR CRUISES
[http://www.starcruises.com]
Star Cruises/Human Resources
Level 3, Shijuku Mitsui 2nd Bldg
3-2-11 Nishi-shinjuku Shinjyuku-Ku
Tokyo, Japan 160-23

Star Cruises/Human Resources
Port Terminal 2F, 4-5
Shinko-Cho, Chuo-ku
Kobe-city, Hyogo, Japan

COPYRIGHT 2001 TICKET TO ADVENTURE

SWAN HELLENIC
[http://www.swanhellenic.com]

TEMPTRESS CRUISES
[http://www.temptresscruises.com]

UNITED STATES LINES
[http://www.unitedstateslines.com]
c/o American Classic Voyages
Human Resources
Robin Street Wharf
1380 Port of New Orleans Place
New Orleans, LA 70130-1890

VICTORIA CRUISES
[http://www.victoriacruises.com]

WINDJAMMER CRUISES
[http://www.windjammer.com]
1759 Bay Road
Box 190120
Miami Beach, FL 33119-0120
(305) 672-6453
FAX (305) 674-1219

WINDSTAR CRUISES
[http://www.windstarcruises.com]
300 Elliott Avenue West
Seattle, WA 98119
(206) 281-3535   (206) 286-3496 (job hotline)

WORLD EXPLORER CRUISES
[http://www.wecruise.com]
555 Montgomery Street
San Francisco, CA 94111-2544

COPYRIGHT 2001 TICKET TO ADVENTURE

INTERNATIONAL DIRECTORY OF CONCESSIONAIRES
(EMPLOYMENT AGENCIES)

JOB DEPARTMENTS
CASINO
CRUISE STAFF
DECK & ENGINE
ENTERTAINMENT
FOOD & BEVERAGE
GENTLEMAN HOST
GIFT SHOP
LECTURER
MEDICAL
PHOTOGRAPHY
SALON & SPA

COPYRIGHT 2001 TICKET TO ADVENTURE

CASINO

Caesars Palace at Sea
3570 Las Vegas Blvd. South
Las Vegas, NV 89109

Carnival Casinos
5225 NW 87th Avenue
Miami, FL 33178-2193
tel. 305-522-7466
FAX: (305) 599-1967.

CRUISE STAFF

Global Ship Services
141 NE 3rd Avenue, Sutie 203
Miami, FL 33132
305-374-8649

DECK & ENGINEERING

BlueSeas International, Inc.
[http://www.jobxchange.com]

CSCS
73 Ruix du Gabin
Gildo Pastor Center
mc98000
Monaco
tel. 011-377-92050248

Global Ship Services
141 NE 3rd Avenue, Suite 203
Miami, FL 33132
305-374-8649

Marine & Mercantile
6925 Biscayne Blvd
Miami, FL 33138
305-759-5900

Seafarers' International Union
606 Kalihi St.
Honolulu, HI 96819
tel. 808-845-5222

DECK & ENGINEERING continued...

Ship Services International
370 West Camino Gardens Blvd. #301
Boca Raton, FL 33432
407-391-5500

Worldwide Ship Services
Pier 2, 1177 South America Way
Miami, FL 33132

ENTERTAINMENT

Bramson Entertainment (Variety Acts/Cabaret Only)
630 9th Avenue, Suite 203
New York, NY 10036
tel. 212-265 3500 FAX 212-265-6615

Jean Ann Ryan Productions, Inc.
308 SE 14th Street
Ft. Lauderdale, FL 33316
tel. 954-523-6399

Kennedy Entertainment
Attn.: Bonnie Brown
244 S. Academy St.
Mooresville, NC 28115
tel. 704-662-3501
Fax: 704-662-3668

Musicianship
tel. 773-728-5956 FAX 773-728-4970

Spotlight Entertainment (Headline Acts Only)
2121 North Bayshore Dr., Suite 909
Miami, FL 33137-5135
tel. 305-576-8626

The Weinstein Agency
PO Box 37725
Honolulu, HI 96837
Contact: Abe Winston
tel. 808-941-9974
Email: AEWjazfest@aol.com

FOOD & BEVERAGE

BlueSeas International, Inc.
[http://www.jobxchange.com]

Seachest Associates
3655 NW 87th Avenue
Miami, FL 33178-2428
305-599-2600

Seafarers' International Union
606 Kalihi St.
Honolulu, HI 96819
tel. 808-845-5222

Zerbone Catering of Italy
Via de Marini 60
16149 Genoa Italy
tel. 011-39010-54831

GENTLEMAN HOST

Lauretta Blake The Working Vacation ® Inc.
The Gentlemen Host ® Program
[http://www.theworkingvacation.com]
345-A West Maple, Suite 1020
New Lenox, Illinios 60451-1611
tel. 815-485-8307, FAX 815-485-7142
info@theworkingvacation.com

GIFT SHOP

Greyhound Leisure
8052 NW 14th Street
Miami, FL 33126 33126
tel. 305- 592-6460

LECTURER

Lauretta Blake The Working Vacation ® Inc.
The Gentlemen Host ® Program
[http://www.theworkingvacation.com]
345-A West Maple, Suite 1020
New Lenox, Illinios 60451-1611
tel. 815-485-8307, FAX 815-485-7142
info@theworkingvacation.com

Golden Speaks Out
[http://www.goldenspeaksout.com]
P.O. Box 1684
Coral Gables, FL 33114

Abarta Media
11900 Biscaye Blvd, Suite #300
Miami, FL 33181-2726
tel. 305-892-6644
FAX 305-892-1005

POSH Talks
Box 2829
Palm Desert, CA 92261
760-323-3205

MEDICAL

Carnival Cruise Lines
[http://www.carnival.com]
Moises Herszenhorn, MD
3655 NW 87th Avenue
Miami, FL 33178-2428
Tel. (305)599-2600 ext 8606
Fax: (305)471-4732

Celebrity Cruises
[http://wwwcelebrity-cruises.com]
Celebrity Cruises
Carlos Gonzales, MD
5201 Blue Lagoon Drive
Miami, FL 33126
tel. (305)262-3526

Commodore Cruise Line
[http://www.commodorecruise.com]
Medical Department c/o Maritime Medical Systems
Box 463
Millerville, MD 21108

MEDICAL continued ...

Cunard
[http://www.cunardline.com]
Cunard
Dr. G. Waddington
Medical Department
Southwestern House
Canute Road, Southampton
Hants SO14 3NR UK
Tel. 011-44-1703716582

Disney Cruise Line
[http://www.disneycruise.com]
Patricia Gilbert, Nurse Supervisor
Medical Department
210 Celebration Place #400
Celebration, FL 34747
Tel. (407)566-3606
Fax: (407)566-7599

Holland America Line (also Windstar Cruises)
[http://www.hollandamerica.com]
Carter Hill, MD, FACEP
300 Elliott Avenue W
Seattle, WA 98119
Tel. (206)281-3535
Fax: (206)285-1168

Norwegian Cruise Line
[http://www.ncl.com]
Oliver DiPietro, MD
Fleet Physician in Chief

c/o Maria Harris
7665 Corporate Center Drive
Miami, FL 33126
Tel. (305) 436-4953
Fax: (305) 436-4138

Royal Caribbean Cruise Line
[http://www.royalcaribbean.com]
Knut A. Grabo, MD
Harbitzalleen Legesenter
PO Box 340 Skoyen
0212 Oslo, Norway
Tel. 011-47-22734611
Fax: 011-47-22733144

Royal Olympic Cruises
[http://www.royalolympiccruises.com]
N. Patiris, MD
87 Akti Miaouli
Piraeus, 185 38, Greece
Tel. 011-30-14291000 Fax: 011-30-14290639 or 0646

You may also wish to contact:
American College of Emergency Physicians
[http://www.acep.org]
PO Box 619911, Dallas, TX 75261-9911
or 1125 Executive Circle, Irving, TX 75038-2522
(972) 550-0911 (800) 798-1822 FAX: (972) 580-2816

PHOTOGRAPHY

Cruise Ship Picture Company
1177 South America Way #200
Miami, FL 33132

Ocean Images
7 Home Farm Business Center
Lockerley, Romsey
Hampshire S051 0JT
United Kingdom
FAX: 44-1794-341415

Trans Ocean Photo
Attn.: Rob Harrow, President
New York Passenger Terminal, Pier 88
711 12th Ave. Berth 1
New York, NY 10019
Tel. 212-757-2707
Fax: 212-265-6943

email: transocean@aol.com
[http://www.transoceanphotos.com]
(Send Cover Letter with FAX- Attn: Rob Harrow,
Position Requested: Ship's Photographer)

SPA & SALON (Health & Fitness)

Steiner Group, Ltd.
1007 North America Way
4th Floor
Miami, FL 33132
Tel. (305) 358 9002
Fax: (305) 372 9310.
Please enclose a passport size photo with your
resume.

Steiner TransOcean
57 The Broadway,
Stanmore, Middlesex, England HA7 4DU
tel. 44 81 954 6121,
fax: 44 81 954 7980.

The Stylists, Inc.
Attn.: Paul Grabb
4644 Kolohala St.
Honolulu, HI 96816
Tel. 808-923-3855
Fax: 808-735-6717
email: Salons@aloha.net

CRUISE GUIDE FOR WORLDWIDE DESTINATIONS

DESTINATION	American Cruise Lines Inc.	American Hawaii Cruises	Cape Canaveral Cruise Line	Carnival Cruise Lines	Celebrity Cruises Inc.	Commodore Cruise Line	Costa Cruise Lines	Crystal Cruises	Cunard Line	Disney Cruise Line	First European Cruises	Holland America Line	Mediterranean Shipping Cruises	Norwegian Coastal Voyage Inc.	Norwegian Cruise Line	Orient Lines	Premier Cruise Lines	Princess Cruises	Radisson Seven Seas Cruises	Regal Cruises	Royal Caribbean International	Royal Olympic Cruises	Seabourn Cruise Line	Silversea Cruises	Windstar Cruises
WORLD CRUISES							•	•				•						•							
WEST COAST				•	•		•	•				•						•				•			
TRANS-PACIFIC							•	•				•						•							
TRANS-ATLANTIC				•		•	•	•			•	•	•		•	•		•	•		•			•	•
SOUTHEAST ASIA							•	•				•			•			•	•			•	•	•	•
SOUTH PAC./TAHITI							•	•				•			•			•	•						•
SOUTH AMERICA				•	•	•	•	•				•			•			•	•					•	
SCANDINAVIA					•		•	•	•		•	•	•	•	•			•	•		•	•	•	•	•
RUSSIA/EUROPE					•		•	•	•		•	•	•		•			•	•		•	•	•	•	•
RIVER (EUROPE)																									
RIVER (CHINA)																								•	
RIVER (AMAZON)					•							•						•			•		•	•	•
RED SEA/SUEZ CANAL							•	•				•						•	•		•	•	•	•	
PANAMA CANAL				•	•		•	•				•	•		•			•	•	•	•	•	•	•	•
NORTH CAPE							•	•				•		•	•			•	•		•	•	•	•	•
E. COAST/N. ENG/CAN	•			•	•		•	•				•			•			•	•		•	•	•	•	•
MEXICO				•	•	•	•	•				•	•		•			•	•		•	•	•	•	•
MEDITERRANEAN					•		•	•			•	•	•		•	•		•	•		•	•	•	•	•
ISRAEL/EGYPT							•	•			•	•	•		•			•	•		•	•	•	•	•
INDIA							•	•				•						•	•		•	•	•	•	
IBERIA				•	•		•	•			•	•			•			•	•		•	•	•	•	•
HAWAII	•	•					•	•				•						•	•		•		•	•	
GREEK ISLES/AEGEAN					•		•	•			•	•			•			•	•		•	•	•	•	
FAR EAST/ORIENT							•	•				•			•			•	•		•		•	•	
EUROPE (EXCL. MED)					•		•	•			•	•	•		•	•		•	•		•	•	•	•	•
CRUISES TO NOWHERE										•							•			•			•		
COSTA RICA					•		•	•	•			•			•			•	•		•	•	•	•	
CARIBBEAN			•	•	•	•	•	•	•	•	•	•			•		•	•	•	•	•	•	•	•	•
CANARY ISLANDS/NORTH AFRICA					•		•	•			•	•			•			•	•		•	•	•	•	•
BRIT ISLES/IRELAND					•		•	•				•			•			•	•		•		•	•	•
BLACK SEA					•		•	•			•	•			•			•			•	•	•	•	
BERMUDA			•						•			•						•	•		•		•	•	
BALTIC					•		•	•			•	•	•		•			•	•		•	•	•	•	
BAHAMAS			•	•	•	•	•	•		•		•			•		•	•		•	•	•		•	
AUSTRALIA/NEW ZEAL.					•		•	•				•						•	•		•			•	
ALASKA			•				•	•				•			•			•	•			•			
AFRICA					•		•	•	•		•	•	•					•	•			•	•	•	

285

CRUISE GUIDE FOR CHILDREN

SPECIAL ACTIVITIES AND SERVICES

	REDUCED CRUISE RATE (w/ 2 full-fare adults) [1]	AIR/SEA RATE (same or less for full fare psgrs.)	BABYSITTING AVAIL. [2]	CRIBS AVAIL. [3]	QUAD/FAMILY CABINS AVAILABLE	ARTS/CRAFTS CLASSES	BASKETBALL	BEACH PARTIES	BRIDGE TOURS	CARTOONS	DAILY PAPERS	DANCING CLASSES	ESCORTED SHORE TOURS	FOREIGN LANGUAGE CLASSES	GAMES/CONTESTS	HISTORY/GEOGRAPHY CLASSES	ICE CREAM BAR/PARTY	MENUS	MOVIES	PARTIES	PING PONG	POOL (JUST KIDS)	SNORKELING	TEEN CTR OR DISCO	TEEN COUNSELORS	VIDEO GAMES	VOLLEYBALL	YOUTH CTR/PLAYROOM	YOUTH COUNSELORS
AMERICAN CRUISE LINES INC.	A	A	A	A	A	A		A	A	A	A	A	A	A	A	A	A	A	A	A	A		A	A				A	A
AMERICAN HAWAII CRUISES	A	A	A	A	A	A		A	A	A	A	A	A	A	A	A	A	A	A	A	A		A	A				A	A
CAPE CANAVERAL CRUISE LINE	A			A	A		S	S		A	A	S	S		A	S	A	A	A	A	A	A		S	A	A	A	A	A
CARNIVAL CRUISE LINES	A	A/H		S	A	H	S	S		A	A/H	A			A		A	A	A	A	A	S		A	A/H	A	A	A	A/H
CELEBRITY CRUISES INC.	A			A	A		S	S	S	S	S	S			S	H	A	A	A	S	A	S		S	H	S	S	S	H
COMMODORE CRUISE LINE	S	A	A/H	A	S/T	H	S	S	A/H	A	S	A		S	A	S	A	H	A	H	A			S	A/H	S		S	A
COSTA CRUISE LINES	A	A	A	A	A	A/H	A	S	A/H	A	A/H	S/H	S	S	A	S	A	A	A	A/H	A	A	S	A	H	A	A	A	A/H
CRYSTAL CRUISES	A	A	A	A	T	S/H	S	A	S/H	A	S	A			A	S	A	A	A	A	A	A		A	A	A	A	A	H
CUNARD LINE	A	A	A	A	S	S	A	A	A	A	A	A	A	A	A		A	A	A	A/H	A	A	S	A	A	A	A	A	A
DISNEY CRUISE LINE	A	A	A	A	A	A	A	A	A	A/H	A	A/S	A	A/H	A	A	A	A	A	A	A	A		A	A	A	A	A	A/H
FIRST EUROPEAN CRUISES	A	A	A	A	A	S	S	S	A	A/H	A	S	S	A	A	A	A	A	A	A	A	S		A	A	A	A	A	H
HOLLAND AMERICA LINE	A	A	A/H	A	A	S	A	A	A	A	A	A	S	S/H	A	S	A	A	A	A	A	S	S	A	A	A	S	S	A
MEDITERRANEAN SHIPPING CRUISES	A	A	A	A	A					S	A	S		S	A		S	S	A	A	A	S	S	A	S	S		S	S
NORWEGIAN COASTAL VOYAGE INC.		S		S	S								A																
NORWEGIAN CRUISE LINE	A	A	A	A	A	S	S	S	A/H	S	S	S/H	S		S		S	S	A	A/S	A		S	S/H	A/H	A		S	A/H
ORIENT LINES	A	A	A	A	A	H	H	H	H	A/H	A/H	A		H	H		A	A	A	H	H			H	H	S		H	H
PREMIER CRUISE LINES	A	A	A	A	A	S/H	S	S	A/H	A/H	A/H	S/H	A	S	A	S/H	A	S	A	A	A	A	S	S	S	A	A	S/H	S/H
PRINCESS CRUISES	A	A	A	S	S	S/H	S	A	S/H	A	A/S	A/S		S	A	S	A	S	A	A/S	A	S	S	S	A/S	S	S	S	A/S
RADISSON SEVEN SEAS CRUISES (4)	S	A	A	A	A							S																	
REGAL CRUISES	A	A	A	A	A	A	A	A	A	A	A	A	A		A		A	A	A	A	A	A		A	A	A	A	A	A
ROYAL CARIBBEAN INTERNATIONAL	A	A	A/H	A	A	S/H	A	S	S	S	S	S/H		S	A	S	A	A	A	A	A	S	S	S	S	A	S	S/H	S/H
ROYAL OLYMPIC CRUISES	A	A	A	A	A	S/H	S	A	A	A	A	A		A	S	S	A	A	A	A	A	S		H	H	A	S	S/H	S/H
SEABOURN CRUISE LINE (4)			A		S																								
SILVERSEA CRUISES (4)	A			T																									
WINDSTAR CRUISES (4)																					H					S			H

KEY

A All ships; S–Some Ships and/or destinations;

T No four-berth cabins available, but some triples;

H Only seasonally: usually Christmas, Easter and summer holiday periods. Whenever children are aboard, most ships go out of their way to accommodate them and their needs...the more children on a sailing, the greater variety of special activities

(1) On most cruise lines, infants travel free. Where applicable, the maximum age for this rate ranges from 1 to 3 years;

(2) Where available, babysitting is arranged on-board, and not-guaranteed

(3) Where available, cribs arranged for at time of booking;

CRUISE GUIDE FOR ACTIVE ADULTS

ON-BOARD

	AEROBICS	BASKETBALL	LOW CAL MENU	GOLF DRIVING	GYM	JOGGING	MASSEUSE	PADDLE TENNIS	SAIL BOATING	SAUNA	SCUBA DIVING	SKEET/TRAP SHOOTING	SNORKELING	SNORKELING LESSONS	SPA POOL	SWIMMING	TOTAL FITNESS PROGRAM	VOLLEYBALL	WATER/JET SKIING	WINDSURFING
AMERICAN CRUISE LINES INC.	A		A	A	A	A	A	A	A/I		A/I		A/I	A/I		A			A/I	A/I
AMERICAN HAWAII CRUISES	A	S	A	A	A	A	A	A		A	—	A	A/I	A/I	A	A	A	A	A/I	
CAPE CANAVERAL CRUISE LINE	A	S	A	A	A	A	A	A	A/I	A	A/I		A/I	A/I	A	A	A	A	—	—
CARNIVAL CRUISE LINES	A	S	A	S	A	S	A	S	—	A	S/I	S	—	—	A	A	A	A	—	—
CELEBRITY CRUISES INC.	A	S	S	A	A	A	S	A	A	A	A	S	A/I	A/I	A	A		A	—	—
COMMODORE CRUISE LINE	A	S	A	A	A	A	A	A	S	A	A/I	S	A/I	S	A	A	A	S	—	—
COSTA CRUISE LINES	A	S	A	S	A	S	A	S	—	S	—	S	S	—	S	A	A	S	S/SP	S/SP
CRYSTAL CRUISES	A		A	S	A	A	A	A	S	A	—	S	A	S	A	A	A	A	—	—
CUNARD LINE	A	S	A	A	A	A	A	A	—	A	A	A	A	A	A	A	S	A	S/SP	S/I
DISNEY CRUISE LINE	A	S	A	S	A	A	A	A	S	A	—		S	—	A	A	A		—	—
FIRST EUROPEAN CRUISES	A	S	A	S	A	A	A	A	—	A	A		A	A/I	A	A	S	S	—	—
HOLLAND AMERICA LINE	A	S	A	A	A	A	A	S	—	A	—	A	A/I	A/I	A	A	S	A	—	—
MEDITERRANEAN SHIPPING CRUISES	A				A	A	A						S			A	A		—	—
NORWEGIAN COASTAL VOYAGE INC.									S											
NORWEGIAN CRUISE LINE	A	S	A	S	A	A	A	S	A	A	A	A	S	A	A	A	A	S	—	
ORIENT LINES	A		A	—	A	A	A	—	—	A	—		A/I	—	A	A	A		—	—
PREMIER CRUISE LINES	A	S/I	A	S/I	A	A	A	S/I	A	A	A	S	S/I	A	S/I	A	S	A	S/I	S/I
PRINCESS CRUISE LINES	A	S	A	S	A	S	A	S	—	S	—	S	S	—	S	A	S	A	S/I	S/I
RADISSON SEVEN SEAS CRUISES	A		A	—	A	A	A	—	A	A	A	A	A	A	A	A	A	S	—	—
REGAL CRUISES	A		A	A	A	A	A	A	—	A	—	A	A/I	A/I	A	A	S	A	—	—
ROYAL CARIBBEAN INTERNATIONAL	A	S	A	A	A	S	A	A	—	A	—	A	S	A/I	A	A	S	S	—	—
ROYAL OLYMPIC CRUISES	S		A		S	S	A		A/I				A/SP		A/SP	S	A/I		A	A/SP
SEABOURN CRUISE LINE	A		A	A	A	A	A	A	A/SP	A	A	A	A/SP	A	A	A	A	S	A/SP	A/SP
SILVERSEA CRUISES	A		A	A	A	A	A	A/SP	A	A	A	—	—	—	A	A	A		A/I	A/I
WINDSTAR CRUISES	S		A	A	A	A	A	A/SP	A/SP	A/SP	A/SP		S	A/SP	A/SP	S	S	S	A/SP/A	A/SP/A

ASHORE*

	BICYCLING	CHARTER FISHING	GOLF	HIKING	HORSEBACK RIDING	SCUBA DIVING	SNORKELING	TENNIS	WATER SKIING	WINDSURFING
AMERICAN CRUISE LINES INC.	A/I	A/I	A/I	A/I	A/I	A/I	A/I	A/I	A/I	A/I
AMERICAN HAWAII CRUISES		—	A/I	A/I	S/I	A/I	A/I	A/I	—	—
CAPE CANAVERAL CRUISE LINE	A/I		A/I	A/I		A/I	A/I	S		
CARNIVAL CRUISE LINES	—	—	A/I	A/I	—	A/I	A/I	—	—	—
CELEBRITY CRUISES INC.	—	—	—	—	—	A/I	A/I	—	—	—
COMMODORE CRUISE LINE	A/I	S	A/I	A/I	S	A/I	A/I	S	—	S
COSTA CRUISE LINES	S	A/I	S	S	—	S	S	S	—	—
CRYSTAL CRUISES	A/I	A/I	A/I	A/I	S	A/I	A/I	A/I	—	—
CUNARD LINE	S	S	S	A	A	A	S	A	S	S
DISNEY CRUISE LINE	A	A	A	A	—	A	A	A	A	A
FIRST EUROPEAN CRUISES	—	—	A	—	—	A	—	—	—	—
HOLLAND AMERICA LINE	S	A	A	S	S	A	A	A	A	S
MEDITERRANEAN SHIPPING CRUISES		—		—	—	—	—	—		
NORWEGIAN COASTAL VOYAGE INC.	—	—	—	—	—	—	—	—	—	—
NORWEGIAN CRUISE LINE	S	S	S	S	S	S	S	S	S	—
ORIENT LINES	—	—	—	—	—	S/I	—	—	—	—
PREMIER CRUISE LINES	S/I	S/I	S/I	S/I	S/I	S/I	S/I	S/I	S/I	—
PRINCESS CRUISE LINES	S	S	S	S	S	S	S	S	S	S
RADISSON SEVEN SEAS CRUISES	—	—	—	—	—	—	—	—	—	—
REGAL CRUISES	S	S	S	S	S	S	S	S	—	—
ROYAL CARIBBEAN INTERNATIONAL	—	—	A	—	—	A	A	—	—	—
ROYAL OLYMPIC CRUISES	—	A	A	A	A	A	A/SP	A	A	A/SP
SEABOURN CRUISE LINE	—	A	A	A	A	A/SP	A/SP	A/A	A/SP	—
SILVERSEA CRUISES	—	A	A	—	S	A/SP	A/SP	A	A/SP	A/SP
WINDSTAR CRUISES	—	—	—	—	S	A/SP	A/SP	A/SP	A/SP	A/SP

KEY
A—All ships
S—Some ships
I—Information on local facilities provided by shipboard staff
SP—Ship(s) equipped with aft water sports platform

NOTE*
(1) There is an additional charge for most shore-side activities. Some shipboard activities such as skeet-shooting, are also extra.
(2) Some water and shore-side sports aren't available in every port or destination (i.e. snorkeling in Alaska)
(3) Unless marked "I", available shore-side activities are provided through shore excursions and sports programs OR arranged at a passenger's request

APPLICATION LOG
Use this log to keep track of your applications and cruise line contacts.

Date:

Cruise Line:

Position desired:

Action:

Follow Up:

Date:

Cruise Line:

Position desired:

Action:

Follow Up:

Date:

Cruise Line:

Position desired:

Action:

Follow Up:

288

Date:

Cruise Line:

Position desired:

Action:

Follow Up:

Date:

Cruise Line:

Position desired:

Action:

Follow Up:

Date:

Cruise Line:

Position desired:

Action:

Follow Up:

Date:

Cruise Line:

Position desired:

Action:

Follow Up:

Date:

Cruise Line:

Position desired:

Action:

Follow Up:

Date:

Cruise Line:

Position desired:

Action:

Follow Up:

BIBLIOGRAPHY

Access Cruise, Access Guides, 1999

Alaska & Canada's Inside Passage Cruise Tour Guide, 1999

Aroyan, Genie and George Aroyan, *Wheels and Waves: A Cruise, Ferry, River and Canal Barge Guide for the Physically Handicapped*

Bolles, Richard Nelson. *What Color is Your Parachute?* Berkeley: Ten Speed Press, 2000
A must. This annual publication will help you gain invaluable personal insight and direction toward the right job for you.

Blum, Ethel. *The Total Traveler by Ship.* New York: Graphic Arts Center Publishing, 1994 (12th Edition)
Savvy observations and advice on choosing your cruise from the pioneer of ship evaluations. Ms. Blum is Cruise Editor for *Cruise Trade Magazine* and a featured speaker on the cruise industry. (An expert evaluation of cruise ships, company histories, ports of call.)

Bow, Sandra *Globetrotter Cruise Guide*, 19999

Bravos, Brooke, *Cruise Hosting*, 1992

Cartwright, Roger and Carolyn Baird, *Development and Growth of the Cruise Industry*, 2000

Cushing, Bill *Travel Agent Guide to Wheelchair Cruise Travel*

Dawson, Phillip, *Cruise Ships: An Evolution in Design*, 2000.
291

BIBLIOGRAPHY

Dervaes, Claudine. *Travel Dictionary.and Complete Guide to Selling Cruises,1999* Tampa: Solitaire Publishing, P.O. Box 14508, Tampa, Fl 33690 1994 813.876.0286/ 800.226.0286 A leader in professional travel agent training. Publishers of travel school text books, workbooks, audio cassettes and software. *The Travel Training Workbook (Set of Six Sections), Complete Guide to Selling Cruises* and *Careers in Travel Video*

Dickinson, Bob and Andy Vladimir, *Selling the Sea: An Inside Look at the Cruise Industry.* New York: John Wiley & Sons, 1997

Frommer, Arthur, *Frommer's 99 Alaska Cruises & Ports of Call.*

Frommer, Arthur and Marilyn Springer and Donald Schultz. *Frommer's Comprehensive Travel Guide: Cruises.* New York: Prentice Hall Travel, 2000
An indispensable resource on choosing your cruise. *Frommer's Travel*
Guides lead the way with detailed descriptions of major cruise lines:
itineraries, programs, accommodations and historical background.

Gershman, Suzy *Frommer's Born to Shop Caribbean Ports of Call,* 1997

Golden, Fran Wenograd and Jerry Brown, *Alaska Cruises & Ports of Call,* 2000, Frommer's Travel Guides

Golden, Fran Wenograd *The Complete Idiots Travel Guide to Cruise Vacations, 2000.,* Macmillan Travel.

Grescoe, Paul and Audrey Grescoe, *Alaska: The Cruise Lover's Guide,* 1998

Griffith, Susan. *Work Your Way Around The World.* Oxford: Vacation Work, 2000

Harman, Jeanne *Harman's Official Guide to Cruise Ships.*

Inside Passage: Alaska & Canada, Coastal Cruise Tour Guides

Israel, Gloria and Laurence Miller, Dictionary of the Cruise Industry., 1999

Krannich Ronald, Ph.D and Caryl, Ph.D. *The Complete Guide to International Jobs & Careers, and The Almanac of International Jobs and Careers.* Manassas Park, VA: Impact Publications, 2000

Ludmer, Larry H. Cruising Alaska: A Traveler's Guide... 1999

Maltzman, Jeffrey *Jobs In Paradise.* New York: HarperCollins, 1993

Mancini, Mark, *Cruising: A Guide to the Cruise Line Industry*, 1999

Maxtone-Graham, John *Crossing & Cruising:From the Golden Era of Ocean Liners to the Luxury Cruise Ships of Today.*

Miller, Capt. Bill, CTC. *The Insider's Guide to Cruise Discounts.* St. Petersburg, FL: Ticket To Adventure, Inc., 1990 813-822-1515

Miller, Wm. H. Jr. *Great Cruise Ships and Ocean LIners from 1954 to 1986: A Photographic Survey.* 1988

Miller, Wm. H. Jr. *Modern Cruise Ships, 1965-1990: A Photographic Record.* 1992

Monaghan, Kelly. *The Insider's Guide to Air Courier Bargains.* New York: The Intrepid Traveler, 2000 also *Home Based Travel Agent* 1999*, The Intrepid Traveler's Guide to Being an Outside Sales Agent*

Peterson, Garth. *Garth's Profile of Ships.* Omaha, NE: Cruising with Garth, 1996

Rapp, Laura and Diane Rapp, *Cruising the Caribbean: A passenger's Guide to the Ports of Call*, 1997

Schwartzman, M. T. *Fodor's 2000:The Best Cruises* Fodor's Travel Publications

Schwartzman, M. T. *Fodor's 2000:Alaska Ports of Call,* Fodor's Travel Publications

Schwartzman, M. T. *Fodor's 2000: Caribbean Ports of Call,* Fodor's Travel Publications

Showker, Kay *Caribbean Ports of Call: Eastern and Southern Regions: A guide for Today's Cruise Passengers,* 1999

Showker, Kay *Caribbean Ports of Call: Northern and Northeastern Regions: A guide for Today's Cruise Passengers,* 1999

Showker, Kay *Caribbean Ports of Call: Western Regions: A guide for Today's Cruise Passengers,* 1999

Showker, Kay and Bob Sehlinger, *The Unofficial Guide to Cruises,* New York: Macmillan Travel, 1995

Slater, Shirley et. al.,.*Fielding's Alaska Cruises and the Inside Passage*

Slater, Shirley et. al.,.*Fielding's Guide to Caribbean Cruises,* 2000

Slater, Shirley et. al.,.*Fielding's Guide to European Cruises,* 2000

Stapen, Candyce, *Cruise Vacations with Kids,* 1999

Stanford, Emma and Thomas Cook *Passport's Illustrated Guide to Caribbean Cruising.* 2000

Stern, Steve B. *Stern's Guide to the Cruise Vacation,* 2000

Steves, Rick *Rick Steve's Guide to Cruises,* 2000

Sugarman, Aaron editor., *Conde Nast Traveler Caribbean Resort and Cruise Ship Finder* 2000

Tanenbaum, Stephen, et. al., *The Cheapskate's Guide to Cruises: The Very Best Trips for the Lowest Cost.,* 1999

Teison, Herbert and Nancy Dunnan, *Travel Smarts*, Globe Pequot Press, 1997

Vipons, Anne, *Alaska by Cruise Ship: The Complete Guide to the Alaska Cruise Experience*, Ocean Cruise Guides,

Vipons, Anne et. al. *Mediterranean by Cruise Ship* 1998.

Vipons, Anne et. al., *The Complete Cruise Handbook, 1996*

Ward, Douglas. *Berlitz Complete Guide to Cruising and Cruise Ships*. New York: Berlitz Publishing Company, Inc. 1999

Wilson, Matthew, et al. *The Bahamas Cruising Guide*, 1998

Periodicals and Serials

ASTA Agency Management. American Society of Travel Agents.

Aware Traveler's Directory, Travel Aware, 7658 Royston St., Annandale, VA 22003-3637

Career Advisor Series: Travel and Hospitality Career Directory, Visible Ink Press/Gale Research Inc., 1993

Conde Nast Traveler.

Cruise Digest, P.O. Box 886, FDR Station, NY, NY 10150
Bi-monthly newspaper published by the International Cruise Passenger Association

The Cruise Industry - An Overview, Cruise Lines International Association, 500 5th Ave. Suite 1407, New York, NY 10110
A semi-annual publication evaluating the growth of the cruise industry, cruise capacity, new ships, demographics of the cruising population, market potential, comparisons in port embarkations and ports of call. Ask your local travel agent if you may read their office copy.

CLIA Annual Cruise Manual. Cruise Lines International Association, 500 5th Ave. Suite 1407, New York, NY 10110

> The annual cruise seller's "Bible." CLIA member lines are profiled with deck plans, menus, activity programs. CLIA guides to passenger programs and facilities. Complete destination guide by location and cruise line, maps of ports of embarkation, glossary, guide to resources on the cruise industry. Ask your local travel agent if you may read their office copy.

Cruise Observer Lehman Publishing Co, 28 Kenilworth Rd., Asheville, NC 28803 800-593-8252 cruzweek@aol.com

Cruise Reports. Slater, Shirley and Harry Basch, Luisa Frey-Gaynor et. al., (973) 605-2442.

Cruise and Vacation Views. Orban Communications, Inc., 60 E. 42nd St., Ste 905, NY, NY 10165

Leisure Travel News. 600 Community Dr., Manhasset, NY 11030

Ocean & Cruise News. P.O. Box 92, Stamford, CT 06901

Official Cruise Guide. 500 Plaza Dr., Secaucus, NJ 07096

> Excellent overview of the cruise passenger fleet, with deck plans, itineraries, programs and facilities. Annual Publication. Ask your local travel agent if you can read their office copy.

Porthole Magazine. 10 Fairway Dr., Suite 200 Deerfield Beach, Fl 33441-1802

Transitions Abroad Magazine. 118 Hulst Rd., PO Box 1300, Amherst, MA 01004

> An invaluable bi-monthly publication providing travelers of all ages, practical, usable information on economical, purposeful international travel opportunities. The source for programs featuring travel, work, living/studying abroad.

Travel Agent. Universal Media Inc. 801 Second Avenue, New York, NY 10017 Weekly publication

Travel Counselor. Tour & Travel News, 600 Community Dr., Manhasset, NY 11030

Travel Holiday.

Travel & Leisure.

Travel Trade: Cruise Trade. Travel Trade Publications, 15 West 44th St., NY, NY 10036 Weekly publication.

Travel Weekly. Reed Publishing, 500 Plaza Dr., Secaucus, NJ 07096

CRUISE LINE CYBERGUIDE

A

Alaska' Glacier Bay Tours & Cruises
[http://www.glacierbaytours.com]

American Canadian Caribbean Line
[http://www.accl-smallships.com]

American Cruise Lines
[http://www.americancruiselines.com]

American Hawaii Cruises
[http://www.cruisehawaii.com]

American Safari Cruises
[http://www.amsafari.com]

American West Steamboat co.
[http://www.columbiarivercruise.com]

Aqua Safaris Worldwide
[http://www.aqua-safaris.com]

B

Bergen LIne
[http://www.bergenline.com]

C

Canodros
[http://www.canodros.com]

Cape Canaveral Cruise Line
[http://www.capecanaveralcruise.com]

Celebrity Cruises
[http://www.celebrity-cruises.com]

Classical Cruises
[http://classicalcruises.com]

Clipper Cruise Line
[http://www.clippercruise.com]

Club Med
[http://www.clubmed.com]

Commodore Cruise Line
[http://www.commodorecruise.com]

Continental Waterways
[http://www.continentalwaterways.com]

Costa Cruises
[http://www.costacruises.com]

Crown Cruise Line
[http://www.applevacations.com]

Cruise West
[http://www.cruisewest.com]

Crystal Cruises
[http://www.crystalcruises.com]

Cunard
[http://www.cunardline.com]

D

Delta Queen Steamboat Co.
[http:www.deltaqueen.com]

DFDS/Scandinavian Seaways
[http://www.seaeurope.com]

Disney Cruise Line
[http://www.disneycruise.com]

E

Ecoventura/Galapagos Network
[http://www.ecoventura.com.ec]

Eurocruises Inc.
[http://www.eurocruise.com]

F

First European Cruises
[http://www.first-european.com]

French Country Waterways
[http://www.>>>

G

Galapagos Cruises
[http://www.ecuadorable.com]

Global Quest (fka OdessAmerica)
[http://www.globalquesttravel.com]

Golden Sun Cruises
[http://goldensuncruises.com]

H

Holland America Lines
[http://www.hollandamerica.com]

I

Imperial Majesty Cruise Line
[http://www.imperialmajesty.com]

Ivaran Lines
[http://www.ivaran.com]

K

KD River Cruises of Europe
[http://www.rivercruises.com]

L

Lindblad Special Expeditions
[http://www.specialexpeditions.com]

M

Marine Expeditions
[http://www.marineex.com]

Maui-Molokai Sea Cruises
[http://www.mauigateway.com]

Mediterranean Shipping Cruises
[http://www.msccruisesusa.com]

N

Neckton Diving Cruises
[http://www.nektoncruises.com]

Norwegian Cruise Line
[http://www.ncl.com]

Nubian Nile Cruises
[http://www.nubiannilecruises.com]

O

Oceanwide Expeditions
[http://www.diveguideint.com/]

Orient Lines
[http://www.orientlines.com]

P

Peter Deilmann EuropAmerica
[http://www.deilmann-cruises.com]

Premier Cruises
[http://www.premiercruises.com]

Prince of Fundy Cruises, Ltd.
[http://www.princeoffundy.com]

Princess Cruises
[http://www.princesscruises.com]

Q

Quark Expeditions
[http://www.quark-expeditions.com]

R

Radisson Seven Seas Cruises
[http://www.rssc.com]

Regal Cruises
[http://www.regalcruises.com]

Regal China Cruises
[http://www.regalchinacruises.com]

Renaissance Cruises
[http://www.renaissancecruises.com]

Riverbarge Excursion Lines
[http://www.riverbarge.com]

Royal Caribbean International
[http://www.royalcaribbean.com]

Royal Olympic Cruises
[http://www.royalolympiccruises.com]

S

St. Lawrence Cruise Lines
[http://www.stlawrencecruiselines.com]

Sea Cloud Cruises
[http://www.seacloud.com]

Seabourn Cruise Line
[http://www.seabourn.com]

Silversea Cruises
[http://www.silversea.com]

Small Ship Cruises
[http://www.smallshipcruises.com]

Society Expeditions
[http://www.societyexpeditions.com]

Spice Island Cruises
[http://www.indo.com/cruises]

Spirit Cruises
[http://www.spiritcruises.com]

Star Clippers Cruises
[http://www.starclippers.com]

Star Cruises
[http://www.starcruises.com]

Swan Hellenic
[http://www.swanhellenic.com]

T

Tall Ship Adventures
[http://www.tallshipadventures.com]

Temptress Cruises
[http://www.temptresscruises.com]

U

United States Lines
[http://www.unitedstateslines.com]

V

Victoria Clipper
[http://www.victoriaclipper.com]

Victoria Cruises, Inc.
[http://www.victoriacruises.com]

Viking River Cruises
[http://www.vikingrivercruises.com]

W

Windjammer Barefoot Cruises
[http://www.windjammer.com]

Windstar Cruises
[http://www.windstarcruises.com]

World Cruise Company
[http://www.worldcruiseco.com]

World Explorer Cruises
[http://www.wecruise.com]

World's Leading Cruise Lines
(Carnival Family of Cruise Lines)
[http://www.leaderships.com]

Glossary

GLOSSARY OF NAUTICAL TERMS

A

ABEAM—Off the side of the ship, at a right angle to length of the ship.

ACCOMMODATION LADDER—External folding stairway for access from ashore or from a tender along side.

AFT—Near, toward or in the rear (stern) of the ship.

ALLEYWAY—A passageway or corridor.

ALOFT—Above the superstructure; in, at or near the masthead.

AMIDSHIPS—In or toward the middle of the ship; the longitudinal center portion of the ship.

ASTERN—Abaft; or beyond the ship's stern.

ATHWARTSHIPS—Across the ship from side to side.

B

BACKWASH—Motion in the water caused by the propeller(s) moving in a reverse (astern) direction.

BAR—Sandbar, usually caused by tidal or current conditions near the shore.

BATTEN DOWN—To secure all open hatches or equipment for worthiness while under way.

BEAM—Width of the ship (amidships) between the widest point of its two sides.

BEARING—Compass direction, usually expressed in degrees, from the ship to a particular destination or objective.

BELLS—Audible sounding of ship's time—one bell for each progressive half hour to a total of eight, commencing at half past the hours of 4, 8, and 12.

BERTH—Dock, pier or quay (key).

BERTH—The bed or beds within the passengers' cabins.

BILGE—Lowermost spaces of the ship's innerstructure.

BINNACLE—The ship's compass.

BOW—Front or forward portion of the ship.

BRIDGE—Navigational and command control center of the ship.

BULKHEAD—Upright partition (wall) dividing the ship into cabins or compartments.

BULWARK—The side of the ship at or near the main deck.

C

CAPSTAN—Vertically mounted motor driven spindle used to wind in hawsers or cables.

CLEAT—Horizontal wedge shaped device to which hawsers or cables are made fast.

COAMING—Raised partition around hatches or between doorways to prevent water from entering.

COLORS—A national flag or ensign flown from the mast or stern post.

COMPANIONWAY—Interior stairway.

CONNING—To superintend the steering of a ship.

COURSE—Direction in which the ship is headed, usually expressed in compass degrees.

CROW'S NEST—Partially enclosed platform at the top of the mast used by a lookout.

D

DAVIT—A device for raising and lowering the ship's lifeboats.

DEADLIGHT—A ventilated porthole cover through which light cannot be emitted.

DOCK—Berth, pier or quay (key).

DRAFT—Measurement in feet from waterline to lowest point of ship's keel.

DRAFT NUMBERS—Located at the bow and the stern to measure draft. Numerals are 6" high and 6" apart.

E

EVEN KEEL—The ship in a true vertical position with respect to its vertical axis.

F

FANTAIL—The rear or aft overhang of the ship.

FATHOM—Measurement of distance equal to 6 feet.

FENDER—Anything serving as a cushion between the side of the ship and the dock or other craft.

FORE—The forward mast or the front (bow) of the ship.

FORWARD—Toward the fore or bow of the ship.

FREEBOARD—That outer part of the ship's hull between the waterline and the main deck.

FREE PORT—A port or place free of customs duty and most customs regulations.

FUNNEL—The smokestack or "chimney" of the ship.

G

GALLEY—The ship's kitchen.

GANGWAY—The opening through the ship's bulwarks (or thru the ship's side) and the ramp by which passengers embark and disembark.

GROSS REGISTERED TON—A measurement of 100 cubic feet of enclosed revenue earning space within a ship. (see Space Ratio)

H

HATCH—The covering over an opening in the ship's deck, usually of considerable size leading to a hold.

HAWSE PIPE—Large pipe(s) in the bow of the ship through which passes the anchor chain or hawser.

HAWSER—A rope of sufficient size and strength to tow or secure a ship.

HELM—Commonly the ship's steering wheel, but more correctly the entire steering apparatus consisting of the wheel, the rudder and their connecting cables or hydraulic systems.

HOLD—Interior space(s) below the main deck for stowage of cargo.

HOUSE FLAG—The flag which denotes the company to which the ship belongs.

HULL—The frame and body (shell) of the ship exclusive of masts, superstructure, or rigging.

I

INBOARD—Toward the centerline of the ship.

J

JACOB'S LADDER—A rope ladder usually with wooden rungs.

K

KEEL—A longitudinal member extending from stem to stern at the bottom center of the ship from which all vertical framing rises.

KING POST—Vertical posts, usually in pairs, to which the ship's cargo cranes are attached.

KNOT—A unit of speed equal to one nautical mile per hour (6080.2 feet) as compared to a land mile of 5 ,280 feet .

L

LATITUDE—Angular distance measured in degrees north or south of the equator. One degree approximates 60 nautical miles.

LEAGUE—A measure of distance approximating 3.45 nautical miles.

LEEWARD—(Pronounced - Lew-ard)—In the direction of that side of the ship opposite from which the wind blows .

LINE—Any rope smaller than a hawser.

LONGITUDE—Angular distance measured in degrees east or west of the prime meridian of Greenwich, England. Due to the earth's curvature, one degree of longitude will vary from approximately 60 nautical miles at the equator to zero at the north and south poles.

M

MANIFEST—A list or invoice of a ship's passengers, crew and cargo.

MIDSHIPS—(See Amidships)

MOOR—To secure a ship to a fixed place by hawsers, cables or anchor.

N

NAUTICAL MILE—6,080.2 feet, as compared to a land mile of 5,280 feet.

O

OUTBOARD—Away from the centerline of the ship, whether toward the ship's sides or beyond them.

P

PADDLEWHEEL—A wheel with boards around its circumference, and, commonly, the sole source of propulsion for riverboats.

PITCH—The alternate rise and fall of a ship's bow which may occur when underway.

PLIMSOLL MARK—One of a series of load lines marked on the side of a ship at the waterline to prevent overloading.

PORT—The left side of the ship when facing forward toward the bow.

PROW—The bow or the stem (the front) of the ship.

Q

QUAY—(Pronounced - "key") A dock, berth or pier.

R

REGISTRY—The country under whose laws the ship and its owners are obliged to comply, in addition to compliance with the laws of the countries at which the ship calls and/or embarks/disembarks passengers/cargo.

RIGGING—The ropes, chains, cables and the like which support the ship's masts, spars, kingposts, cranes and the like .

ROLL—The alternate sway of a ship from side to side which may occur when underway.

RUDDER—That fin-like device astern and below the waterline which when turned to port or starboard will cause the bow of the ship to respond with a similar turn.

RUNNING LIGHTS—Three lights (green on the starboard side, red on the portside and white at the top of the mast) required by international law to be lighted when the ship is in motion between sunset and sunrise.

S

SCREW—The ship's propeller.

SCUPPER—An opening in the bulwarks of a ship through which water accumulated on deck can flow freely overboard.

SOUNDING—Determining the depth of the water either by a weighted rope soundline in shallow waters or by electronic echo in deep waters.

SPACE RATIO—A measurement of cubic space per passenger. Gross Registered Tonnage divided by number of passengers (basis two) equals Space Ratio (rounded to two figures).

STABILIZERS—A gyroscopically operated fin-like device extending from both sides of the ship below the waterline to provide a more stable motion.

STACK—The funnel or "chimney" from which the ship's gasses of combustion are freed to the atmosphere.

STAGE—the gangway of a paddlewheel steamboat.

STARBOARD—Right side of the ship when facing forward toward the bow.

STEERAGEWAY—A rate of forward or reverse motion necessary to allow the ship to "answer" a repositioning of the rudder (helm).

STEM—The extreme bow or prow of the ship.

STERN—The extreme rear of the ship, or toward the rear.

STOW—To fill or load a ship with cargo or provisions.

SUPERSTRUCTURE—The structural part of the ship above the main deck.

T

TENDER—A smaller vessel, sometimes the ship's lifeboat, used to move passengers to and from the ship and shore when the ship is at anchor.

W

WAKE—The track of agitated water left behind a ship in motion.

WATERLINE—The line at the side of the ship's hull which corresponds with the surface of the water.

WEATHER SIDE—That side of the ship exposed to the wind or to the weather.

WEIGH—to raise, e.g., to "weigh" the anchor.

WINCH—Usually a power operated machine with a horizontal spindle used to operate the ship ' s cranes and/or davits .

WINDWARD—Toward the wind, to the direction from which the wind blows.

Y

YAW—To erratically deviate from the ship's course, usually caused by heavy seas.

DS—Diesel ship

MS—Motor ship

MTS—Motor turbine ship

MV—Motor vessel

NS—Nuclear ship

RHMS—Royal Hellenic Mail Ship (old)

RMS—Royal Mail Ship

SS—Steamship

STR—Steamer

TS—Twin Screw

TSS—Turbine steamship

USS—United States Ship (U.S. Navy)

GLOSSARY OF BOOKING TERMS

A

ACCOMMODATION—(See Room)

ADD ON—A supplementary charge added to the cruise fare, usually applied to correlated air fare and/or post cruise land tours.

AFT—Near, toward or in the rear (stern) of the ship.

AIR/SEA—A package consisting of the two forms of travel, i.e ., air to and from the port of embarkation as well as the cruise itself.

B

BAGGAGE ALLOWANCE—That amount of baggage, generally consisting of the passenger's personal effects, carried by the cruise line free of charge.

BASIS TWO—The cabin rate per person applicable to a cabin capable of accommodating at least two persons. Also referred to as double occupancy.

BOOKING—A telephone request to a line's reservations department to secure an option on a cabin.

C

CABIN—(See Room)

CATEGORY—A price gradient of similar cabins from the most expensive to the least expensive, or vice versa.

CLASS—Extinct on most cruises. On some trans-ocean voyages denotes an overall level of ambience and cost, such as "First Class", "Tourist Class" or "Transatlantic Class." Cruises are generally termed: one-class service.

CONDUCTOR'S TICKET—A free cruise ticket usually associated with groups of passengers traveling together, the entitlement to which is governed by each Line's policy.

CRUISE FARE—The actual cost of the cruise excluding all extras such as taxes, port charges, airfare, gratuities and the like.

D

DEBARKATION—Exiting from the ship.

DECK CHAIR—Open deck chaise lounge which is generally provided on a complimentary basis.

DECK PLAN—An overhead diagram illustrating cabin and public room locations in relation to each other.

DEPOSIT—A part payment of the cruise fare required at the time of booking to secure the cabin being reserved.

E

EMBARKATION—Entering or boarding the ship.

F

FORWARD—Toward the fore or bow (front) of the ship.

FINAL PAYMENT—Payment of the full cruise fare plus any necessary or agreed extras, such as taxes, air add on, preparatory to issuance of correlated travel documents.

FIRST SITTING—The earlier of two meal times in the ship's dining room.

FLY/CRUISE—(See Air/Sea)

G

GRATUITIES—The passenger's personal expression of thanks (tips) to the ship's service personnel for services received.

GRT—Gross registered tonnage, i.e., a measurement of 100 cubic feet of enclosed revenue earning space within a ship.

GUARANTEE—The cruise line's promise that the passenger will sail on a stated voyage in a specified price category or type of cabin, at an agreed rate no higher than would ordinarily apply for that voyage, which may result in an improvement of accommodations at no additional cost.

GUARANTEE SHARE FARE—Acceptance by some lines of a single booking at the cost-saving double occupancy rate, with the understanding that the client is willing to share use of the cabin with a stranger of the same sex.

I

INSIDE—A cabin having no windows or portholes to offer a view of the sea, or of the river.

L

LOWER BED—A single bed placed at the conventional height from the floor.

M

MIDSHIPS—In or toward the middle of the ship; the longitudinal center portion of the ship.

O

OFFER—The cruise line's commitment for accommodations then available which may be suitable to the passenger's needs or wishes.

OPEN SITTING—Free access to unoccupied tables in the ship's dining room, as opposed to specific table assignments.

OPTION—The cruise line's offering of a specific cabin (or guarantee) for a specified period of time during which the passenger decides whether or not to accept. Acceptance is confirmed either by a deposit or final payment.

OUTSIDE—A cabin having window(s) or porthole(s) offering a view of the sea, or of the river. 'Oceanview'

318

P

PASSAGE CONTRACT—Detailed terms of responsibility and accountability found in the cruise ticket.

PETS—Any ordinary domesticated bird of animal. None are carried aboard cruise voyages.

PORT—The left side of the ship when facing forward.

PORT CHARGES—An assessment which also includes port taxes, collected by the line and paid to a local government authority.

PORTHOLES—Circular "windows" in the side of the ship's hull or superstructure.

PORT TAXES—A charge levied by local government authority to be paid by the passenger. In some air/sea packages port taxes are included in the final price.

Q

QUAD RATE—An economical per person rate available to individuals for quadruple occupancy on a guarantee share basis.

R

REVIEW DATES—A periodic evaluation of the progress of the sale and promotion of a group combined with attendant cabin utilization.

ROOM—The passenger's room, stateroom or personal accommodation.

S

SAILING TIME—The actual hour at which the ship is scheduled to clear the dock and sail.

SECOND SITTING—The later of two meal times in the ship's dining room.

SHARE BASIS—(See Guarantee Share Fare)

SHORE EXCURSIONS—Off-the-ship tours at ports of call for which an extra charge is usually applied.

SINGLE OCCUPANCY—Sole occupancy of a cabin which is designed to accommodate two or more passengers in which instance a premium is ordinarily charged.

SPACE RATIO—A measurement of cubic space per passenger. Gross Registered Tonnage divided by number of passengers (double occupancy) equals Space Ratio. (rounded to nearest whole number)

STARBOARD—The right side of the ship facing forward.

STATEROOM—(See Room)

STOPOVER—Leaving the ship at a port of call and rejoining it at a subsequent port of call or upon the ship ' s return to the earlier port of call.

T

TENDER—A smaller vessel, sometimes the ship's lifeboat, used to move passengers to and from the ship and shore when the ship is at anchor.

TBA—To be assigned.

TRANSFERS—Conveyances between the ship and other modes such as airports, hotels or departure points for shore excursions.

TRIPLE RATE—An economical per person rate available to individuals for triple occupancy on a guarantee share-fare basis.

TYPE—(See Category)

U

UPPER BED—A single size bed higher from the floor than usual (similar to a bunk bed) often recessed into the ceiling or wall by day.

W

WAITLIST—Not a guarantee, but the cruise line's endeavor to obtain accommodations for passengers on a first-come-first-served basis when all cabins are presently either sold, under deposit or under option.

Glossaries reprinted from the *Cruise Manual,* Cruise Lines International Association.

A

Accounting • 4, 14, 60, 61, 63, 84, 85
Administration • 4, 83, 84
Administrative assistants • 14, 85
Aerobics • 74, 75, 76, 92, 134, 217, 257
Alaska's Glacier Bay Tours & Cruises • 207
Alders International • 58
America World City • 200
American Classic Voyages • 123, 199
American Cruise Lines • 123
American Hawaii Cruises • 99, 101, 123 - 125, 128
American Maritime Officers • 128
American Society of Travel Agents (ASTA) • 254, 255
American West Steamboat • 129
Application • 96
Apply, 10 Best Ways to • 107
Assistant Cruise Director • 13, 21- 23, 27, 33, 104, 128
Assistant Hotel Manager • 60
Assistant shore excursion manager • 45
Asst. Food & Beverage Manager • 56
Asst. Restaurant Manager • 55

B

Baby-sitting • 237
Banking • 4, 107, 237
Bars • 4
Bartender • 50
Beautician • 8
Benefits • 8, 14, 69, 129, 250, 255
Bergen Line, Inc. (Norwegian Coastal Voyages) • 130
Big Four • 5
Busboy • 50, 53

C

Caesars Palace at Sea • 147
Cape Canaveral Cruise Line • 131
Captain • 97
Carnival Cruise Lines • 5, 6, 7, 24, 41, 61, 72, 90, 95, 102, 108, 132, 133, 134, 148, 157, 174-176, 194, 195, 198, 199, 212, 215, 218, 220, 224, 227, 238, 239
Cashier • 20
Casino • 14, 17
Casino Manager • 8, 19
Celebrity Cruises • 6, 38, 51, 61, 72, 82, 107, 109, 135- 137, 171, 173, 195, 211, 213
Chaine des Rotisseurs • 54
Chandris • 33, 61, 62, 72

World Explorer Cruises •
250
World of ResidenSea • 201
Y
Youth counselor • 6, 7, 21,
35, 87, 88, 104, 111,113,
121, 125, 237, 238, 241

Are you ready for Travel, Adventure, Romance & a Steady Paycheck?

● **You need this book.** ●

Leave the 9-5 routine behind! Get the inside story from *How to Get a Job with a Cruise Line, 5th Ed.*

● Available in book stores

● Visit www.cruisechooser.com

● or purchase from publisher:

**Toll-free 24 hour Order Hotline
1-800-929-7447** Visa/Mastercard

Customer Service: 727-822-5029

USA & Canada US$20.95.
All others US$29.
(includes Shipping & Handling)
Visa/Mastercard/Check/Money Order
Ticket to Adventure, Inc.
PO Box 41005
St. Petersburg, FL 33743-1005

Name_____

Address_____

City_____

State_____ Zip/Postal Code_____

Tel. # (   ) _____

e mail_____

Don't delay...get this book & get paid to travel!

Are you ready for Travel, Adventure, Romance
& a Steady Paycheck?

● **You need this book.** ●

Leave the 9-5 routine behind! Get the inside story from
How to Get a Job with a Cruise Line, 5th Ed.

●Available in book stores

●Visit www.cruisechooser.com

●or purchase from publisher:

Toll-free 24 hour Order Hotline
1-800-929-7447 Visa/Mastercard

Customer Service: 727-822-5029

USA & Canada US$20.95.
All others US$29.
(includes Shipping & Handling)
Visa/Mastercard/Check/Money Order
Ticket to Adventure, Inc.
PO Box 41005
St. Petersburg, FL 33743-1005

Name_____

Address_____

City_____

State_____ Zip/Postal Code_____

Tel. # (   ) _____

e mail_____

Don't delay...get this book & get paid to travel!

Are you ready for Travel, Adventure, Romance & a Steady Paycheck?

● **You need this book.** ●

Leave the 9-5 routine behind! Get the inside story from *How to Get a Job with a Cruise Line, 5th Ed.*

- ●Available in book stores
- ●Visit www.cruisechooser.com
- ●or purchase from publisher:

Toll-free 24 hour Order Hotline
1-800-929-7447 Visa/Mastercard

Customer Service: 727-822-5029

USA & Canada US$20.95.
All others US$29.
(includes Shipping & Handling)
Visa/Mastercard/Check/Money Order
Ticket to Adventure, Inc.
PO Box 41005
St. Petersburg, FL 33743-1005

Name_____

Address_____

City_____

State_____ Zip/Postal Code_____

Tel. # (   ) _____

e mail_____

Don't delay...get this book & get paid to travel!